Digital Scenography in Opera in the Twenty-First Century

Digital Scenography in Opera in the Twenty-First Century is the first definitive study of the use of digital scenography in Western opera production. The book begins by exploring digital scenography's dramaturgical possibilities and establishes a critical framework for identifying and comparing the use of digital scenography across different digitally enhanced opera productions. The book then investigates the impacts and potential disruptions of digital scenography on opera's longstanding production conventions, both on and off the stage. Drawing on interviews with major industry practitioners, including Paul Barritt, Mark Grimmer, Donald Holder, Elaine J. McCarthy, Luke Halls, Wendall K. Harrington, Finn Ross, S. Katy Tucker, and Victoria 'Vita' Tzykun, author Caitlin Vincent identifies key correlations between the use of digital scenography in practice and subsequent impacts on creative hierarchies, production design processes, and organisational management. The book features detailed case studies of digitally enhanced productions premiered by Dutch National Opera, Komische Oper Berlin, Opéra de Lyon, The Royal Opera, Covent Garden, San Francisco Opera, Santa Fe Opera, Théâtre Royal de la Monnaie, The Metropolitan Opera, Victorian Opera, and Washington National Opera.

Caitlin Vincent researches the future of work in the arts. Key areas of focus include opera, cultural labour, performance and technology, and equity, diversity, and inclusion. An acclaimed opera librettist, Vincent has been commissioned for Washington National Opera, the Schubert Club of Minnesota, the University of Connecticut, and Carnegie Hall.

Ashgate Interdisciplinary Studies in Opera
Series Editor: **Roberta Montemorra Marvin**, *University of Massachusetts, USA*

The *Ashgate Interdisciplinary Studies in Opera* series provides a centralized and prominent forum for the presentation of cutting-edge scholarship that draws on numerous disciplinary approaches to a wide range of subjects associated with the creation, performance, and reception of opera (and related genres) in various historical and social contexts. There is great need for a broader approach to scholarship about opera. In recent years, the course of study has developed significantly, going beyond traditional musicological approaches to reflect new perspectives from literary criticism and comparative literature, cultural history, philosophy, art history, theatre history, gender studies, film studies, political science, philology, psychoanalysis, and medicine. The new brands of scholarship have allowed a more comprehensive interrogation of the complex nexus of means of artistic expression operative in opera, one that has meaningfully challenged prevalent historicist and formalist musical approaches. This series continues to move this important trend forward by including essay collections and monographs that reflect the ever-increasing interest in opera in non-musical contexts. Books in the series are linked by their emphasis on the study of a single genre - opera - yet are distinguished by their individualized and novel approaches by scholars from various disciplines/fields of inquiry. The remit of the series welcomes studies of seventeenth-century to contemporary opera from all geographical locations, including non-Western topics.

Curating Opera
Reinventing the Past Through Museums of Opera and Art
Stephen Mould

Digital Scenography in Opera in the Twenty-First Century
Caitlin Vincent

For more information about this series, please visit: www.routledge.com/music/series/AISO

Digital Scenography in Opera in the Twenty-First Century

Caitlin Vincent

Routledge
Taylor & Francis Group

LONDON AND NEW YORK

First published 2022
by Routledge
2 Park Square, Milton Park, Abingdon, Oxon OX14 4RN

and by Routledge
605 Third Avenue, New York, NY 10158

Routledge is an imprint of the Taylor & Francis Group, an informa business

© 2022 Caitlin Vincent

British Library Cataloguing-in-Publication Data
A catalogue record for this book is available from the British Library

Library of Congress Cataloging-in-Publication Data
A catalog record has been requested for this book

ISBN: 978-0-367-55392-0 (hbk)
ISBN: 978-0-367-55393-7 (pbk)
ISBN: 978-1-003-09330-5 (ebk)

DOI: 10.4324/9781003093305

Typeset in Times New Roman
by codeMantra

For Nathan, Vivien, and Elinor

Contents

Figures

Acknowledgements

I signed the contract for this book just a few weeks after Australia entered national lockdown to control the spread of COVID-19. Subsequent revisions and rewrites were set against the framework of the pandemic: watching case numbers rise and opera companies close, all while working from home, losing childcare, and eventually enduring more than 100 days of lockdown restrictions after a second wave in the state of Victoria.

I imagine the process of writing a book is always something of a trial by fire, but in this case, there is no question that this book would have been impossible without the support of my family: my husband Nathan Wyatt, who cooked, cleaned, read drafts, and tackled Adobe Illustrator on my behalf; my parents Larry Vincent and Sharon Tyers, who took on daily childcare duties and copy editing requests with equal aplomb and good humour; my sister Jordan Beth Vincent, who provided a steady hand alongside advice and edits; my daughter Vivien, who benevolently agreed to watch (short) snippets of digitally enhanced opera productions with me in her post-nap hours; and baby Elinor, who graciously timed her first appearance a few weeks after I submitted the final manuscript.

During a time of such uncertainty in the opera industry, it has been my privilege to be able to highlight opera productions, designers, and directors that are leveraging digital technology in unique and innovative ways. My sincere gratitude to the many opera professionals who were so generous in sharing their time and insights with me at various stages of the process, including Yarmila Alfonzetti, Paul Barritt, Nancy Black, Aaron Blake, Mark Campbell, Carolyn Chard, Peter Divers, Mark Grimmer, Luke Halls, Wendall K. Harrington, Jake Heggie, Roger Hodgman, Donald Holder, Elaine J. McCarthy, Katie Mitchell, Beth Moxon, Sven Ortel, Grégoire Pont, Tobias Ribitzki, Finn Ross, Sabine Theunissen, S. Katy Tucker, Vita Tzykun, and Japhy Weideman.

Additional thanks to Katya Johanson, who helped to guide the PhD version of this book into fruition; the publishing team at Routledge, particularly my editor Heidi Bishop; the anonymous peer reviewers who provided such thoughtful consideration of my work in its early forms; the Deakin Motion.Lab and Fika Entertainment; Victorian Opera; the State Opera of

South Australia; West Australian Opera; the Australian International Opera Company; Alice Xerri; Zachary Xerri; Paul Xerri; Isabelle Anderson; Paul Mathews; Justine McNamara; and my colleagues at the University of Melbourne, especially Guy Morrow, Kirsten Stevens, Christiaan De Beukelaer, and Brian Long.

Introduction to digital scenography in opera

In 1998, composer Philip Glass and stage director Robert Wilson premiered their new opera, *Monsters of Grace*, at Wolf Trap Opera in Virginia. The production was highly anticipated for its use of digital technology. Live music was synced with 13 3D computer-animated films, each projected on a screen above the performers and viewed by the audience through polarised glasses. Touted by its creators as 'a digital opera,' the work promised a theatrical experience that would immerse its audience in the world of technology (Dixon 2007, 25). The 'much-hyped' event, notes Dixon (2007), was 'one of the most publicized digital performances of all time' (25).

Unfortunately for the creative team, reviews were scathing. Many rebuked the lack of integration between the live performers and the 3D digital projections, which heightened a 'perceived mismatch' between two opposing aesthetic forms (Dixon 2007, 28). 'Relative brevity would appear to be the opera's most salient virtue,' wrote John von Rhein (1999) for the *Chicago Tribune*. 'The ultimate impression left by "Monsters of Grace" is that of a rummage through the discards of creative artists who approached the new project at less than full strength,' noted Alan Rich (1998) in *Variety*. Stacey Kors (1999) more diplomatically described the opera as 'an interesting experiment' in her review for *Salon* but concluded that 'until artists have a better understanding of technology and its capabilities—and limitations—… the future's still a long way off.' Even co-creator Robert Wilson eventually distanced himself from the work, admitting in an interview for the *New York Times*, 'it was one of the most embarrassing things in my life' (Midgette 1999). With this inauspicious start, opera officially entered the digital age.

More than two decades later, digital projections are now commonplace at most major opera companies. Barbour (2011a) describes the twenty-first century as the 'age of projections,' noting that digital elements are no longer a 'boutique item for the well-heeled' but an integral element of stage production that spans 'all sensibilities and budget lines' (28). The use of digital technology is also increasing. An examination of programming at New York's The Metropolitan Opera shows that 46 per cent of new productions between the 2011/12 and 2015/16 seasons credited a video or projection

DOI: 10.4324/9781003093305

designer, compared to only 13 per cent in the previous five seasons (2006/7 to 2010/11) (Vincent et al. 2017). At The Royal Opera, Covent Garden (hereafter, The Royal Opera), six out of ten new productions presented in the 2019/20 season credited a video or projection designer—more than in any of the previous 14 seasons (Royal Opera House Collections Online n.d.).

Some opera productions use projections as the digital equivalent of background scenery, akin to the large-scale painted sets of previous centuries. Teatro Real de Madrid's *Turandot* (2018), Beijing's National Centre for the Performing Arts' *Il Trovatore* (2019), and Opéra National de Paris' *La Bohème* (2017) each use digital technology to create spectacular background settings and environments that shift with the narrative of the opera (Guth 2017; Wilson 2018; De Ana 2019). Such use of digital scenography can be alternatively subtle and dynamic, helping to evoke the passage of time, establish a certain mood, or transition between scenic locations. In The Metropolitan Opera's *La Donna del Lago* (2015), for example, a projected background of a scenic vista gradually morphs from dawn to dusk over the course of the performance (Curran 2015).

Digital elements are also commonly used to realise supernatural effects, as the technology can provide a solution to challenging staging requirements. Productions of W.A. Mozart's fantastical opera *The Magic Flute* are frequently staged with digital scenography,[1] which is often employed to dramatise the trials of fire and water in the second act. Richard Wagner's *The Flying Dutchman*[2] and *Der Ring des Nibelungen* (*Ring* cycle)[3] are also frequently produced with digital projections, which help meet Wagner's staging demands for ghost sailors and a rainbow bridge to Valhalla, among other effects. Out of 128 digitally enhanced productions reviewed by industry magazine *Opera News* between 2010 and 2018, nearly half explicitly feature supernatural or fantastical elements in their narratives (*Opera News* n.d.).

In more extreme examples of digital scenography in practice, directors and designers are leveraging advancements in media servers, motion capture, projection mapping, and game engines to create cutting-edge interpretations of operatic works (Vincent et al. 2016; Love 2017). In The Royal Opera's *Don Giovanni* (2014), omnipresent projections shift in concert with the title character's psychological demise (Holten 2014). In Robert Lepage's *Ring* cycle (2010–2012) for The Metropolitan Opera, projection mapping is used to create lavish spectacles that are functionally interactive in real time (Barbour 2011b). Digital technologies are even being used to create autonomous virtual entities, capable of interacting with live performers and even replacing them on stage, as seen in Opéra de Lyon's *L'Enfant et les Sortilèges* (2016) and The Cleveland Orchestra's *The Cunning Little Vixen* (2014) (Pont and Bonas 2016; McClung 2017).

So what happened? Has Kors' (1999) hope that artists have a 'better understanding of technology and its capabilities—and limitations—' finally come to pass?

Without question, digital technology has become a viable tool for opera companies of varying size and budgets. Major institutions like The Metropolitan Opera and Opera Australia are devoting significant financial resources to commission new productions in which digital elements play a substantial role. The Metropolitan Opera invested more than USD 20 million in Lepage's digitally enhanced *Ring* cycle in 2010 (Stewart 2015), while Opera Australia launched a highly publicised series of new digital productions starting with its *Aida* in 2018 (Bailey 2018).

Smaller opera companies are also actively incorporating digital projections into their repertory, often by renting existing productions or forming coalitions to offset the cost of commissioning new works. Komische Oper Berlin's digitally enhanced production of *The Magic Flute* has been rented and restaged by more than 20 different opera companies worldwide since its premiere in 2012 (1927 n.d.). In an example of the coalition approach, composer Jake Heggie and librettist Gene Sheer's digitally enhanced *Moby-Dick* (2010) was jointly commissioned by five companies—The Dallas Opera, San Francisco Opera, San Diego Opera, State Opera of South Australia, and Calgary Opera—each of which presented the production's regional premiere (Wallace 2013). Another popular strategy is to use digital technology as part of a larger strategic investment into new works. Between its 2005/6 and 2018/19 seasons, for example, Minnesota Opera commissioned and produced eight world-premiere operas, five of which featured extensive digital elements (Operabase n.d.).

The use of digital technology in opera has notably been encouraged and facilitated by government bodies, which see an opportunity to create a more sustainable organisational model. In 2016, Australia's National Opera Review recommended that Australia's four federally funded opera companies actively incorporate digital elements into their productions (Department of Communications and the Arts 2016). The report's authors claimed that this shift would allow companies to innovate the art form and appeal to diverse audiences, while also reducing the costs associated with building and touring physical sets. 'Potential economies of scale may be offered through the development and use of digital staging,' they noted, 'which could generate additional financial benefits and make opera more accessible over time' (56).

Digital technology has thus been framed as the solution to many deep-seated issues facing the opera industry. Over the past century, the operatic canon has become increasingly fixed in what Till (2012) terms a 'museum repertory,' in which the tried-and-true classics of long-dead composers like Mozart, Wagner, Puccini, and Verdi remain the staples of the opera house (240). This reliance on the canon requires a continuous source of new and improved productions of historical repertoire that will appeal to modern audiences (Sgourev 2013). Digital scenography is seen as an ideal way to revitalise these classic works to suit a contemporary perspective.

Opera companies are also anxious to attract younger operagoers who have come of age in a technology-driven world. Industry organisation Opera

America highlighted this priority in its 2017 report on audience engagement, aptly titled, 'What Do Millennials Want?' (Opera America 2017). Digital technology is seen as part of a critical strategy to lure the so-called *Game of Thrones* generation into the opera house. Describing Opera Australia's shift towards digital opera productions, artistic director Lyndon Terracini explains, 'We live in a visual age and, particularly with young people, we need to find something they find stimulating visually' (Morgan 2017). Giesekam (2007) confirms the popularity of this view, noting, 'it is believed that such work will appeal to the media-savvy younger audiences which theatres are desperate to attract' (4).

Finally, with many opera companies struggling to remain financially viable, digital technology is seen as a way to save money. Opera is notoriously expensive to produce, and with rising austerity measures, elaborate physical sets are increasingly framed as an unnecessary expense (Trevisan 2017). Consider Seattle Opera, which in 2017 eliminated the scene shop that had built its physical sets for three decades. Citing the closure as a cost-saving measure prompted by budget cuts, then artistic director Aidan Lang noted that the expense of maintaining the physical shop did not align with advancing technologies and the 'new wave of opera design' (Sillman 2017). 'Digital effects cut costs, lift wow factor' concurred a headline from a review of Opera Australia's *Aida* in 2018 (Westwood 2018). Digital projections are 'the high-tech future of opera,' added another reviewer of *Aida*, that will 'inevitably be more cost effective' (Galvin 2018).

Whether digital technology actually resolves any of these issues remains to be seen. Digital technology can certainly be used as a tool to reinterpret canonical operatic works, but the same is arguably true of any new production design that uses physical materials. The relationship between digital technology and audience appeal is also unclear. There is an absence of quantitative data that shows a direct correlation between the use of digital technology and increased box office sales or younger audiences. Most importantly, digital scenography is not necessarily a cost-effective replacement for physical sets. Digital sets still need to be built, updated for new software, and stored. They also require extensive technical hardware and experienced practitioners; all of this 'comes at a price' (Payne 2005, 25).

Nevertheless, the narrative persists, and opera companies around the world are keen to jump on the digital bandwagon. Yet, there is little evidence to suggest that companies now have the 'better understanding' of digital technology that Stacey Kors anticipated following the premiere of *Monsters of Grace* in 1998. Instead, there remains a disconnect between perceptions of digital technology and the practical implications of its use. This includes aesthetic and dramaturgical considerations, such as how digital elements can be integrated with live performers on stage, as well as impacts on backstage processes, including creative hierarchies and production workflows.

As a result, many opera companies are turning to digital technology without a clear understanding of its dramaturgical implications or the potential consequences to their existing creative and administrative processes. With the use of digital technology continuing to increase, this may have repercussions within the wider industry. Major institutions like The Metropolitan Opera, The Royal Opera, Teatro alla Scala, and Opera Australia have sufficient financial stability to experiment with digital technology. For smaller, regional companies, an uninformed investment in digital tools could have serious consequences for their budgets, audience base, and long-term sustainability. If opera's future is indeed 'digital,' it is critical to establish a baseline of knowledge and practice across the international opera community.

This book aims to build this understanding by undertaking the first extensive analysis of the current use of digital scenography in Western opera production. In doing this, it is necessary to address not only the dramaturgical effects of digital technology in opera production but also the ways in which scenographic designs are created, since visual elements interact in complex ways within the real-world setting of production. The discussion first establishes a framework for identifying and comparing the use of digital scenography across different digitally enhanced productions. In subsequent analysis, I then consider the impacts of digital technology across its varying potentials and the degree to which it poses a 'disruption' to opera's existing production conventions, both on and off the stage.

What is digital scenography?

Aronson (2008) describes 'scenography' as both 'an ancient and recent term,' with origins stemming from the Greek *skēnē*, or 'scene building,' as well as Aristotle's references to *skenografia*, or 'scenic writing' (8). In the twentieth century, understandings of scenography evolved beyond the kinds of two-dimensional pictorial stage settings historically associated with theatrical performance. Theatrical practitioners Edward Gordon Craig and Josef Svoboda are frequently cited for their influence on the concept of scenography as one that both encompasses and blurs independent design practices (Hann 2019). Yet, the exact meaning of the term remains subject to considerable debate (Collins and Nisbet 2010).

In her introduction to *What is Scenography?*, Pamela Howard (2002) asks nearly 50 different theatrical designers to define the term. Not surprisingly, each practitioner proposes a different definition. This ambiguity also extends to scholarly considerations of scenography. Aronson (2018) suggests that scenography is multidisciplinary and 'implies something more than creating scenery or costumes or lights' (7). McKinney and Butterworth (2009) define scenography as 'a dynamic and kinaesthetic contribution to the experience of performance' and cite an affinity with other theatrical terms like 'mise en scène,' 'theatre design,' and 'visual dramaturgy' (3). Howard (2002) takes a more quantitative approach and defines scenography as the 'synthesis' of seven individual factors—'space, text, research, art, actors, directors and spectators'—each of which is equally integrated within the theatrical space (130).

A common thread in these explanations is the idea that scenography encompasses every aspect of the theatrical experience, including performers *and* spectators. Howard (2002) argues that scenography requires an active relationship between the performer and the spectator and is, in fact, incomplete until the performer is physically on stage and 'engages with the audience' (xix). McKinney and Butterworth (2009) and McAuley (2000) echo this requirement for audience engagement, as does Aronson (2018), who describes 'the observer and the thing observed' within the shared time and space of the theatrical experience (8). The emphasis on the role of the spectator as a crucial part of scenography recalls Peter Brook's oft-cited definition of theatre: 'a man walks across this empty space whilst someone else is watching him' (Brook 1996, 7).

These scholars and practitioners describe an idealised vision of scenography, in which independent theatrical elements are successfully integrated to create an emotive experience that is more than the sum of its parts. Moreover, the spectator does not serve as a passive observer but actively engages with both the performer and the scenic elements as part of the theatrical experience. This idea of an intrinsic relationship between the performer, the stage setting, and the spectator served as a starting point for my own exploration of digital scenography in opera and, in particular, my consideration of how current trends in the genre might be identified and evaluated.

Like scenography, the term 'digital' also poses something of a challenge due to its ambiguity. In the context of 'digital scenography,' the term broadly refers to the kind of technology being used to create projections on stage (i.e., digital), rather than the projected effects themselves (Palmer 2018). 'Digital' thus encompasses a vast range of computer-based technologies that function through digital means. This makes it difficult to distinguish between, for example, Opera Australia's 'entirely digital' *Aida* (2018), San Francisco Opera's 'all-digital' *The Magic Flute* (2012), and the 'digital scenery' of Atlanta Opera's *Porgy and Bess* (2011), each one employing different forms of digital technology in different scenographic ways (Brock 2011; Winn 2015; Galvin 2018).

I draw on Dixon's (2007) definition of 'digital performance' to establish a basic premise for digital scenography that is not limited by or linked to any specific technology in practice. Dixon describes digital performance as one in which 'computer technologies play a *key* role rather than a subsidiary one in content, techniques, aesthetics, or delivery forms' (3). He notes that the term can encompass a multitude of computer technologies, including video, projection, animation, motion capture, and real-time interactivity, and should be understood as a reflection of the prominence of digital elements within a production's design.

Applying Dixon's definition to digital scenography, I use the term 'digital' to refer to any form of digital media that is used on stage in a way that is arguably integral to the scenographic design. This encompasses the hand-drawn animation of Opéra de Lyon's *L'Enfant et les Sortilèges* (2016), the 3D stereoscopic imagery of Victorian Opera's *The Flying Dutchman* (2015), and the functionally interactive projections of The Metropolitan Opera's *Das Rheingold* (2010), among other variations of digital scenography in practice. For the purposes of this book, then, 'digital scenography' can be understood as a theatrical experience that involves active engagement between the performer, a scenic setting in which digital technologies play a 'key role,' and the spectator.

Many of the technologies that underpin the current use of digital scenography in opera are new developments. Love (2017) highlights media server technology, which can store and control projected imagery, as a particular 'game-changer' for designs using digital elements, as well as advances in projection mapping techniques, which allow digital imagery to be projected onto different surfaces on the stage. Shaw (2012) lists a number of other technological advancements that have expanded the artistic possibilities for digital elements in performance design, including motion capture techniques, live-driven video game engines, virtual and augmented reality, and networked real-time systems.

While these kinds of technologies are recent innovations, the scenic effects they create—large-scale projections within a proscenium theatrical environment—are not. Giesekam (2007) refers to 'a commonly found historical amnesia that suggests the use of recorded media in theatre is a recent phenomenon' (1). In the case of digital scenography, this amnesia reflects an assumption that digital projections are a fundamentally new scenographic tool. Consider Michael Billington, former drama critic of *The Guardian*, who declared 'it would be crazy for theatre not to embrace new technology, especially video projections' in a 2012 interview (Shaw 2012). Such misunderstandings of historical precedent even extend to opera companies. In 2018, Opera Australia claimed to be the first company to 'stage an entirely digital production,' two decades after the premiere of 'digital opera' *Monsters of Grace* (Galvin 2018).

Projection has a long history in theatrical performance, one that can be traced back to the magic lantern device of the seventeenth century and the earliest forms of projected images used in concert with physical sets.[4] The relationship between performance and technology is even more longstanding. In his survey of twentieth-century scenography, Baugh (2013) contends that 'stage technology, machinery and special effects have always been a part of the experience of theatre and performance' and cites examples dating from Greek antiquity (1). McKinney and Butterworth (2009) concur, noting that scenographic innovation has been directed by the 'gradual and continual incorporation of materials and technologies' (128).

Traditionally, the relationship between performance and technology has not been an easy one. Baugh (2013) cites a recurring anxiety about the role of the performer in technology-driven stage settings that stems from theatre's earliest origins. More recently, integrations of live performers and media technologies have inspired a certain uneasiness in the minds of the public. Writing more than two decades ago, Auslander (1999) describes 'the air of a melodrama in which virtuous live performance is threatened, encroached upon, dominated, and contaminated by its insidious Other, with which it is locked in a life-and-death struggle' (42). Giesekam (2007) similarly cites 'border disputes' between seemingly opposed artistic mediums (5), while Palmer (2006) suggests that technology is seen as 'detracting from the very "liveness" of the performance event, an unnecessary adjunct, and diversion from the primacy of the performer' (106). All three scholars were writing at a time that predated many of the digital technologies currently in use, but each refers to concerns about the status of the performer that remain relevant to modern-day discussions of digitally enhanced production.

Why opera?

Opera is the combination of a tangible written score (in itself, the combination of music and text) and an intangible live performance. Abbate (2003) identifies the relationship between the score and its performative manifestation as 'intrinsically antagonistic,' and anticipates unavoidable conflicts in the course of composition, realisation, interpretation, and reproduction (xvi). While the musical and textual aspects of an opera can be notated and thus achieve a relatively permanent form, stage interpretations are unfixed and changeable, shaped by performers, directors, designers, venue, budget, and audience. As a result, regardless of the artistic intentions of the original composer, librettist, or producer, opera is susceptible to deviations and even desecrations, particularly once beyond the lifetime and control of its creators.

In grappling with this conflict, Ridout (2012) suggests a two-pronged definition for opera: first, 'the work,' which denotes the compositional achievement (i.e., the musical score), and second, 'work,' which denotes the piece after it has gone into theatrical production (i.e., the musical score as interpreted on stage). Up until the 1960s, opera scholars prioritised 'the work' in their research, viewing the tangible musical score as more legitimate than any performative manifestations (Till 2012). Even by the 1990s, most critical writing about opera continued to emphasise the score alone, rather than the score within the context of staged performance (Littlejohn 1994). Regardless of how a score is analysed or perceived, however, opera ultimately requires performers, a stage, and an audience in order to be complete.

In the twenty-first century, opera as a genre remains largely defined by its historical repertoire and traditional production conventions. The operatic canon—a collection of works written by white male composers in the eighteenth, nineteenth, and early twentieth centuries—remains the mainstay of major opera companies worldwide. At The Royal Opera, for example, 74 per cent of all operas staged between the 2005/6 and 2019/20 seasons were written before the turn of the twentieth century (Royal Opera House Collections Online n.d.). While there are exceptions, opera is also most commonly produced in proscenium-based venues, in which the audience is seated at a distance while the action of the narrative occurs on stage (Agid and Tarondeau 2010).

Opera may seem to be an unlikely case study for an examination of digital scenography in the twenty-first century. Yet, spectacle, and in particular, technology-driven spectacle, has been a fundamental part of the genre since it first emerged as a commercial enterprise in the 1630s (Baker 2013). The genre has also long been defined by its scale, both in terms of the emotional arcs of its dramatic narratives and its scenographic requirements. As projection designer Elaine J. McCarthy explains, 'There's an emotion to it and a largesse that can handle projections. Opera tells the big stories. It can handle a 40-foot tall volcano exploding without upstaging the singers' (personal communication, May 23, 2020).

From an analytical perspective, opera's reliance on canonical works and historical production conventions also represents a unique opportunity to establish a benchmark of common practice around digital scenography. In opera, both genre and repertoire are reinterpreted and redefined by digital technologies, even while remaining entrenched in a traditional theatrical framework. This establishes a space-specific artistic constant around opera production, which enables a clear comparison and analysis of digital scenography in practice. With the conventions of music, venue, performers, and even repertoire firmly established, the disruptions caused by digital technology can be readily identified.

Digital scenography in opera has unquestionably been shaped by developments in theatre more broadly, particularly as creative practitioners often work across multiple fields. While acknowledging the impact and influence of theatre, it is important to outline some critical differences between the two genres. These differences directly affect the ways in which digital scenography is being realised on operatic stages, as well as the consequences for opera's production conventions.

The most obvious distinction between opera and theatre is that opera is inherently a musical art form. 'The genre is dominated by the work of the composer and then the interpretation of such by the director,' explains projection designer Sven Ortel (personal communication, May 21, 2020). In contrast to theatre, the musical director plays a major role in the realisation of the operatic work, with direct implications for opera's production requirements. As lighting designer Donald Holder notes, 'Many staging and production design decisions are driven by the needs of the maestro, singers and orchestra. In the theatre, it's usually all about the text' (personal communication, June 27, 2020).

Opera is also distinct from theatre in terms of its venues and production timelines. Operatic productions are generally produced in much larger spaces than standard theatre, with Donald Holder suggesting that most traditional opera stages are twice the size of a typical 'playhouse' venue (personal communication, June 27, 2020). Elaine J. McCarthy notes that opera is also characterised by a longer lead-time for design commissions. Commissions can be received as much as two or three years in advance, almost twice as long as commissions for theatre or Broadway productions (personal communication, May 23, 2020).

Finally, opera has a more limited timeframe for technical rehearsals in the lead-up to a production's premiere. 'A Broadway production of a play or musical may have several weeks of technical rehearsal time with the full cast, followed by 3–4 weeks of preview performances,' notes Holder. 'In most opera productions, stage time with the full company is limited to very few rehearsal days.' Holder cites The Metropolitan Opera as an example, noting that available stage time with the cast can be limited to as little as 15–20 hours total before a production premiere (personal communication, June 27, 2020).

While both design practitioners and practices can overlap from theatre, the conventions of the operatic genre require a very different benchmark for considering digital scenography in practice. Yet, there has been limited scholarship that specifically examines the use of digital scenography in opera. Digital scenography in performance more generally has been the subject of attention by scholars such as Auslander (1999), Baugh (2013), Causey (2006), Dixon (2007), and Salter (2010). These scholars primarily focus on multimedia theatrical performance, such as experimental works by The Wooster Group, Merce Cunningham, The Builders Association, Robert Lepage, and Dumb Type. Yet, none explore digital scenography within the unique context of opera or examine the relationship between digital scenography, opera's historical production conventions, and contemporary arts management.

The majority of existing scholarship that does consider opera focuses on non-scenographic digital topics, such as opera on high-definition (HD) broadcasts, in cinemas, or on television. Pérez (2012), for example, discusses opera's presentation on Italian television and in Italian film but does not discuss the use of digital technology specifically within operatic stagings. Citron (2010), Esse (2010), and Ward-Griffin (2014) similarly focus on the relationship between opera production and film, rather than digitally enhanced scenic designs.

Scholars that do examine digital scenography in opera production generally focus on experimental or avant-garde examples that are not applicable to wider industry practices. For example, Morris (2010) considers the hierarchy of live versus recorded opera performances, and Leipert (2017) analyses an experimental non-narrative video-opera that premiered in 2003. Notable exceptions include Morris' (2011) 'Wagnervideo,' which considers the future of opera mediality through a close analysis of Peter Sellar's digitally enhanced *The Tristan Project*. Wilson Smith (2012) and Poll (2018) also both explore digital scenography in their work on stage director Robert Lepage and his production of the *Ring* cycle for The Metropolitan Opera.

Given the limitations of existing scholarship around digital scenography in opera production, there is clearly a need for further research in this area. From an industry perspective, the stakes are also high. Digital technology is being framed as a solution to many of opera's deep-rooted problems, yet there is no scholarly framework for evaluating its use or consequences across the industry. This book aims to establish a much-needed benchmark of practice for digital scenography in opera that supports an analytical exploration of its broader implications for the genre.

Research methods

My investigation of digital scenography in opera production in the twenty-first century encompasses two key research questions. First, how is digital scenography currently being used on operatic stages? Second, does this use constitute a 'disruption' to existing operatic conventions, either on or off the stage?

This two-pronged approach involves a consideration of digital scenography not only as a dramaturgical outcome but in terms of its practical impacts on opera's production logistics. The research for this book therefore draws on a mixed methods approach that considers the dramaturgical and logistical processes of scenography, as well as the nature of the audience experience, the relationship between digital elements and live performers, and the historical developments specific to opera and multimedia performance.

The modes of synthesis

Given the importance of identifying trends around digital scenography in practice, my first methodological task for this book was to establish a means for mapping the use of digital elements in opera. My intent was to create a framework for assessing and comparing different digitally enhanced opera productions that would be fundamentally objective, distinct from any consideration of stylistic interpretation or aesthetic creative decisions.

Outlined in Chapters 1 and 2, the resulting classification system, *the modes of synthesis*, is based on the visual relationship that emerges between the live performer and any digital elements from the perspective of the spectator. The presence or absence of what I term 'causal interplay'—or a seemingly reciprocal relationship between live and digital elements—determines the specific mode of synthesis: non-synthesis, partial-synthesis, or full-synthesis. Because the modes of synthesis relate specifically to the visual relationship between the performer and digital elements from the perspective of the spectator, the classification system constitutes a practical means for evaluating and comparing productions that are drastically different in terms of repertoire and design.

My use of the term 'synthesis' intentionally aligns to the writings of twentieth-century practitioners Adolphe Appia and Josef Svoboda, both of whom posited an idealised theatrical experience that integrated the performer and stage setting for the benefit of the audience. In his 1921 essay on stage scenery, *Living Art or Dead Nature?*, Appia wrote, '... once the movement of the performers lends life to these spaces, and when they fuse before the visitor's eyes into a living *synthesis*, his doubt and former prejudice will be dispelled' (Beacham 2013, 120; italics mine). Svoboda outlined a similar goal for integrating film and live performers, writing, 'One thing is not the background for the other; instead you have a simultaneity, a *synthesis* and fusion of actors and projections' (McKinney and Butterworth 2009, 134; italics mine).

Both Appia and Svoboda are central figures in the development of theatrical scenography and are discussed at length in Chapters 3 and 4, along with Ferdinando Galli-Bibiena, Richard Wagner, Edward Gordon Craig, Enrico Prampolini, and Günther Schneider-Siemssen. As I argue, these historical antecedents play a critical role in our understanding of the functionality of digital scenography in opera in the present day, as well as the degree to which it constitutes a digital 'disruption' to production conventions. As such, the use of the term 'synthesis' as a central tenet of my classification system represents an acknowledgement of digital scenography's historical lineage and the ideals of past innovators in the field.

A number of other scholars and practitioners have proposed terminology to define the use of media or digital technology in performance. In 1966, Michael Kirby coined the term 'filmstage' to describe the integration of electronic media in theatre (Giesekam 2007). Performance art group Forkbeard Fantasy refers to 'crossing the celluloid divide' for their work that involves seeming interactivity between stage and screen (Forkbeard Fantasy n.d.). Auslander (1999) refers to the 'mediatisation' of live performance, while Chapple and Kattenbelt (2007) propose 'intermediality' to describe the layering of live and digital within a theatrical space. They further define the term's meaning as 'a meeting point in-between the performers, the observers, and the confluence of media involved in a performance at a particular moment in time' (12). In these cases, we can see how the interplay between the performers and any digital entities is consistently highlighted as a key component of media-enhanced performance.

However, with the exception of Dixon (2007) and Giesekam (2007), these discussions rarely extend to a consideration of the practical implications of using digital scenography. There is no connection made between, for example, Chapple and Kattenbelt's 'intermediality' or Auslander's 'mediatisation' and practical theatrical production, including dramaturgical impacts, backstage processes, or organisational management. Indeed, Giesekam (2007) highlights the absence of such discussions, citing the 'limited systematic exploration' of how projected technologies 'radically alter approaches to *mise-en-scene*, dramaturgy, performance, modes of production and spectatorship' (7).

This is where the modes of synthesis are useful for analysing the practical considerations of integrating digital scenography into opera production. The modes of synthesis function as a template for mapping the potential digital disruption to opera's onstage scenographic conventions. Outlined in Chapters 3 and 4, this analysis relies on a historiographic approach to establish a lineage of precedents for modern-day digitally enhanced opera, from the genre's earliest origins in seventeenth-century Italy to the end of the twentieth century. The discussion draws upon themes of historical research more generally, in which scholars acknowledge the importance of understanding the 'trajectory of circumstances' that has led to 'a phenomenon or a situation' (O'Brien, Remenyi, and Keaney 2004, 135).

The modes of synthesis then serve as a means for tracking the digital disruption to opera's offstage conventions, including creative hierarchies and production design processes. Drawing on interviews with practitioners in the field and detailed case studies of digitally enhanced productions, the discussion traces the correlation between the use of certain modes of synthesis in practice and subsequent variations to opera's longstanding production conventions. Design choices are not driven solely by administrative or economic structures but *are* ultimately limited by these. It is within these contexts that we can identify the greatest impacts and disruptions from the use of digital scenography in opera.

Examples of practice

Establishing the framework of the modes of synthesis required an extensive analysis of digitally enhanced opera productions. It was critical to examine the specific ways in which digital scenography is currently being employed by opera companies, particularly in terms of the visual relationship with live performers. In order to establish a cohort of recent examples of practice, I identified those productions presented by major opera companies worldwide since 2005 that explicitly credited a projection design practitioner within their creative team listings (e.g., projection designer, video designer, animator, etc.). The make-up of this cohort was then informed by each production's accessibility for analysis, via live, pre-recorded, or streamed performance.

Overall, I reviewed 63 different opera productions presented between 2005 and 2020 by 33 different opera companies, not including co-commissioning companies (see Appendix 1). The 33 companies vary by budget and size, with both major industry leaders and smaller regional companies represented. The total cohort of reviewed productions also spans a wide range of countries,[5] including the United States, Australia, France, Italy, England, Germany, Austria, Spain, and Belgium. Repertoire is similarly varied, representing 52 different operatic works from the Western opera tradition. A number of canonical works are represented multiple times, including

Mozart's *The Magic Flute* (five productions), Wagner's *Das Rheingold* (four productions), and Mozart's *Don Giovanni* (two productions).

Each production was presented in a traditional proscenium-based venue. These included black box theatre spaces, as well as more formal opera houses. In all cases, spectators assumed non-participatory roles and remained seated in the auditorium for the duration of the performance. While the modes of synthesis are equally applicable to productions in unconventional performance spaces, the shared use of traditional venues across the productions reviewed in this research enabled a clear comparison of digital scenography's use in practice, which aided the development of the modes of synthesis.

My process of content analysis involved viewing each opera production multiple times and tracking all instances of causal interplay evident in the production design. I assessed the nature of these instances to devise the three variants of causal interplay outlined in Chapter 2: agency, augmentation, and autonomy. Through this approach, I established a comparative benchmark for assessing digitally enhanced productions of varying scope and scale.

Out of the full cohort, I also selected 12 productions to function as in-depth case studies and examples of practice (see Appendix 2). These productions were chosen based on the degree to which they demonstrated a particular mode of synthesis or variant of causal interplay in practice. A further consideration was the availability of secondary material related to each production's use of digital scenography, including behind-the-scenes video footage or documentaries, industry features, critical reviews, and associated publications or catalogues. This combination of primary and secondary sources provided multifaceted perspectives of the creative motivations for scenographic decisions and the impacts of the modes of synthesis on hierarchies and production design processes. Selection of each case study was also informed by the availability of creative practitioners who were involved in each production to participate in semi-structured interviews.

Within this smaller cohort of case study productions, 11 different opera companies and seven different countries are represented. As with the larger sample, the United States is strongly represented, with five of the 12 productions presented by opera companies based in New York, Ohio, California, New Mexico, and Washington, DC. The case study opera companies also vary by budget and size, with several productions presented by regional organisations. The case study group is significantly less varied in terms of repertoire, with productions almost exclusively limited to operas that contain fantastical or supernatural elements. Productions of Mozart's *The Magic Flute*, for example, make up a third of productions included in this case study group.

The majority of the 63 digitally enhanced opera productions were viewed via video recording or streaming services. This enabled repeat viewings, as well as a close analysis of the relationship between the live performers and digital elements. While such recordings provide visual records of a live production in terms of its scenographic design, they are unquestionably limited in their ability to preserve an ephemeral performance experience. Much scholarly discussion has outlined the problematic nature of using recorded or streamed performance as a source of analysis due to the detachment of the viewer from the live experience and restrictions on the viewer's gaze (Esse 2010; Read 2014). Given these limitations, I supplemented these production recordings with first-hand interviews from creative practitioners (as noted above and discussed further below), as well as production photographs, critical reviews, and other secondary source materials.

The reliance on recorded formats initially created a substantial imbalance in the kinds of productions that could be included in the discussion. Only top-tier opera companies generally produce professional recordings of their performances, as this expenditure is generally outside budgetary scope for smaller companies. As a result, the sample is dominated by productions from well-funded companies that maintain live streaming or HD broadcast programmes. These include The Metropolitan Opera and The Royal Opera, Covent Garden, as well as European companies that are partnered with the free streaming service OperaVision.

This imbalance was somewhat resolved by the COVID-19 pandemic in 2020. With the closure of many physical venues in Europe, the United States, and Australia, numerous opera companies shifted to online streaming models and posted archival footage of past productions on YouTube and other social media channels (Vincent 2020). This enabled the inclusion of several additional productions by smaller companies into the overall sample, which would not have been otherwise accessible for review. These included digitally enhanced productions by Beth Morrison Projects, Philadelphia Opera, Sydney Chamber Opera, and Glyndebourne Festival, among others.

Another limitation of the study is the low representation of opera companies outside of the United States, Western Europe, and Australia. Only two productions from Asia are included in the sample—one in Hong Kong and one in China—while none are included from South America or Russia. This absence is largely due to a lack of access to the necessary production footage, either via live performance or streaming platforms, as well as language obstacles that prevented the review of relevant secondary source materials.

Despite these limitations, the overarching data sample represents a wide range of companies and countries operating within the Western opera tradition, particularly across Europe and the United States. While the reviewed productions cannot be said to be representative of every dramaturgical potential for the use of digital scenography, they provided a sufficiently broad sample of current practice in the field to establish the modes of synthesis as a framework for critical comparison.

Interviews

Interviews have traditionally comprised a major part of research methodologies in the field of scenography. 'Much of the existing knowledge and understanding about scenography is bound up with its practice and with the tacit knowledge of scenographers,' note McKinney and Iball (2011, 119). As projection design is still an emerging field in performance studies, it was critical to rely on first-hand accounts from creative practitioners as a way of tracking current activity in the field. These interviews provided crucial insight into the practical inner workings of digital scenography and the disruption posed by advancing technologies from the perspective of practitioners themselves.

Each of the creative practitioners interviewed for this book maintains McKinney and Iball's 'tacit knowledge' of opera production, codified over the course of their professional careers. This includes an understanding of aesthetic opportunities and challenges, as well as the effects of digital technology on creative workflows and production design processes. Their experiences also presented an opportunity to consider broader trends across the opera industry, as many of the creative practitioners have been employed by some of the most prominent opera companies in the world.

I interviewed 18 creative practitioners currently active in the opera industry (see Appendix 3). This included 10 projection designers, video designers, or animators; four stage directors; one set designer; one production designer who works across set, costume, and video design; and two lighting designers. Potential participants were identified by two characteristics: (1) high profiles in the opera industry, and (2) involvement in digitally enhanced productions at major opera companies over the course of their careers. To supplement the perspectives of strictly creative practitioners, I also interviewed two performers who were involved in digitally enhanced productions and could speak to the impact on their personal practice, as well as two executive directors who produced touring productions of Komische Oper Berlin's digitally enhanced *The Magic Flute* in 2019. Interviews were conducted between September 2016 and September 2020, with a number of follow-up discussions with individual practitioners via email.

Given my focus on digital scenography, projection design practitioners comprised the majority of the interview subjects. There are only a small number of prominent projection and video designers working in the field, and many of the same practitioners are repeatedly hired by the same opera companies. For example, video and projection designer S. Katy Tucker has worked on five productions for Washington National Opera at the Kennedy Center since 2014, video designer Finn Ross has worked on eight different productions at English National Opera since 2010, and 59 Productions (led by Mark Grimmer and Leo Warner) has provided video imagery for at least eight different productions at The Metropolitan Opera since 2008 (Metropolitan Opera Archives n.d.; Ross n.d.; Tucker n.d.). Many of these practitioners have also established strong collaborative relationships with specific designers or directors and have worked on multiple digitally enhanced productions as part of the same creative team. Filmmaker Luke Halls, for example, regularly collaborates with set designer Es Devlin and director Kasper Holten, while S. Katy Tucker has worked with director

Francesca Zambello at least 12 times since 2008 (Luke Halls Studio n.d.; Tucker n.d.).

The purpose of each interview was two-fold: first, to collect each individual's perspective around the experience of working with digital scenography in opera, and second, to identify commonalities that could help quantify larger trends around the technology's use in the field. During the interviews, participants were asked to describe the backstage processes employed for specific digitally enhanced opera productions, including creative hierarchy, timeline, and design process. For productions that incorporated causal interplay between live performers and digital elements (see Chapters 1 and 2), practitioners were also asked to describe the process of conceiving and designing key moments of interactivity. All interview transcripts were coded to establish commonalities across participant responses. These findings directly informed the analytical discussions of creative hierarchies and production design processes in Chapters 5 and 6, as well as key case study examples.

In order to expand the scope of qualitative data and, in particular, to source perspectives from stage directors and designers who were unavailable for interviews, I also drew on existing secondary source material. This included publications written by artists William Kentridge and Jun Kaneko relating to their respective digitally enhanced productions of *The Magic Flute*, as well as published interviews with stage directors Barrie Kosky, Simon McBurney, Robert Lepage, Leonard Foglia, and Kasper Holten; and designers Es Devlin, Leo Warner, and Zachary Borovay.

Although the interviews cover a variety of creative and administrative roles, there are some absences. On the creative side, no costume designers are represented, with the exception of Victoria 'Vita' Tzykun, who works across set, costume, and video design. There are also no perspectives from musical conductors, who are significantly involved in the artistic realisation of an operatic work (see Chapter 5). On the administrative side, no artistic directors are represented, and the two executive directors, Carolyn Chard and Yarmila Alfonzetti, represent Australian opera companies that presented touring productions of Komische Oper Berlin's *The Magic Flute* but did not produce digitally enhanced productions themselves. Similarly, there is no representation of backstage practitioners, such as stage managers or stage crew, and only two interviews with performers. Interviews with individuals in these additional roles would provide further insight into the use of digital scenography and could support future research on the implications of integrating digital technology into opera production.

Chapter outline

This book aims to provide a critical understanding of current trends in digital scenography across Western opera production. The modes of synthesis provide a means for comparing different digitally enhanced productions through an objective scenographic lens, regardless of variations of budget, practitioners, or repertoire. This, in turn, allows for a consideration of the potential disruption of digital scenography to opera's longstanding production conventions, both on and off the stage.

Outlined in **Chapter 1**, the modes of synthesis meet the need for an analytical framework—or Giesekam's (2007) 'systematic exploration'—that considers the different dramaturgical potentials of digital scenography when incorporated into live performance (7). The classifications of non-synthesis, partial-synthesis, and full-synthesis each reflect a particular relationship between the live and the digital that is fundamental to the scenographic design and can be used to quantify the nature of what is happening on stage. To explore the interpretive opportunities and limitations of each mode in practice, I examine the digital designs used for three different digitally enhanced productions of Mozart's *The Magic Flute.*

In **Chapter 2**, I expand the classification system to consider three variants of causal interplay that address particular aspects of the relationship between the live and the digital. These variants—agency, augmentation, and autonomy—speak to some of the additional aesthetic opportunities for digital scenography on stage, which are informed by the choices of the creative team, as well as technical capabilities. Collectively, the modes of synthesis and variants of causal interplay help to establish a spectrum of possibilities for digital scenography and the integration of live performers with digital elements from the perspective of the audience.

In **Chapter 3**, I begin to explore the potential disruption of digital scenography to opera's onstage production conventions by mapping the historical lineage of opera's scenographic developments. Starting from the earliest paradigm of Baroque opera in the seventeenth century, the analysis traces opera's progression through subsequent scenographic innovations introduced by Ferdinando Galli-Bibiena, Richard Wagner, and Adolphe Appia. Each innovation represents a different approach to the interplay between the performer, stage setting, and spectator and anticipates pre-digital forms of the modes of synthesis in practice.

In **Chapter 4**, I continue to outline opera's scenographic lineage through the multimedia innovations of the twentieth century, including the avant-garde theories of Edward Gordon Craig and Enrico Prampoli, the kinetic stage of Josef Svoboda, and the early holographic experiments of Günther Schneider-Siemssen. This lineage establishes a framework for understanding digital scenography's contemporary context through the past innovations that informed and shaped its development. In the course of the analysis, I find that the use of digital scenography in modern-day opera production does not ultimately function as a disruption but rather as the latest iteration of technology-driven developments in opera design.

In the final two chapters of the book, I explore the potential disruption of digital scenography to opera's backstage processes. In **Chapter 5**, I consider opera's creative hierarchies and the consequences of introducing both projection design and projection designers into the traditional hierarchical structures that have historically dominated opera production. Drawing on interviews with creative practitioners, I identify the nature of this digital disruption and outline a correlation between the modes of synthesis and varying impacts on standard creative hierarchies.

In **Chapter 6**, I examine production design processes and draw on in-depth analyses of five case studies in order to map commonalities across different productions and practitioners. The analysis reveals that backstage processes vary widely and are most often shaped by the preferences of those involved. However, as with creative hierarchies, there is evidence of a clear disruption prompted by the use of digital technologies. Drawing on practitioner interviews, I identify a correlation between the use of causal interplay and the need for a shift in existing production conventions.

In the Conclusion, I consider some extreme forms of digital scenography and the modes of synthesis, including extended realities and digital performance platforms. I propose certain recommendations for how the modes of synthesis might be leveraged to improve organisational understandings of digital scenography and enable the continued experimentation and evolution of digitally enhanced opera production in the future.

Notes

1 Examples include digitally enhanced productions at the University of Kansas (2003), the Théâtre Royal de la Monnaie (2005), San Francisco Opera (2012), Komische Oper Berlin (2012), Festspielhaus Baden-Baden (2013), Dutch National Opera (2013), Opera Colorado (2015), Lyric Opera of Chicago (2016), Opera Maine (2019), and the Salzburg Festival (2020) (Operabase n.d.; *Opera News* n.d.).
2 Examples include digitally enhanced productions at Opernhaus Zürich (2012), English National Opera (2012), San Francisco Opera (2013), Scottish Opera (2013), Calgary Opera (2014), Victorian Opera (2015), Finnish National Opera (2016), Teatro Real de Madrid (2016), Houston Grand Opera (2018), and Opera San José (2018) (*Opera News* n.d.).
3 Examples include digitally enhanced productions at Teatro alla Scala (2010), The Metropolitan Opera (2010–2012), San Francisco Opera (2011), Houston Grand Opera (2013), Washington National Opera (2016), Bayreuth Festspielhaus (2016), Opera North (2016), and Arizona Opera (2018) (*Opera News* n.d.).
4 These early effects were not the equivalent of modern-day digital scenery, but aspects of their use are analogous to current manifestations.
5 These figures do not include any revival stagings or tours to other countries following initial performance runs, which significantly extend the international reach of these productions.

References

1927. n.d. "The Magic Flute." Accessed August 13, 2020. https://www.19-27.co.uk/the-magic-flute.

Abbate, Carolyn. 2003. *In Search of Opera*. Princeton: Princeton University Press.

Agid, Philippe, and Jean-Claude Tarondeau. 2010. *The Management of Opera: An International Comparative Study.* Basingstoke: Palgrave Macmillan.

Aronson, Arnold. 2008. *Looking Into the Abyss: Essays on Scenography.* Ann Arbor: University of Michigan Press.

Aronson, Arnold, ed. 2018. *The Routledge Companion to Scenography.* Abingdon: Taylor & Francis.

Auslander, Philip. 1999. *Liveness: Performance in a Mediatized Culture.* New York: Routledge.

Bailey, Michael. 2018. "Opera Goes Digital: Lyndon Terracini Plan to Attract Millennials." *Financial Review,* August 17, 2018. https://www.afr.com/life-and-luxury/arts-and-culture/opera-goes-digital-lyndon-terracini-plan-to-attract-millennials-20180815-h140ni.

Baker, Evan. 2013. *From the Score to the Stage: An Illustrated History of Continental Opera Production and Staging.* Chicago: University of Chicago Press.

Barbour, David. 2011a. "The Prevalence of Projections: Projection in the Theatre is Nearly as Old as Theatre Itself, but Recent Technological Advances Have Made It Easier to Use—and Misuse." *American Theatre Magazine* 28, no. 10 (December): 28–33.

Barbour, David. 2011b. "The Road to Valhalla." *Lighting and Sound America,* January 2011. http://www.lightingandsoundamerica.com/metoperaringcycle.pdf.

Baugh, Christopher. 2013. *Theatre, Performance and Technology: The Development of Scenography in the Twentieth Century.* New York: Palgrave Macmillan.

Beacham, Richard C. 2013. *Adolphe Appia: Texts on Theatre.* London: Routledge.

Brock, Wendall. 2011. "Atlanta Opera to Mount High-Tech 'Porgy and Bess.'" *Atlanta Journal-Constitution,* February 10, 2011. https://www.atlantaopera.org/media/pdf/Access_02.10.11pdf.pdf.

Brook, Peter. 1996. *The Empty Space.* New York: Touchstone.

Causey, Matthew. 2006. *Theatre and Performance in Digital Culture: From Simulation to Embeddedness.* London: Routledge.

Chapple, Freda, and Chiel Kattenbelt, eds. 2007. *Intermediality in Theatre and Performance.* 3rd ed. Amsterdam: Editions Rodopi B.V.

Citron, Marcia J. 2010. *When Opera Meets Film.* Cambridge: Cambridge University Press.

Collins, Jane, and Andrew Nisbet, eds. 2010. *Theatre and Performance Design: A Reader in Scenography.* London: Routledge.

Curran, Paul, dir. 2015. *La Donna Del Lago,* by Gioachino Rossini and Andrea L. Tottola. DVD. The Metropolitan Opera. Warner Classics/Parlophone.

De Ana, Hugo, dir. 2019. *Il Trovatore,* by Giuseppe Verdi and Salvadore Cammarano. Streaming video. National Centre for the Performing Arts, Beijing, China. https://operavision.eu/en/library/performances/operas/il-trovatore-ncpa-beijing.

Department of Communications and the Arts. 2016. *National Opera Review Final Report.* Commonwealth of Australia. https://www.arts.gov.au/sites/g/files/net1761/f/national_opera_review_final_report.pdf.

Dixon, Steve. 2007. *Digital Performance: A History of New Media in Theater, Dance, Performance Art, and Installation.* Cambridge: MIT Press.

Esse, Melina. 2010. "Don't Look Now: Opera, Liveness, and the Televisual." *The Opera Quarterly* 26, no. 1: 81–95. https://doi.org/10.1093/oq/kbq014.

Forkbeard Fantasy. n.d. "Forkbeard's Use of Film." Accessed November 15, 2018. http://www.forkbeardfantasy.co.uk/useoffilm1.php.

Galvin, Nick. 2018. "Facing the Music: Opera Australia Makes Its Boldest Move." *Sydney Morning Herald*, July 13, 2018. https://www.smh.com.au/entertainment/opera/facing-the-music-opera-australia-makes-its-boldest-move-20180709-h12f6j.html.

Giesekam, Greg. 2007. *Staging the Screen: The Use of Film and Video in Theatre.* Basingstoke: Palgrave Macmillan.

Guth, Claus, dir. 2017. *La Bohème*, by Giacomo Puccini, Giuseppe Giacosa, and Luigi Illica. Streaming video. Opéra National de Paris, France. https://www.medici.tv/en/operas/puccini-la-boheme-opera-de-paris/.

Hann, Rachel. 2019. *Beyond Scenography.* Routledge: Abingdon.

Holten, Kasper, dir. 2014. *Don Giovanni*, by Wolfgang A. Mozart and Lorenzo da Ponte. DVD. The Royal Opera House, London. Opus Arte.

Howard, Pamela. 2002. *What Is Scenography?* New York: Routledge.

Kors, Stacey. 1999. "Monsters of Grace." *Salon*, July 21, 1999. https://www.salon.com/1999/07/21/monsters.

Leipert, Trent. 2017. "The Submerged Subject of Video-Opera: Fausto Romitelli's *An Index of Metals.*" *The Opera Quarterly* 33, no. 2: 161–183. https://doi.org/10.1093/oq/kbx028.

Littlejohn, David. 1994. *The Ultimate Art: Essays Around and About Opera.* Berkeley: University of California Press.

Love, Catherine. 2017. "Why Video Is Getting a Bigger Part in Theatre." *The Stage*, February 20, 2017. https://www.thestage.co.uk/features/2017/video-getting-bigger-part-theatre/.

Luke Halls Studio. n.d. "About." Accessed November 22, 2018. http://lukehalls.com/about/.

McAuley, Gay. 2000. *Space in Performance: Making Meaning in the Theatre.* Ann Arbor: University of Michigan Press.

McClung, Don, dir. 2017. *Opera Reimagined: Animating the Cunning Little Vixen.* Documentary, 26:47. WVIZ/PBS Ideastream.

McKinney, Joslin, and Philip Butterworth. 2009. *The Cambridge Introduction to Scenography.* Cambridge: Cambridge University Press.

McKinney, Joslin, and Helen Iball. 2011."Researching Scenography." In *Research Methods in Theatre and Performance*, edited by Baz Kershaw and Helen Nicholson, 111–136. Edinburgh: Edinburgh University Press.

Metropolitan Opera Archives. n.d. Accessed April 2017. http://archives.metoperafamily.org.

Midgette, Anne. 1999. "Theater; A Procession of Elusive Images From the Merlin of Surreal Form." *New York Times*, July 4, 1999. https://www.nytimes.com/1999/07/04/theater/theater-a-procession-of-elusive-images-from-the-merlin-of-surreal-form.html.

Morgan, Joyce. 2017. "Changing the Tune: Opera Companies Find New Ways to Draw Audiences." *Sydney Morning Herald*, August 9, 2017. https://www.smh.com.au/entertainment/opera/changing-the-tune-opera-companies-find-new-ways-to-draw-audiences-20170808-gxrhba.html.

Morris, Christopher. 2010. "Digital Diva: Opera on Video." *The Opera Quarterly* 26, no. 1: 96–119. https://doi.org/10.1093/oq/kbq002.

Morris, Christopher. 2011. "Wagnervideo." *The Opera Quarterly* 27, no. 2–3 (Spring–Summer): 235–255. https://doi.org/10.1093/oq/kbr016.

O'Brien, John, Dan Remenyi, and Aideen Keaney. 2004. "Historiography—A Neglected Research Method in Business and Management Studies." *Electronic Journal of Business Research Methods* 2, no. 2: 135–144.

Opera America. 2017. "What Do Millennials Want? Findings from The Wallace Foundation." *Opera America Magazine*, July 11, 2017. https://medium.com/@OPERAAmerica/what-do-millennials-want-69623590d458.

Operabase. n.d. "Production Archives—Companies." Accessed 20 August 2020. https://www.operabase.com/en.

Opera News. n.d. "Archives—In Review." Accessed 15 July 2018. https://www.operanews.com/operanews/templates/archives.aspx.

Palmer, Scott. 2006. "A Place to Play: Experimentation and Interactions Between Technology and Performance." In *The Potentials of Space: The Theory and Practice of Scenography and Performance*, edited by Alison Oddey and Christine White, 105–120. Bristol: Intellect.

Palmer, Scott. 2018. "Light and Projection." In *The Routledge Companion to Scenography*, edited by Arnold Aronson, 48–61. Abingdon: Taylor & Francis.

Payne, Nicholas. 2005. "Opera in the marketplace." In *The Cambridge Companion to Twentieth-Century Opera*, edited by Mervyn Cooke, 306–320. Cambridge: Cambridge University Press.

Pérez, Héctor Julio, ed. 2012. *Opera and Video: Technology and Spectatorship*. Bern: Peter Lang.

Poll, Melissa. 2018. *Robert Lepage's Scenographic Dramaturgy: The Aesthetic Signature at Work*. Cham: Palgrave Macmillan.

Pont, Grégoire, and James Bonas, dir. 2016. *L'Enfant et les Sortilèges*, by Maurice Ravel and Colette. Streaming video. Opéra de Lyon, France. https://www.france.tv/france-5/passage-des-arts/1385465-l-enfant-et-les-sortileges.html.

Read, Claire. 2014. "'Live, or Almost Live…': The politics of Performance and Documentation." *International Journal of Performance Arts and Digital Media* 10, no. 1: 67–76.

Rich, Alan. 1998. "Monsters of Grace." *Variety*, April 20, 1998. https://variety.com/1998/music/reviews/monsters-of-grace-1117467398/.

Ridout, Nicholas. 2012. "Opera and the Technologies of Theatrical Performance." In *The Cambridge Companion to Opera Studies*, edited by Nicholas Till, 159–178. Cambridge: Cambridge University Press.

Ross, Finn. n.d. "Finn Ross." Accessed November 22, 2018. https://www.behance.net/finnross.

Royal Opera House Collections Online. n.d. Accessed August 2018. http://www.rohcollections.org.uk/Performances.aspx.

Salter, Chris. 2010. *Entangled: Technology and the Transformation of Performance*. Cambridge: MIT Press.

Sgourev, Stoyan V. 2013. "The Dynamics of Risk in Innovation: A Premiere or an Encore?" *Industrial and Corporate Change* 22, no. 2: 549–75. https://doi.org/10.1093/icc/dts021.

Shaw, Dougal. 2012. "Digital Drama: The Technology Transforming Theatre." *BBC News*, March 27, 2012. http://www.bbc.com/news/technology-17079364.

Sillman, Marcie. 2017. "At Seattle Opera, the Real Drama Is Offstage." *Kuow*, March 29, 2017. http://archive.kuow.org/post/seattle-opera-real-drama-offstage.

Stewart, James B. 2015. "A Fight at the Opera." *New Yorker*, March 23, 2015. https://www.newyorker.com/magazine/2015/03/23/a-fight-at-the-opera.

Till, Nicholas. 2012. "The Operatic Work: Texts, Performances, Receptions and Repertories." In *The Cambridge Companion to Opera Studies*, edited by Nicholas Till, 225–256. Cambridge: Cambridge University Press.

Trevisan, Paola. 2017. *Reshaping Opera: A Critical Reflection on Arts Management.* Newcastle upon Tyne: Cambridge Scholars Publishing.

Tucker, S. Katy. n.d. "Biography." Accessed November 22, 2018. http://www.skatytucker.com/biography/.

Vincent, Caitlin. 2020. "Giving It Away For Free—Why the Performing Arts Risks Making the Same Mistake Newspapers Did." *The Conversation*, June 4, 2020. https://theconversation.com/giving-it-away-for-free-why-the-performing-arts-risks-making-the-same-mistake-newspapers-did-139671.

Vincent, Caitlin, Jordan Beth Vincent, Katya Johanson, and Kim Vincs. 2017. The Intersection of Live and Digital: New Technical Classifications for Digital Scenography in Opera." *Theatre and Performance Design* 3, no. 3: 155–171. https://doi.org/10.1080/23322551.2017.1400764.

Vincent, Jordan Beth, Caitlin Vincent, Kim Vincs, and John McCormick. 2016. "Navigating Control and Illusion: Interactivity Versus 'Faux-Interactivity' in Trans-Media Dance Performance." *International Journal of Performance Arts and Digital Media* 12, no. 1: 44–60. https://doi.org/10.1080/14794713.2016.1161955.

von Rhein, John. 1999. "'Monsters of Grace': One Performance, Two Vastly Different Reviews." *Chicago Tribune*, March 8, 1999. https://www.chicagotribune.com/news/ct-xpm-1999-03-08-9903080037-story.html.

Wallace, Robert K. 2013. *Heggie and Scheer's Moby Dick: A Grand Opera for the Twenty-First Century.* Denton: University of North Texas Press.

Walne, Graham. 1995. *Projection for the Performing Arts.* Waltham: Focal Press.

Ward-Griffin, Danielle. 2014. "Virtually There: Site-Specific Performance on Screen." *The Opera Quarterly* 30, no. 4: 362–368. https://doi.org/10.1093/oq/kbv001.

Westwood, Matthew. 2018. "Opera Australia's *Aida:* Digital Effects Cuts Costs, Lift Wow Factor." *The Australian*, July 14, 2018. https://www.google.com.au/amp/s/amp.theaustralian.com.au/arts/review/opera-australias-adia-digital-effects-cuts-costs-lift-wow-factor/news-story/bb2c74410cf2525bd346d299d8a15e8b.

Wilson, Robert, dir. 2018. *Turandot*, by Giacomo Puccini, Giuseppe Adami, and Renato Simoni. Streaming video. Teatro Real de Madrid, Spain. https://www.france.tv/spectacles-et-culture/1142637-turandot-de-puccini-par-robert-wilson-au-teatro-real-de-madrid.html.

Wilson Smith, Matthew. 2012. "Gesamtkunstwerk and Glitch: Robert Lepage's 'Ring' across Media." *Theater* 42, no. 2: 65–77. https://doi.org/10.1215/01610775-1507793.

Winn, Steven. 2015. "Sight and Sound at Odds in Colorful Take on *The Magic Flute.*" *San Francisco Classical Voice*, October 21, 2015. https://www.sfcv.org/reviews/san-francisco-opera/sight-and-sound-at-odds-in-colorful-take-on-lt-em-gt-the-magic-flute-lt-/em-gt.

1 A new classification system for digital scenography

The modes of synthesis

The extent to which digital technologies can be integrated into an operatic production varies, as do the dramaturgical and administrative implications. The scope of possible variations presents a major obstacle to any attempt to classify different digitally enhanced productions. How can one approach a comparison of the projected backgrounds in Teatro alla Scala's *Madama Butterfly* (2016) with the live video feeds used in Beth Morrison Projects and LA Opera's chamber opera *Dog Days* (2015) (Woodruff 2015; Hermanis 2016)? Or the fantastical animated drawings in the Théâtre Royal de la Monnaie's *The Tale of Tsar Saltan* (2019) with Violetta and Alfredo's projected social media conversation in Opéra National de Paris' *La Traviata* (2019) (Stone 2019; Tcherniakov 2019)? Each production is a reflection of a different creative team, a different venue and presenting company, and a different operatic work. Most importantly, each represents a very different use of digital technology within a scenographic design.

Given the perception of digital technology as a seeming magic bullet for the opera industry, a basic framework to identify and standardise some of these dramaturgical possibilities is necessary. Such a framework will allow for the critical comparison and analysis of digitally enhanced productions, regardless of repertoire, aesthetic, or other variables.

A number of efforts have been made to categorise productions that use projected elements across varying performance genres (see Auslander 1999; Chapple and Kattenbelt 2007; Jacquemin and Gagneré 2007; Oliszewski and Fine 2018). However, the majority of these classifications are not aligned with dramaturgical impacts or practical considerations from an administrative perspective. One exception is Giesekam (2007) who suggests that digitally enhanced theatrical productions can be classified as either 'multimedial' or 'intermedial' (10).

In a multimedial production, Giesekam argues, projected elements assume a similar role to sets and lighting and help to establish a particular visual environment that supports the narrative of the work. In contrast, an intermedial production employs significant interplay between digital components and performing bodies to the extent that neither can be said to exist independently within the theatrical space. Giesekam acknowledges that

DOI: 10.4324/9781003093305-1

some productions may draw on both techniques simultaneously. As such, he suggests that 'multimedial' and 'intermedial' are best considered 'ends of a spectrum' of scenographic possibilities (8).

Applying Giesekam's framework to opera, we can compare The Metropolitan Opera's *La Donna del Lago* (2015), with its digital scenic vista that morphs from dawn to dusk over the course of the performance, to English National Opera's *The Sunken Garden* (2013), which incorporates extensive video sequences, 3D stereoscopic effects, and virtual performers (Smith 2013; Curran 2015). In this context, Giesekam's classification system provides an effective means for quantifying the differences between the two productions. *La Donna del Lago* clearly functions as a more conventional 'multimedial' production, which uses projections as the modern-day equivalent of a painted backdrop. *The Sunken Garden* operates as an 'intermedial' piece, integrating digital media with its live performers as part of an avant-garde and non-narrative aesthetic.

The dichotomy of 'multimedial' and 'intermedial' presents a useful starting point for a discussion of digital scenography in opera production. Given the scope of technological advancements since the publication of Giesekam's work, however, there is opportunity to expand upon his approach and examine some of the further possibilities for interactivity and exchange that now underpin digital processes. This opportunity also extends to a consideration of the practical implications of these dramaturgical decisions on backstage processes and opera's longstanding production conventions.

This chapter proposes an expansion of Giesekam's approach in which the classification of multimedial and intermedial is reconceived as *the modes of synthesis*. The modes of synthesis encompass three distinct categories—*non-synthesis, partial-synthesis,* and *full-synthesis*—each based on the relationship between the performer, the stage setting, and the spectator that is fundamental to understandings of scenography in practice. Each mode specifically considers the visual relationship, or 'synthesis,' that emerges between the live performer and the digital elements within the shared theatrical space.

This framework enables a more detailed analysis and comparison of different digital scenographies that may not be readily apparent from using only Giesekam's categories. This, in turn, provides a means for identifying trends in the way digital scenography is currently being used on operatic stages. With these benchmark categories in place, it becomes possible to consider the larger implications of digital scenography for the operatic genre, including its potential disruption to existing conventions, both on and off the stage.

This chapter begins by defining each mode of synthesis and outlining both scenographic characteristics and common dramaturgical uses. The chapter then applies the classification system to an analysis of three digitally enhanced productions of W.A. Mozart's *The Magic Flute*. Each production features extensive digital elements but exhibits a different mode of synthesis in practice. The analysis will demonstrate the practicality of the modes as a way of differentiating between digitally enhanced productions and contextualising the artistic choices made by their creative teams. In addition, the chapter will consider some of the challenges posed by each technique and explore the critical responses to their use.

Articulating the modes of synthesis: non-synthesis, partial-synthesis, and full-synthesis

Whether digitally enhanced or not, theatrical productions are traditionally framed for the gaze of the audience member, who perceives the convergence of performer, set, lighting, costumes, and projections within the context of the work. This is particularly evident in genres like opera that uphold the primacy of the proscenium stage, in which the spectator is visually engaged but physically detached from the world of the narrative. Only the performers share the same physical space and fictional setting as the various elements of the scenic design. Because of this physical overlap, the particular relationship between the live performers and digital elements can change in digitally enhanced productions, depending on the dramaturgical requirements of the work and the creative decisions of its director and designers. As this relationship evolves and develops on stage, so too does the resulting visual experience for the audience.

The modes of synthesis qualify this potential by identifying three forms of visual 'synthesis,' each of which stems from the visual relationship established between the live performers and digital elements. The specifics of this relationship are based on two broad functionalities, which I term 'visual correlation' and 'causal interplay.' Both of these functionalities prioritise the gaze of the spectator while also addressing the scope of interactivity that can develop between live performers and digital elements.

In *visual correlation*, live performers and digital elements function as coordinated 'layers' without either a sensory fusion (an 'immersive' experience) or an interactive one (a demonstration of agency or causality). A narrative connection between the two components frequently exists, but there is never evidence of an interactive relationship within the context of the narrative itself. As an example, in the first act of Polish National Opera's *Tosca* (2019), Cavaradossi sings an aria in which he compares the black eyes of his lover Tosca to a painting of Mary Magdalene (Wysocka 2019). As the performer sings, a video projection of Tosca's eyes (i.e., pre-recorded footage of the performer playing the role) appears on the set piece behind him. While there is clearly a narrative connection between the subject of Cavardossi's aria and the video imagery behind him, he never directly interacts with or acknowledges Tosca's projected eyes. Instead, the two elements function solely as coordinated visual layers for the audience.

In *causal interplay*, live performers and digital elements explicitly interact. The most common example of this kind of interaction is when one entity's behaviour (either digital or live) appears to prompt a corresponding response in the other. This establishes a shared spatial realm where the live and digital not only meet but co-exist as performers. The initial prompt for this reciprocal relationship between the live and the digital is frequently grounded in physical movement, such as when a live performer gestures and digital elements appear to respond accordingly. Instances of causal interplay can also be situational—achieved through the live performer's presence within immersive digital environments—or internalised, located within the live performing body itself.

The implication of causality differentiates this relationship from visual correlation, as the performer appears to 'cross the celluloid divide' from the perspective of the audience and engage directly with the digital elements (Forkbeard Fantasy n.d.). Consider, for example, the final scene in Glyndebourne Festival's *Vanessa* (2018), when Erika orders the Footman to cover the mirrors in the house (Warner 2018). The Footman reaches up to the side of the stage, makes an unhooking movement, and then appears to 'pull' a digital curtain across the back of the set and 'cover' the mirrors. This moment evokes an intentional causality between the live and the digital, in which one appears to physically engage with the other.

Another comparison of the difference between visual correlation and causal interplay can be seen in the use of projected live video footage in both Beth Morrison Projects and LA Opera's *Dog Days* (2015) and the Théâtre Royal de la Monnaie's *Lucio Silla* (2017). In the second act of *Dog Days*, the character Lisa sings to her reflection in a large mirror. Meanwhile, a video camera affixed to the mirror projects a close-up of the performer's face onto the back wall of the set, allowing the audience to observe Lisa's emotional distress through a cinematic lens (Woodruff 2015). In *Lucio Silla*, a similar technique is used to project live footage from a 'security camera' that is placed in Giunia's bedroom. This footage is projected onto a series of television screens on the lower level of the set, which the character Silla appears to review and 'rewind' in order to secretly watch Giunia (Kratzer 2017). In both productions, the audience is able to perceive the live video footage as a critical and intentional element of the scenographic design. Yet, it is only in *Lucio Silla* that causal interplay takes place; here, through the use of the 'security footage,' the live performer playing Silla appears to actively interact with the digital elements within the context of the narrative.

Like Giesekam's 'multimedial' and 'intermedial,' the modes of synthesis are not fixed benchmarks but function as a spectrum of dramaturgical possibilities, depending on the extent of visual correlation or causal interplay employed (see Figure 1.1). The classification of *non-synthesis* is essentially a variation of Giesekam's 'multimedial' classification and represents the most traditional permutation of digitally enhanced scenography. Digital elements can be used in a number of ways from a dramaturgical perspective: establishing a projected scenic environment, evoking a certain mood, reflecting the passage of time, providing psychological insight into key characters, and

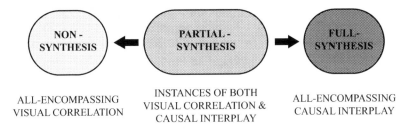

Figure 1.1 The modes of synthesis.

realising special effects, among other functions (Oliszewski and Fine 2018). However, the relationship between the live performers and digital elements is defined by all-encompassing visual correlation. Digital elements play a significant aesthetic role but remain detached from the performers. They are layered with the performers' physical presence from the perspective of the audience but never actively interact with them in a causal way.

In Finnish National Opera and Ballet's *Don Giovanni* (2020), for example, the staging for Leporello's catalogue aria takes place in front of a series of video projections of women's faces (Nikkilä 2020). The audience associates this visual overlay with Leporello's 'catalogue' of Don Giovanni's past conquests, but none of the performers on stage have any explicit interaction with the projected imagery. They neither acknowledge the projected faces nor prompt the faces' appearance through any physical behaviour. In another example, the Australian International Opera Company's *The Magic Flute* (2016) features seven projected scenic environments, including a fantastical jungle and palace courtyard (Vincent, McCormick, and Vincs 2016). As in *Don Giovanni*, however, the performers do not interact with the digital imagery in any way. Instead, their physical presence is simply overlaid with the digital environments projected behind them.

In both productions, the creative teams present the audience with a prepared experience that relies on their ability to recognise the visual correlation between the two elements. In the examples given above, there is a clear logic to the connection between performer and setting. The projected faces in *Don Giovanni* illustrate the premise of Leporello's aria as well as the licentious history of the titular character, while the jungle and courtyard in *The Magic Flute* establish the environmental setting required by the narrative. Importantly, the category of 'non-synthesis' does not necessarily require any such narrative connection between the live and the digital. The classification is intentionally independent of the degree of literality or abstraction in a production's scenography in order to avoid qualitative comparisons. Instead, the mode of non-synthesis reflects *any* scenographic design in which the relationship between the live performers and digital elements consists solely of layered visual correlation.

In a *partial-synthesis* production, the overall scenographic design actively integrates both physical and digital components on stage. While the relationship between the live and the digital can be defined by visual correlation at times, there are always instances of 'causal interplay' between the two components. At the beginning of The Metropolitan Opera's *Das Rheingold* (2010), the Rhinemaidens appear to emit cascades of digital bubbles (Lepage 2012). Creating the illusion that the performers are singing under water, the bubbles shift in size, location, and speed depending on each performer's physical movement. Similarly, in the penultimate scene of Dallas Opera's *Moby-Dick* (2010), three digital whale boats are projected along the curved back wall of the stage, while the sailors of the *Pequod* appear to sit inside them (Foglia 2010) (see Figure 1.2). When the boats are swamped by the digital white whale, the performers jump out of the 'capsized' boats, slide down the back wall, and appear to plunge into the depths of the projected ocean.

In these productions, the physical behaviour of the performers prompts or responds to specific actions programmed into the digital elements. This establishes the illusion of a shared spatial realm. The human-digital connection can be literal, as in *Das Rheingold,* with the bubbles reflecting a real-time interactivity prompted by sensory data captured during the live performance (Barbour 2011). Alternatively, this connection can be conceptual, as in *Moby-Dick*, grounded in what Vincent et al. (2016) term 'faux-interactivity,' or an illusion achieved through the combination of pre-rendered imagery and pre-determined choreography. The use of 'functional' versus 'faux' interactivity has implications for the backstage processes of these productions (see Chapter 2), but the resulting visual experience is the same for the audience.[1]

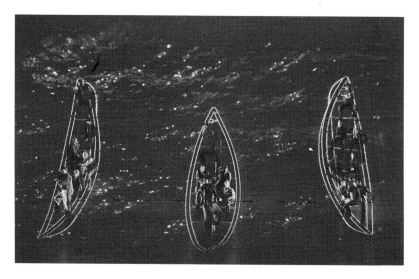

Figure 1.2 The sailors of the *Pequod* in Dallas Opera's *Moby-Dick*. Photograph © Karen Almond 2016 for Dallas Opera.

Both methods create a seemingly interactive exchange between the live and the digital that surpasses the juxtaposition of non-synthesis productions.

In partial-synthesis productions, digital elements are integral but not central to the overall experience. They extend the expressive possibilities of the stage setting and heighten the production's theatricality but augment rather than supplant the scenographic design. Instances of causal interplay may be used intermittently to highlight a significant narrative moment, emphasise a mood, convey a certain relationship, or resolve particular staging challenges. These moments require the audience to suspend disbelief as the scenic design shifts between causal interplay and visual correlation during the production's progression. As such, partial-synthesis productions are built on a fluidity of approach, in which digital enhancement is significant but not necessarily the defining dramaturgy of the entire work.

The final mode of synthesis represents the most extreme form of digital scenography in practice. What I term *full-synthesis* productions are characterised by the total integration of the live and the digital, both in terms of the nature of the scenographic design and in the scope of causal interplay employed between both elements. Komische Oper Berlin's *The Magic Flute* (2012), for example, uses a combination of interactive digital environments and animated digital characters to establish the total integration of its live performers and digital components. In the first act, the live performer playing Monostatos appears to hold the digital leash for three digital dogs while the live performer playing Pamina cowers on the digital landing of a digital staircase (Minnesota Opera 2014). Later in the opera, Sarastro appears to ride a digital elephant, Papageno uses a digital straw to drink out of a digital martini glass, and Tamino summons a digital magic flute as a shield against torrents of digital fire.

In addition to extensive interplay between the live performers and digital entities, full-synthesis productions often utilise instances of causal interplay that are grounded within the live performing body. In Komische Oper Berlin's *The Magic Flute,* the live performers playing the Three Spirits 'transform' into digitalised butterflies, while the Queen of the Night performs her vengeance aria with the digital body of a skeletal spider (Minnesota Opera 2014). Similarly, in Opéra de Lyon's *L'Enfant et les Sortilèges* (2016), the live performer playing the Squirrel is superimposed with a digital tail, and the figure of Maman is characterised as a giant digital hand (Pont and Bonas 2016). In these cases, the live performing body is inextricably linked and defined by the digital components from the perspective of the audience, and the worlds of live and digital become one. This connection is integral to the dramaturgy of a full-synthesis work.

It is useful to consider these three modes in the context of a single operatic work in order to better understand the dramaturgical impact of each in practice. The next section will examine three digitally enhanced productions of W.A. Mozart's *The Magic Flute*: Jun Kaneko's production for San Francisco Opera (2012), William Kentridge's production for the Théâtre

Royal de la Monnaie (2005), and Barrie Kosky and 1927's production for Komische Oper Berlin (2012). The analysis will consider how the use of different scenographic techniques and, in particular, the relative synthesis of the live and digital can change the aesthetic of a production and the resulting theatrical experience.

While a number of canonical operas are now commonly staged with digital elements, *The Magic Flute* was selected as a case study for two reasons. First, the plot of the opera involves a number of supernatural effects that naturally lend themselves to digital technology, including Tamino's opening battle with a serpent and the trials of fire and water in the second act. Second, the opera has an uncertain scenographic legacy in terms of production conventions and staging expectations (Eckelmeyer 1991; Hunter 2008). This has traditionally allowed for significant dramaturgical experimentation across different productions of the work.[2] As Liebner (1972) states, '*The Magic Flute* is like a mirror: anyone who looks into it, sees himself; and he will find in it whatever he is looking for' (228). This tradition of interpretative freedom provides an opportunity to apply the modes of synthesis to a wide range of artistic readings, in which the only scenographic commonality is the use of digital technology.

These particular productions of *The Magic Flute* were chosen because of the scale of the digital elements employed within their scenographic designs. Each production has also been staged by multiple opera companies worldwide since first premiering, which suggests a wide reach across both audiences and companies in the opera industry. As of 2020, Komische Oper Berlin's production had been staged by at least 20 different companies across Europe, China, the United States, and Australia (1927 n.d.). The Théâtre Royal de la Monnaie's production had been subsequently staged by ten different companies (Theunissen n.d.), and San Francisco Opera's production had been staged by at least four (San Francisco Opera Archives n.d.). Each production is also supported by extensive secondary materials, including critical reviews, practitioner interviews, and production design publications, all of which aided a critical analysis of their use of digital scenography in practice.

Non-synthesis—San Francisco Opera, *The Magic Flute* (2012)

In 2009, San Francisco Opera, with partner companies Washington National Opera, Lyric Opera of Kansas City, Opera Carolina, and Opera Omaha, commissioned Japanese ceramic artist Jun Kaneko to design a new production of *The Magic Flute* for a premiere in June 2012 (Rowe 2012). Kaneko's previous scenography for *Madama Butterfly* (2006) and *Fidelio* (2008) for Opera Omaha and Opera Company of Philadelphia, respectively, had also incorporated digital elements (Kaneko 2006; Kaneko 2008), but his designs for *The Magic Flute* drew on digital technology in a far more prominent way. The production incorporated 160 minutes of digital animation and 1,200 pieces of individual media, all projected onto nine screens over the course of the three-hour work (Kaneko 2012; Martinfield 2012). Kaneko's digital designs were the cornerstone of the production's publicity campaign, with San Francisco Opera billing *The Magic Flute* as the company's first 'all-digital' opera (Winn 2015).

Based on overlapping projections of colourful lines and geometric shapes, the scenography for *The Magic Flute* evokes an abstract sculpturalism that several critics compared to the work of Piet Mondrian (Vincent et al. 2017). As the opera begins, a single line of colour slowly moves across the projection surface, gradually followed by additional lines of colour, some moving parallel and perpendicular, others breaking off into sudden angles, until the entire screen is populated with a mass of grids, overlapping shapes, and blocks of colour. This aesthetic continues throughout the production, with digital lines, shapes, and colour blocks used as both scenic focal points and simple background animations. These designs also provide visual inspiration for the production's sculpturally abstract costumes and props, which Kaneko directly oversaw (Kaneko 2012).

When developing his scenographic design, Kaneko used hand-drawn storyboards to map out a series of fixed tableaus that traced the intended visual progression of the entire work. The process of animating the designs and linking the tableaus together was then outsourced to Clark Creative Group, an animation company in Nebraska, USA, with which Kaneko had previously collaborated on both *Madama Butterfly* and *Fidelio*. Head Video Editor Kevin Reiner highlighted Kaneko's fastidiousness in determining each aspect of the digital design, explaining, 'Jun is very specific in what he wants to see on the screen … He gives us the snapshots of what the video should look like and we fill in the blanks to make everything move' (Kaneko 2012, 32). In order to account for possible tempo changes from performance to performance, the majority of the animations were built on repeating 'loops,' so that each new animation could be triggered in real time by the stage manager.

Given the dominance of digital components in Kaneko's design, it would be tempting to classify San Francisco Opera's production as an example of full-synthesis. However, *The Magic Flute* does not employ any instances of causal interplay between its live performers and digital elements. Instead, the correlation between the two is purely visuo-temporal, based on a layering of live performing bodies and digital components, rather than any illusion of an interactive relationship.

In the Queen of the Night's first aria, for example, the live performer stands at a central point on the stage. As she sings, colourful lines spur out from a central position on the projection surface behind her (see Figure 1.3). The overlay of these two components creates a visual correlation for the audience, in which the Queen of the Night's physical presence is linked to an optical correlate in the projected scenery (Kaneko 2012). The live performer does not make any physical movements to prompt the response in

Figure 1.3 The Queen of the Night's first entrance in Jun Kaneko's *The Magic Flute.* Production premiered by San Francisco Opera (2012). Photograph © Scott Suchman for Washington National Opera.

the digital scenography nor does she acknowledge or react to the lines advancing across the projection surface behind her. Instead, the scenography employs the layering effect of the two components as a means for focusing the audience's gaze on the Queen of the Night at the origin point of the symmetrical design.

Similarly, in the final scene of the opera, a large orb of swirling orange lines is projected above the performers on stage. The image is clearly a reference to the words of the final ensemble, in which the chorus celebrates the triumph of the day (e.g., Sarastro, here characterised as a sun) over the night (e.g., the Queen of the Night) (Kaneko 2012). Again, the performers have no causal relationship with the projected digital effects, but the audience is able to understand the narrative connection between the singers and the sun-like orb projected behind them. In both scenes, the connection between the live and the digital is structured as a juxtaposition of image, performance, and sound. The digital design provides a distinct visual layer that runs parallel to the other elements of the opera but does not bridge the live–digital divide.

The use of all-encompassing visual correlation in the production is a reflection of Jun Kaneko's artistic intentions. Describing his inspiration for the work, Kaneko notes that he explicitly prioritised the music of the opera rather than its narrative when conceiving the digital imagery (Kaneko 2012). 'Developing an opera design starts simply by listening to the music until a visual image begins in my mind,' Kaneko (2012) explains. 'The design

I create needs to integrate with the music naturally and spontaneously so that we feel the music and design as one unified expression' (22). Kaneko's designs are not meant to distinguish between different scenic settings in a traditional way or to support the dramatic narrative of the opera. Instead, his designs relate to the harmonies and rhythms of Mozart's music: Papageno sings his opening aria against a field of horizontal lines, for example, while his duet with Papagena is set against a series of small black discs (Kaneko 2012).

Because Kaneko's projected backgrounds are abstract, rather than scenically realistic, and align to the music rather than the narrative of the opera, his digital scenography remains detached from the dramatic situations unfolding onstage. Accordingly, critic Anne Midgette (2014) described Kaneko's production as 'emotionally neutral' and noted that the performers are responsible for 'bring[ing] the characters to life and get[ting] the story across.' This 'neutrality' naturally aligns to the use of visual correlation, in which Kaneko's live performers and digital elements are visually layered but physically unintegrated.

Partial-synthesis—Théâtre Royal de la Monnaie, *The Magic Flute* (2005)

In contrast to San Francisco Opera's non-synthesis production, the Théâtre Royal de la Monnaie's production (hereafter La Monnaie) represents a clear demonstration of partial-synthesis through its use of both visual correlation and causal interplay. South African artist William Kentridge was commissioned to design the production in 1998 by then La Monnaie general director Bernard Foccroulle as a co-production of La Monnaie, Opéra de Lille, Théâtre de Caen, and Teatro di San Carlo in Naples (Law-Viljoen 2007). As an artist, Kentridge is known for his monochromatic drawings and prints, as well as his unique single-frame animation technique (Stevens 2006). Rather than drawing a series of cells as in traditional animation, Kentridge creates animated sequences from a single charcoal drawing, which he erases and redraws over a series of photographs (Midgette 2007). The resulting aesthetic, characterised by its blacks, whites, greys and mechanistic stop motion animation, evokes the early days of film and German expressionist artists such as Otto Dix and Max Beckmann (Stevens 2006).

Kentridge's scenographic concept for *The Magic Flute* centred on the theme of photography and the contrast between light and shadow, which he framed as a representation of the two narrative foils of Sarastro and the Queen of the Night (Rosenthal 2009). Kentridge's design utilises a significant physical set, which includes painted backdrops, perspective flats, and a moving walkway built into the stage floor. The flats and backdrops are modelled after Baroque opera productions and depict generic scenic landscapes. The flats also serve as front and rear projection surfaces for Kentridge's animations, as well as for shadow puppetry and an excerpt of Robert Schumann's 1911/12 film *Rhinoceros Hunting in German East Africa*

Figure 1.4 The Three Spirits guide Tamino in William Kentridge's *The Magic Flute.* Production premiered by Théâtre Royal de la Monnaie (2005). Photograph by Brescia and Amisano for Teatro alla Scala. © Teatro alla Scala.

(Roussel 2007). While the shadow puppetry is used to denote specific characters during scenic transitions, such as a puppet version of Papageno clambering over a mountain before the live performer's first entrance, the projected animations depict geometric shapes, diagrams, and scientific objects such as metronomes, hot-air balloons, and cameras (Holland 2007) (see Figure 1.4).

A number of Kentridge's scenographic designs rely on visual correlation. Sarastro's activity on stage, for example, is frequently layered against projections of scientific diagrams and instruments. The live performer has no interaction with the images projected behind him. Instead, the visual correlation of the two components is used to provide insight into Sarastro's character and his prioritisation of rational scientific thought. In these scenes, Kentridge employs visual correlation as a way of providing psychological context that supports the narrative for the audience: 'the image on the screen is what we imagine the singer seeing or thinking,' he explains (Kentridge 2007, 68).

The production also features several instances of causal interplay between its live performers and digital components. The most prominent example of this is the use of the physical moving walkway in tandem with projected scenic environments. When Pamina and Papageno escape from Monostatos in the first act, the performers begin to walk on the moving platform (Kentridge 2012). As they move, the projected scenery behind them also 'travels,' advancing through Kentridge's animations of a lush jungle environment until reaching the exterior of Sarastro's temple.

Here the digital scenography serves a logistical function by enabling a transition between scenic locations in the narrative. The parallel movement of the live performers and digital environment also positions the two components as part of a shared spatial realm. As the performers walk, the scenic background moves: an explicit demonstration of a physical prompt and response. Drawing on this simultaneous behaviour, Kentridge effectively establishes an interactive link between the live performers and their digital environment based on a causal relationship.

Kentridge's designs also involve a number of instances of causal interplay between live performers and specific digital entities. In the opening scene of the opera, the Three Ladies stand in front of a prop *cinématographe* and weave their arms in a beam of projected light, creating the illusion of a writhing serpent on the projected background (Kentridge 2012). Tamino's opening aria is then based on his fear of this shadowy virtual serpent, which the Three Ladies 'slay' by simply removing their arms from the light. The image of the shadow serpent is fully animated and not created by the Ladies in real time, but the staging of the scene is designed to imply a corresponding relationship between the Ladies' physical behaviour and the digital serpent's subsequent appearance.

Describing his rationale for this kind of interactive relationship, Kentridge (2007) explains, 'What makes the story come alive is when the singer leads the image, as if they are making it … When this happens successfully there is a sense of agency, of power, of making' (68). None of these instances of causal interplay are driven by real-time interactivity. Instead, they are achieved through a combination of pre-rendered imagery and predetermined staging. While only an illusion, however, the physical impetus and corresponding responses built into Kentridge's designs successfully establish a shared theatrical realm from the perspective of the audience.

Importantly, while Kentridge's live performers are often staged to summon or prompt digital elements through their physical behaviour, they never openly acknowledge the images on the projection surface behind them (Kentridge 2007). The Three Ladies, for example, never look directly at the serpent they create, instead focusing on their own hands within the beam of light. This is an intentional staging decision that Kentridge cites as a way of enabling the use of both causal interplay and visual correlation in practice. By limiting the scope of causal interplay for his performers, Kentridge is able to extend the dramaturgical possibilities of his scenograpahic design to allow for both the illusion of interactivity and the opportunity for visuo-temporal layering. Accordingly, the partial-synthesis production easily shifts between both functionalities, and the mode of interaction between performers and digital components remains in flux throughout the work.

Full-synthesis—Komische Oper Berlin, *The Magic Flute* (2012)

Komische Oper Berlin's production of *The Magic Flute* is similar to San Francisco Opera's production in terms of sheer scale of digital scenography. Like the nine projection screens used by San Francisco Opera, the set for Komische Oper Berlin's production consists entirely of projection surfaces, in this case a white wall with six hatches and ledges placed at various heights (Minnesota Opera 2014). While San Francisco Opera's production is limited to visual correlation, however, Komische Oper Berlin's *The Magic Flute* is built on the total integration of the live and the digital in the shared theatrical space.

Created in collaboration with Suzanne Andrade and Paul Barritt of London-based animation and production studio 1927, the aesthetic for *The Magic Flute* is very much a reflection of 1927's visual style, with two-dimensional animations that are inspired by the 1920s and suggestive of the Gothic work of Edward Gorey (Dobrin 2017). The production intentionally alludes to the silent film era: the opera's traditional spoken dialogue is replaced with projected text plates, and several characters are reimagined as figures from the era of silent film, including Pamina as Louise Brooks, Papageno as Buster Keaton, and Monostatos as Nosferatu (Kettle 2015) (see Figure 1.5).

In the production design, the total integration of the live and the digital is first established through all-encompassing digital environments. These not only serve as scenic backdrops but establish a spatial realm in which the live performers appear to interact with their virtual surroundings. This

Figure 1.5 Monostatos threatens Pamina in Barrie Kosky and 1927's *The Magic Flute*. Production premiered by Komische Oper Berlin (2012). Photograph © Scott Masterton for the Edinburgh International Festival.

interplay is enabled by the design of the physical set. The hatches and ledges allow the performers to assume spatial positions of varying heights within the projected scene. When Papageno and Pamina escape from Monostatos in the first act, for example, the two performers are positioned on the ledge of the central upper hatch. Their digital surroundings transform into a digital rooftop while Monostatos' digital henchmen lurk below. As the live performers begin their 'escape,' they kick their feet out from the ledge and appear to 'jump' onto a series of subsequent digital rooftops. The live performers remain stationary throughout the scene—fixed to the ledge with harnesses—but the combination of physical choreography and digital animation creates the illusion of a frenzied escape across the rooftops (Minnesota Opera 2014).

Tamino's opening scene with the serpent—in this case, a digital dragon—employs a similar combination of choreography and animation to establish the illusion of interactivity. Positioned on the stage floor, the live performer playing Tamino is partially obscured by a curved set piece that covers his legs and midsection. When the digital dragon appears on the projected surface behind him, the live performer begins to move his arms rapidly, and digital 'running' legs are projected onto the curved set piece (see cover image). As the dragon pursues, the projected forest environment begins to whirl in time with Tamino's running legs (Minnesota Opera 2014). The scenographic design first augments Tamino's physical body with digital elements, then links his physical movement—both the actual movement of his arms and the virtual movement of his digital legs—to the movement of his digital surroundings.

In addition to the digital environment and digitalised performing body, a third layer of causal interplay extends to the relationship between the live performer (here, the combination of live arms and virtual legs) and an external digital character (the dragon). The dragon is 'chasing' Tamino, which prompts Tamino's physical reaction, which, in turn, prompts the movement of the projected forest environment behind him. By simultaneously combining multiple forms of causal interplay, Barrie Kosky, Suzanne Andrade, and Paul Barritt ensure that their live performers are inextricably linked to every aspect of their digital surroundings. Physical set, digital imagery, and live performing body are linked by multiple modes of connection. The resulting effect is not a uni-directional causality (e.g., performer to digital element or digital element to performer), but a multi-layered interactivity in which the digital elements and live performer emerge as co-creative.

The digitalisation of Tamino's legs speaks to another prominent technique used in the production: fully and partially digitalised performing bodies. Several subsidiary characters are fully digitalised in the production, including Papageno's cat, Monostatos' dogs, Papageno and Papagena's fictional children, and the magic flute itself, which is characterised as a nude fairy. The live performers frequently interact with their digital counterparts, often appearing to physically touch or hold them. In their duet in the first act, for example, Papageno and Monostatos appear to physically restrain their digital pets from fighting each other, and Monostatos is eventually 'dragged' away by his dog.

A number of live performers are also partially digitalised at various points in the opera. Like Tamino, Papageno is presented with digitalised legs at a key narrative moment, and both Pamina and the Three Spirits appear to 'fly' with digital butterfly wings. The characterisation of the Queen of the Night is the most extreme example of this technique. Throughout the entire opera, only the live performer's head is visible to the audience. Meanwhile, her body is obscured in a white cocoon-like costume and superimposed with different digital forms depending on the context of the scene.

The production design requires the live performers to adhere to detailed choreography in order to maintain the constant illusion of causal interplay. In an interview, assistant stage director Tobias Ribitzki notes that every element of stage activity was fixed within the digital imagery long before the first staging rehearsal took place (personal communication, September 13, 2016). Staging was then a matter of teaching the performers the specific details of their pre-determined choreography (see Chapter 6 for a more extensive discussion of this production process).

Ribitzki highlights the scene with Monostatos and his digital dog as a particularly difficult moment in terms of staging. The performer playing Monostatos must 'hold' a taut digital leash with an extended arm and pretend to be dragged off stage in time with the digital dog's pre-determined pace and movement. As an additional challenge, the live performers in the production cannot look directly at the digital images with which they are interacting or they risk disrupting the illusion of visual integration (Kettle 2015). Instead, they must adhere to carefully coordinated movements to achieve the desired visual effects, while the audience alone witnesses the full-synthesis of the two components on stage. As the impact of the performer's embodiment of the role (i.e., the effort required to 'hold the leash taut') becomes embedded in the physicality of the performance itself, a further interactive layer between performers and digital elements is ingrained in the performance.

A comparison of critical responses to the three productions

All three productions of *The Magic Flute* employ digital technology as a fundamental aspect of their scenographic designs. Each application also demonstrates a different technique for integrating digital elements with live performers that directly affects the audience perspective. In many ways, Jun Kaneko's use of non-synthesis techniques for San Francisco Opera's production represents a fairly traditional permutation, in which digital scenography is used to establish an abstract background that is layered with the live performers through visual correlation. William Kentridge's partial-synthesis production for La Monnaie uses a more fluid approach, maintaining a certain detachment between the live performers and digital components but also employing instances of causal interplay at key moments. Barrie Kosky and 1927's full-synthesis production for Komische Oper Berlin reflects the most extreme use of digital scenography in dramaturgical terms. The result is a fully integrated theatrical experience in which the live performers are inextricably linked to and dependent on their digital counterparts.

The critical responses to the three productions examined in this chapter align with the kinds of reactions that typically accompany theatrical productions that use projected elements or media technology. Positive reviews generally laud the visual spectacle, while negative critiques reference a perceived threat to the primacy of the live performer. The following critical responses represent only a few of many that have been published since each production first premiered. Accordingly, it is difficult to draw definitive conclusions about the modes of synthesis and subsequent critical reception, particularly as reviewers are basing their critiques on the entire production experience, rather than solely the integration of live performers and digital technology. However, based on the select number of reviews examined for each production across their subsequent stagings, certain patterns emerge.

Critical responses to the visual components of San Francisco Opera's *The Magic Flute* were largely positive. Critics described the production as 'visually ravishing' (Scheinin 2012), 'explosively colorful' (Kosman 2012), and 'at once friendly and frenetic to the eyes' (Winn 2015). Yet, several expressed concerns about the seeming subordination of the live performers within Kaneko's digital designs. Midgette (2014) politely contended that the performers 'managed at least a draw' on the audience's focus, while Winn (2015) noted that the digital components 'dwarfed' the live singers. Downey (2014) was particularly negative about the visual dominance of the digital elements and complained that the production looked 'as if Kaneko just sprayed neon graffiti all over something.'

Non-synthesis productions represent the most traditional permutation of digital scenography in that they do not actively integrate the live performers and digital elements through causal interplay. Instead, digital elements are generally used to provide scenic background, atmospheric effects, or psychological context, all of which is layered with the action of the narrative. As such, one might expect the use of non-synthesis to be the least invasive in terms of the impact on live performers. Interestingly, the critical responses to Kaneko's production suggest the opposite: non-synthesis productions have the potential to utilise digital scenography in its most interfering form.

Because the live performing body and digital components are only linked through visual correlation, they can easily become competitive elements. This is exacerbated by problems of scale, in which the physical presence of any live performers is minimised by projections that fill the visual field of the stage, as well as by stylistic decisions, which may visually distract from the story and its characters. These issues are circumvented by the gentle aesthetic of some non-synthesis productions, such as The Metropolitan Opera's *La Donna del Lago* with its subtle scenic vista that gradually shifts from day to night over the course of the opera. Kaneko's bold, abstract style and intentional detachment from *The Magic Flute*'s narrative elements highlighted this disconnect, emphasising an inherently competitive relationship between the live performers and visual effects.

The scenography for La Monnaie's partial-synthesis *The Magic Flute* appears to have been received more positively overall. Schwartz (2007) described Kentridge's production as a 'beguiling meditation on the theme of Enlightenment,' while another critic complimented the use of digital elements to 'introduce the character, to put the background, to draw the towers, or to depict the images that run through the heads of protagonists' ('The Magic Flute' 2011). Nevertheless, as with Kaneko's designs, the production received negative comments related to the visual integration of the live and the digital.

One reviewer complained that the evening was 'stolen' by Kentridge's designs, and 'at any given time 90% of the audience were ignoring the singers on a visual level' (Spicer 2011). Another noted the lack of engagement between the performers and digital elements and described a 'nagging feeling of disconnect … the sense of distance between singers "in living color," and backgrounds of light and shadow only—all giving the impression of parallel but distinct worlds' (Holland 2007). Although the relationship between the live and the digital was not perceived to be as antagonistic as in San Francisco Opera's production, these critical responses still suggest a dissatisfaction with Kentridge's scenographic vision and its approach to integrating live performers with digital elements.

Of the three productions, Komische Oper Berlin's *The Magic Flute* received the most enthusiastic accolades. Maddocks (2015) described it as a 'tour de force,' Swed (2013) 'a hit,' and Farber (2016) 'a must see,' while Zasada (2014) contended that 'somewhere, up in musical heaven, Wolfgang is smiling.' Several reviewers referenced the constrained role of the live performers due to the dominance of the digital elements. Maddocks (2015) particularly noted how the partial digitalisation of the Queen of the Night and the Three Spirits required the performers to 'submit to the bigger stage picture.'

Overall, however, the comments remained largely removed from the 'air of melodrama' that Auslander (1999) anticipates in discussions of theatrical productions that showcase media technology. Critics Swed (2013) and Woolfe (2013), for example, both mentioned the demands posed by the detailed choreography, but neither classified the relationship between the live performers and digital components as one of competition or interference. Instead, Woolfe simply noted that the performers are 'fitted into a fanciful vision of animation,' while Swed suggested the piece is best suited to young performers who can tackle the staging challenges.

Based on these select reviews, the full-synthesis demonstrated by Komische Oper Berlin's production appears to establish a more equitable relationship between the live and the digital than San Francisco Opera's

non-synthesis production or even La Monnaie's partial-synthesis production. Because of the close integration of the two components in Komische
Oper Berlin's *The Magic Flute*, neither is distinguishable as an independent
or opposing force within the scenographic design.

Still, in order to achieve this complete integration, the extreme of full-
synthesis places significant demands on the performer. The digital components in Komische Oper Berlin's production are 'faux-interactive':
pre-determined and not responsive in real time (Vincent et al. 2016). This
means that the illusion of interactivity depends on the actions of the live performers, who must sacrifice their physical autonomy for the sake of the audience's visual synthesis. 'Critics would say we reduce our performers to mere
puppets within the animated world. This is of course entirely true,' notes
1927 animator Paul Barritt (Babbs 2012). Even though full-synthesis might
be perceived as the least competitive form of digital scenography due to its
close integration of live and digital elements, the technique still exemplifies
concerns that live performers will become puppets in the digital realm.

Conclusion

The classifications of non-synthesis, partial-synthesis, and full-synthesis
provide an initial framework for assessing the possibilities of digital scenography in performance. The classification system marks the distinction
between the technological scale and sophistication used in a production and
the dramaturgical construction of the performance–technology relationship. By basing this system on the scope of causal interplay between the live
and the digital from the audience perspective, it becomes possible to categorise and compare digitally enhanced productions from a position of critical
distance, without resorting to subjective considerations.

However, there is clearly a need to interrogate additional nuances of digital scenography and, in particular, the underlying characteristics of the
modes of synthesis. If we frame the modes as a 'spectrum' of scenographic
possibilities, as Giesekam (2007) suggests, then the use of causal interplay
can serve as a focal point for this further analysis (8). The next chapter will
examine some of the potential variants of causal interplay in practice. Combined with the modes of synthesis, these variants help to establish a nuanced
benchmark of trends and dramaturgical possibilities for digital scenography. This benchmark then serves as an analytical launching point for the
second and third parts of this book, which consider the extent of 'disruption' posed by digital scenography, both on and off the stage.

Notes

1 The dichotomy between faux-interactivity and functional interactivity is a fairly
  recent phenomenon, one that is directly linked to the advancement of technologies that enable the use of functional interactivity in real time. Robert Lepage's
  production of *La Damnation de Faust*, which premiered in 1999 in Matsumoto,

Japan, represents one of the earliest examples of this kind of technology being used in large-scale repertoire opera (Poll 2018). Mark Reaney is another early forerunner in the integration of real-time computer-generated imagery and live performers, including in a production of *The Magic Flute* for the University of Kansas in 2003 (Reaney 1995; Dixon 2007; Kuksa and Childs 2010). Accordingly, while historical productions can be retrospectively classified as 'faux-interactive' due to the way they incorporate projected or visual effects, the reality is that no 'functional' alternative existed.

2 Premiered nearly four decades before the heyday of staging manuals, Mozart's *The Magic Flute* lacks the secondary source materials that accompany later operas by Verdi, Wagner, and other nineteenth-century composers. The precise origins and timeline of the libretto are unknown, and details surrounding the premiere performance are also vague: no record of any scenery, costumes, props, or stage equipment survived (Chailley 1971; Eckelmeyer 1991; Hunter 2008). Given these uncertainties, the original intentions of the work's composer and librettist are largely open for debate, which has led to a tradition of flexible stage interpretations.

References

1927. n.d. "The Magic Flute." Accessed August 13, 2020. https://www.19-27.co.uk/the-magic-flute.

Auslander, Philip. 1999. *Liveness: Performance in a Mediatized Culture.* New York: Routledge.

Babbs, Helen. 2012. "The Theatre Film hybrid—An Interview with Paul Barritt." *Animations Online*, December 19, 2012. http://www.puppetcentre.org.uk/animations-online/features/theatre-film-hybrid/.

Barbour, David. 2011. "The Road to Valhalla." *Lighting and Sound America*, January 2011. http://www.lightingandsoundamerica.com/metoperaringcycle.pdf.

Chailley, Jacques. 1971. *The Magic Flute, Masonic Opera: An Interpretation of the Libretto and the Music.* Translated by Herbert Weinstock. New York: Da Capo Press.

Chapple, Freda, and Chiel Kattenbelt, eds. 2007. *Intermediality in Theatre and Performance.* 3rd ed. Amsterdam: Editions Rodopi B.V.

Curran, Paul, dir. 2015. *La Donna Del Lago*, by Gioachino Rossini and Andrea L. Tottola. DVD. The Metropolitan Opera. Warner Classics/Parlophone.

Dixon, Steve. 2007. *Digital Performance: A History of New Media in Theater, Dance, Performance Art, and Installation.* Cambridge: MIT Press.

Dobrin, Peter. 2017. "O17's 'Magic Flute'—Mozart by Way of Monty Python and Edward Gorey." *Philadelphia Inquirer*, September 16, 2017. https://www.inquirer.com/philly/entertainment/arts/o17-magic-flute-review-opera-philadelphia-20170916.html.

Downey, Charles T. 2014. "'Magic Flute' at Washington National Opera." *Ionarts*, May 7, 2014. https://ionarts.blogspot.com/2014/05/magic-flute-at-washington-national-opera.html.

Eckelmeyer, Judith A. 1991. *The Cultural Context of Mozart's Magic Flute: Social, Aesthetic, Philosophical.* Lewiston: Edwin Mellen Press.

Farber, Jim. 2016. "Review: L.A. Opera's Version of Mozart's 'Magic Flute' Remains Magical." *Los Angeles Daily News*, February 17, 2016. https://www.dailynews.com/2016/02/17/review-la-operas-version-of-mozarts-magic-flute-remains-magical/.

Foglia, Leonard, dir. 2010. *Moby-Dick*, by Jake Heggie and Gene Scheer. DVD. San Francisco Opera. EuroArts.

Forkbeard Fantasy. n.d. "Forkbeard's Use of Film." Accessed November 15, 2018. http://www.forkbeardfantasy.co.uk/useoffilm1.php.

Giesekam, Greg. 2007. *Staging the Screen: The Use of Film and Video in Theatre.* Basingstoke: Palgrave Macmillan.

Hermanis, Alvis, dir. 2016. *Madama Butterfly*, by Giacomo Puccini, Giuseppe Giacosa, and Luigi Illica. Streaming video. Teatro alla Scala, Italy. https://www.youtube.com/watch?v=8oV6jVXqRw8.

Holland, Bernard. 2007. "The Flute Is Awfully Nice, Tamino, but Check Out That Astral Sketchbook." *New York Times*, April 11, 2007. http://www.nytimes.com/2007/04/11/arts/music/11flut.html?_r=0.

Hunter, Mary. 2008. *Mozart's Operas: A Companion.* New Haven: Yale University Press.

Jacquemin, Christian, and Georges Gagneré. 2007. Revisiting the Layer/Mask Paradigm for Augmented Scenery." *International Journal of Performance Arts and Digital Media* 2, no. 3: 237–257.

Kaneko, Jun. 2006. *Madama Butterfly*. Omaha: Joslyn Art Museum.

Kaneko, Jun. 2008. *Fidelio Leonore*. Philadelphia: Opera Company of Philadelphia.

Kaneko, Jun. 2012. *The Magic Flute*. London: Laurence King.

Kentridge, William. 2007. "Drawing the Stage." In *William Kentridge: Flute*, edited by Bronwyn Law-Viljoen, 66–78. Johannesburg: David Krut Publishing.

Kentridge, William, dir. 2012. *Die Zauberflöte*, by Wolfgang A. Mozart and Emanuel Schikaneder. DVD. Teatro alla Scala, Milan. Opus Arte.

Kettle, David. 2015. "Interview: Belin's [sic] Komische Oper Intendant, Barrie Kosky, on The Magic Flute." *The List*, June 30, 2015. https://edinburghfestival.list.co.uk/article/72057-interview-belins-komishche-oper-intendant-barrie-kosky-on-the-magic-flute/.

Kosman, Joshua. 2012. "'Magic Flute' Review: S.F. Opera's Fanciful Vision." *San Francisco Chronicle*, June 15, 2012. http://www.sfgate.com/music/article/Magic-Flute-review-S-F-Opera-s-fanciful-vision-3635445.php.

Kratzer, Tobias, dir. 2017. *Lucio Silla*, by Wolfgang A. Mozart, Giovanni de Gamerra, and Pietro Metastasio. Streaming video. The Théâtre Royal de la Monnaie, Belgium. https://www.lamonnaie.be/en/streaming/1680-lucio-silla.

Kuksa, Iryna, and Mark Childs. 2010. "But a Walking Shadow: Designing, Performing and Learning on the Virtual Stage." *Learning Media and Technology* 35, no. 3: 275–291.

Law-Viljoen, Bronwyn, ed. 2007. *William Kentridge: Flute*. Johannesburg: David Krut Publishing.

Lepage, Robert, dir. 2012. *Das Rheingold*, by Richard Wagner. DVD. The Metropolitan Opera. Deutsche Grammophon.

Liebner, János. 1972. *Mozart on the Stage*. London: Calder and Boyars.

Maddocks, Fiona. 2015. "The Magic Flute at Edinburgh Festival Review— Unforgettable and Exhausting." *The Guardian*, August 30, 2015. https://www.theguardian.com/stage/2015/aug/30/magic-flute-edinburgh-festival-review-barrie-kosky-1927-komische-oper-berlin.

"The Magic Flute by William Kentridge Finally Came to Paris." 2011. *Operacake*, December 26, 2011. http://opera-cake.blogspot.com.au/2011/12/magic-flute-by-william-kentridge.html.

Martinfield, Sean. 2012. "Jun Kaneko's 'Magic Flute' Is Stunningly Visual." *Huffington Post*, June 28, 2012. http://www.huffingtonpost.com/sean-martinfield/magic-flute-jun kaneko_b_1633445.html.

Midgette, Anne. 2007. "Artist's Video Adds Magic to 'Flute.'" *New York Times*, April 9, 2007. http://www.nytimes.com/2007/04/09/arts/music/09flut.html?_r=0.

Midgette, Anne. 2014. "Washington National Opera Offers 'The Magic Flute' in a Color-Saturated Production." *Washington Post*, May 4, 2014. https://www.washingtonpost.com/entertainment/music/wno-offers-magic-flute-in-color-saturated-jun-kaneko-production/2014/05/04/e83e0b7c-d3a7-11e3-aae8-c2d44bd79778_story.html.

Minnesota Opera. 2014. "Behind the Curtain: The Magic Flute." Video Feature, 1:15:12. https://www.youtube.com/watch?v=QpgI_opQG-4.

Nikkilä, Jussi, dir. 2020. *Don Giovanni*, by Wolfgang A. Mozart and Lorenzo da Ponte. Streaming video. Finnish National Opera and Ballet, Finland. https://www.youtube.com/watch?v=f2GumUO9Lbk.

Oliszewski, Alex, and Daniel Fine. 2018. *Digital Media, Projection Design, & Technology for the Future*. New York: Routledge.

Poll, Melissa. 2018. *Robert Lepage's Scenographic Dramaturgy: The Aesthetic Signature at Work*. Cham: Palgrave Macmillan.

Pont, Grégoire, and James Bonas, dir. 2016. *L'Enfant et les Sortilèges*, by Maurice Ravel and Colette. Streaming video. Opéra de Lyon, France. https://www.france.tv/france-5/passage-des-arts/1385465-l-enfant-et-les-sortileges.html.

Reaney, Mark. 1995. "Virtual Reality on Stage." *VR World* III, no. 3 (May/June): 28–31.

Rosenthal, Mark, ed. 2009. *William Kentridge: Five Themes*. New Haven: Yale University Press.

Roussel, Stéphane. 2007. "Drawing with Light." Translated by Andrew Ayers. In *William Kentridge: Flute*, edited by Bronwyn Law-Viljoen, 80–126. Johannesburg: David Krut Publishing.

Rowe, Georgia. 2012. "In Review: *Attila* (6/12/12), *The Magic Flute* (6/13/12)." *Opera News*, September 2012. https://www.operanews.com/Opera_News_Magazine/2012/9/Reviews/SAN_FRANCISCO__Attila_Flute.html.

San Francisco Opera Archives. n.d. Accessed April 2017. http://archive.sfopera.com.

Scheinin, Richard. 2012. "Review: San Francisco Opera's Visually Stunning 'Magic Flute' Too Often Verges on Mozart as Sit-Com." *Mercury News*, June 14, 2012. http://www.mercurynews.com/2012/06/14/review-san-francisco-operas-visually-stunning-magic-flute-too-often-verges-on-mozart-as-sit-com/.

Schwartz, Stan. 2007. "The Modern 'Magic Flute.'" *New York Sun*, March 26, 2007. http://www.nysun.com/arts/modern-magic-flute/51189/.

Smith, Steve. 2013. "A Fantastical Tale to Set the Ears and Eyes Popping." *New York Times*, April 16, 2013. https://www.nytimes.com/2013/04/17/arts/music/sunken-garden-by-the-english-national-opera.html.

Spicer, Graham. 2011. "William Kentridge's Animations Are the True Stars of The Magic Flute at Milan's La Scala." *Gramilano*, April 4, 2011. https://www.gramilano.com/2011/04/william-kentridges-animations-are-the-true-stars-of-the-magic-flute-at-milans-la-scala/.

Stevens, Mark. 2006. "Moral Minority: Why Is the Art World So Drawn To William Kentridge? Because He's the Rarest of Political Artists: A Subtle, Funny

One." *New York Magazine*, February 20, 2006. http://nymag.com/arts/art/profiles/15946/#.

Stone, Simon, dir. 2019. *La Traviata*, by Giuseppe Verdi and Francesco Maria Piave. Streaming video. Opéra National de Paris, France. https://www.medici.tv/en/operas/verdis-la-traviata-simon-stone/.

Swed, Mark. 2013. "Review: Brilliant Transformation of 'The Magic Flute.'" *Los Angeles Times*, November 25, 2013. http://articles.latimes.com/2013/nov/25/entertainment/la-et-cm-la-opera-flute-review-20131125.

Tcherniakov, Dmitri, dir. 2019. *The Tale of Tsar Saltan*, by Nikolai Rimsky-Korsakov and Vladimir Belsky. Streaming video. The Théâtre Royal de la Monnaie, Belgium. https://www.lamonnaie.be/en/streaming/1450-the-tale-of-tsar-saltan.

Theunissen, Sabine. n.d. "Scene: *The Magic Flute*." https://sabinetheunissen.weebly.com/scene.html.

Vincent, Caitlin, Jordan Beth Vincent, Katya Johanson, and Kim Vincs. 2017. "The Intersection of Live and Digital: New Technical Classifications for Digital Scenography in Opera." *Theatre and Performance Design* 3, no. 3: 155–171. https://doi.org/10.1080/23322551.2017.1400764.

Vincent, Jordan Beth, John McCormick, and Kim Vincs. 2016. *The Magic Flute (Scenographic Visualisations) for Australian International Opera Company*. Melbourne: Australian International Opera Company.

Vincent, Jordan Beth, Caitlin Vincent, Kim Vincs, and John McCormick. 2016. "Navigating Control and Illusion: Interactivity versus 'Faux-Interactivity' in Trans-Media Dance Performance." *International Journal of Performance Arts and Digital Media* 12, no. 1: 44–60. https://doi.org/10.1080/14794713.2016.1161955.

Warner, Keith, dir. 2018. *Vanessa*, by Samuel Barber and Gian Carlo Menotti. Streaming video. Glyndebourne Festival Opera, England. https://www.medici.tv/en/operas/samuel-barbers-vanessa/.

Winn, Steven. 2015. "Sight and Sound at Odds in Colorful Take on *The Magic Flute*." *San Francisco Classical Voice*, October 21, 2015. https://www.sfcv.org/reviews/san-francisco-opera/sight-and-sound-at-odds-in-colorful-take-on-lt-em-gt-the-magic-flute-lt-/em-gt.

Woodruff, Robert, dir. 2015. *Dog Days*, by David T. Little and Royce Vavrek. Streaming video. Beth Morrison Projects and LA Opera, USA. https://www.bethmorrisonprojects.org.

Woolfe, Zachary. 2013. "The Happy Results of a Speedy Shift: 'The Magic Flute' at the Los Angeles Opera." *New York Times*, November 25, 2013. https://www.nytimes.com/2013/11/26/arts/music/the-magic-flute-at-the-los-angeles-opera.html.

Wysocka, Barbara, dir. 2019. *Tosca*, by Giacomo Puccini, Giuseppe Giacosa, and Luigi Illica. Streaming video. Polish National Opera, Poland. https://www.youtube.com/watch?v=-G341HC0hp8.

Zasada, Marc Porter. 2013. "Review: The Magic Flute at L.A. Opera." *Huffington Post*, December 2, 2013. https://www.huffingtonpost.com/marc-porter-zasada/the-magic-flute-at-la-opera_b_4341376.html.

2 The variants of causal interplay

The modes of synthesis establish a framework for comparing digitally enhanced productions by evaluating the visual integration of live performers and digital elements from the perspective of the audience. Yet, the modes are only a starting point for classifying the different kinds of relationships that can emerge. The presence of causality between live and digital components enables an initial categorisation: if a production employs causal interplay, it can be classified as either partial-synthesis or full-synthesis, depending on the extent of live–digital interaction within the production design. If a production does not employ any causal interplay but relies only on visual correlation, it can be classified as non-synthesis.

However, the potential functionality of 'causal interplay' is extremely broad. In any digitally enhanced production, various gradations of interplay might occur. Teatro alla Scala's *Das Rheingold* (2010), for example, only invokes a single instance of causal interplay. In the opening scene, the Rhinemaidens appear to cast digital shadows onto the projected water on the background (Cassiers 2013). In contrast, Gran Teatre del Liceu's *Turandot* (2019) makes frequent use of causal interplay, ranging from Princess Turandot's initial characterisation as a giant digital avatar to Liù's death by bolts of digital electricity in the third act (Aleu 2019). In Florida Grand Opera's production of *Florencia en al Amazonas* (2018), causal interplay is limited to an environmental relationship, in which the characters on the river boat appear to be 'travelling' in concert with shifting video projections of the Amazon river (Condemi 2018).

All three productions rely on causal interplay in concert with visual correlation and unequivocally fall in the category of partial-synthesis. But an analysis of their digital scenographies is incomplete without additional consideration of the particular dramaturgical effects enabled. What is the dramaturgical objective of the relationship that is being established between the live and the digital, and is this relationship actually 'real' or just a theatrical illusion?

To speak to these questions, this chapter outlines three variants of causal interplay which reflect additional nuance within this scenographic functionality. I term these variants: *agency, augmentation,* and *autonomy.*

DOI: 10.4324/9781003093305-2

These variations allow for a more detailed classification of the live–digital relationship emerging on stage, which, in turn, enables a closer comparison of different digitally enhanced productions. Each variant is based on the overarching premise of causal interplay, in which one component, either digital or live, prompts a corresponding response in the other. While the modes of synthesis are framed around the audience perception of this relationship, the variants of causal interplay examine the nature of the relationship itself. The potential scope and functionality of causal interplay varies depending on the role designated to the respective performers and digital elements. This reflects a strategic artistic decision made by the creative team in the process of design conception and staging but is also informed by the technological capabilities of the production.

The variant of *agency* examines the delineation of power in the relationship between the live and the digital and considers which entity drives, or appears to drive, instances of causal interplay. This functionality encompasses action-based forms of interplay that are realised through one-on-one live–digital interactions, such as Liù's death by electricity in *Turandot*, as well as large-scale environmental effects, such as the moving river in *Florencia en al Amazonas*, which encompasses all of the performers on stage simultaneously.

Augmentation considers forms of causal interplay that impact the live performing body. This augmentation can be realised through the extension of the live performer's physical presence, their partial transformation through digitalised body parts, or, in extreme examples, their total replacement with a digital counterpart. Both agency and augmentation are variants of causal interplay that can be framed as dramaturgical effects, which impact the visual synthesis from the perspective of the audience.

The third variant of causal interplay, *autonomy,* speaks to the technical inner workings of the relationship between the live and the digital and whether instances of causal interplay reflect true interactivity or merely the illusion of it, termed 'faux-interactivity' by Vincent et al. (2016). Regardless of whether causal interplay is the result of functional or faux-interactivity, the resulting visual synthesis does not necessarily change for the audience. Instead, autonomy speaks to the experience of the performers and the degree to which they possess physical independence within the theatrical space.

This chapter explores these variants of causal interplay through a close analysis of six digitally enhanced opera productions. Each production was selected as a case study due to its demonstration of one particular variant as a major component of its scenographic design. As with the three productions of *The Magic Flute* described in the previous chapter, each production is the result of a different creative team and overarching aesthetic, as well as different forms of digital technology in practice.

Agency: the screen as 'performer'

In discussions of digital performance, Vincent et al. (2016) outline three common components of an 'interactive' relationship: first, a technical/

digital interfacing component; second, the sharing of data between live and digital entities; and third, and most importantly, causality (46). Dixon (2007) describes 'causality' in this sense as 'the satisfying power to take meaningful action and see the result of our decisions and choices' (560). Packer and Jordan (2001) also define 'interactivity' around the premise of causality and reference a user's ability to 'alter' digital media (see also Smuts 2009). They explain: 'reading a text is not an interaction experience; interactivity implies changing the words of the text in some way—adding to them, reorganizing them, engaging with them in a way that affects their appearance on the screen' (xxxvi).

For both Dixon and Packer and Jordan, the concept of interactivity is framed as something of a one-sided relationship. Packer and Jordan cite 'the ability of the user to alter media she comes in contact with, either alone or in collaboration with others' (xxxvi). They note that the 'text' on the screen can be 'altered,' 'changed,' 'reorganized,' and 'affected,' but only as a result of a user's personal engagement. On its own, the 'text' remains inactive. Dixon similarly highlights the primacy of the user and the idea of interactivity as the opportunity to see the result of 'our decisions and choices,' rather than the other way around. Digital elements can participate in an 'interactive' relationship, but the user serves as the driving force.

This understanding of interactive relationships can be applied to the kinds of causal interplay we see in digitally enhanced opera production. Consider William Kentridge's designs for La Monnaie's *The Magic Flute*, in which he intentionally instils his performers with the illusion of control over the digital imagery. In the Queen of the Night's first aria, the live performer makes a sweeping, circular motion with her arm, and two digital planets begin to move in orbit on the projection surface behind her (Kentridge 2012). Kentridge (2007) specifically instructed the performer to 'draw lines, not at the speed they appear on screen, but faster, ahead of the image, more decisively' (68). The resulting effect implies that the Queen of the Night has personally summoned the digital imagery and possesses a 'sense of agency, of power, of making' over the projected elements (Kentridge 2007, 68). Reframed within Packer and Jordan's terminology, the 'user,' represented by the Queen of the Night, engages with the digital scenography in a way that manifests in her seeming power to 'alter' and change the planetary 'text' on the projection screen.

In digitally enhanced productions, however, causal interplay is not one-sided. Instead, we can recognise the relationship between the live and the digital as one of reciprocity. Both live performers and digital elements have the ability to prompt a corresponding behavioural response in the other. The premise of mutuality between the live and the digital frames the 'text' of the screen as a 'user' in its own right. Rather than waiting to be 'altered' by the live performers, digital elements can actively drive and modify the behaviour of the performers within the scenic setting.

This potential agency represents a key variant of causal interplay because it helps to establish a shared theatrical realm for the audience. Neither live nor digital assumes a position of primacy over the other. Instead, digital elements can function as true dramatic partners for the live performers. The following section examines the role of agency in two digitally enhanced productions. In both Dutch National Opera's *The Magic Flute* (2012) and Victorian Opera's *Four Saints in Three Acts* (2016), digital elements predominate as the driving force in instances of causal interplay across both environmental and one-on-one interactions.

Dutch National Opera, The Magic Flute (2012)—partial-synthesis

Co-commissioned by Dutch National Opera, English National Opera, and Festival d'Aix-en-Provence, Simon McBurney's 2012 production of *The Magic Flute* relies on a number of unconventional staging techniques, including elevating the orchestra to the level of the stage, reimagining the Three Spirits as shadow puppets, and utilising a sonic artist to create sound effects in real time (McBurney 2015). Within this fluctuating aesthetic, McBurney uses digital scenography in varying ways over the course of the production and actively shifts between visual correlation and causal interplay. The majority of instances of causal interplay are built around digital agency, in which the behaviour of the live performers appears to be driven by the digital elements.

In the opening scene, Tamino appears amid flashes of lightning and real-time thunder booms, while a digital projection of writhing snakes is projected onto the scrim in front of him. Tamino attempts to flee, each time recoiling as he appears to encounter the digital snakes (McBurney 2015). The performer playing Tamino is positioned behind the scrim that serves as the projection surface, so there is little question that the interplay between the live and the digital is an illusion based on pre-determined staging. Yet, Tamino's activity on stage is designed to imply a causal relationship and, in particular, a relationship in which the live performer responds and reacts to the digital components.

McBurney takes a similar approach for his staging of Tamino's aria 'Dies Bildnis,' in which Tamino falls in love with a portrait of Pamina. Stagings of this scene often involve an actual portrait, but McBurney instead projects an animated video of Pamina's face onto various projection surfaces, including white sheets held intermittently by the Three Ladies (McBurney 2015). Each time Tamino sees the digital portrait, he moves to reach it. Each time, just as the performer is about to touch Pamina's face, the projection shifts to a new surface and prompts Tamino to change direction once again. With every shift of the portrait, Tamino's behaviour is responsive, designed in reaction to the movement of the portrait as a way of reflecting his longing for Pamina. Although the video image of Pamina's face never responds to Tamino's presence—functioning more as a 'live' photograph than a dynamic digital character—the digital element directs Tamino's activity and positions the live performer as a passive force in their relationship.

In his staging of the trials of fire and water in the second act, McBurney employs a more extreme technique to assign agency to the digital elements, in this case, the all-encompassing digital environment. When the first trial begins, Tamino and Pamina are standing on an elevated platform that tilts to obscure them from view as digital flames are projected on the scrim in front of them. When the flames die away and the platform resumes its original position, a surge of digital water appears to engulf the two performers (see Figure 2.1). The platform drops away, and Tamino and Pamina, now strapped into wire harnesses, appear to be caught in a surge of projected water (McBurney 2015).

The closely timed coordination of the falling platform, animated digital water, and wire harnesses creates the illusion that Tamino and Pamina have been swept away by the water. Here, the use of harnesses is key to establishing a shared spatial realm in which the live performers appear to be immersed in their virtual environment. Because McBurney's live performers are also hoisted above the stage floor and cannot move independently, they are fixed in a passive role in their relationship with the digital elements: affected by—but unable to affect—the digital surging waves.

In each of these scenes, McBurney's stage directions intentionally position the digital elements as the driving force in the relationship between the live and the digital. In Tamino's opening scene, the live performer's staging is designed in response to the movement of the digital snakes projected in front of him, just as his behaviour is later directed by the shifting location of Pamina's digital portrait. In the trial of water, the live performers possess

Figure 2.1 Tamino and Pamina face the trial of water in Simon McBurney's *The Magic Flute*. Production premiered by Dutch National Opera (2012). Photograph © Robbie Jack for English National Opera.

even less agency, literally strapped into harnesses while the stage floor drops away beneath them. If we consider McBurney's production within the context of Packer and Jordan's (2001) definition of interactivity, the live performers assume the role of the text, which is 'altered,' 'changed,' 'reorganized,' and 'affected' by the specific engagement of the 'user,' or in this case, the digital scenography.

Each of these instances relies on choreographed staging and pre-rendered digital imagery in order to achieve the illusion of causal interplay. If Tamino does not recoil from the digital snakes at the right time or the Three Ladies hold the projection surface for Pamina's portrait at the wrong angle, the visual illusion is ruined. Similarly, if Tamino and Pamina have technical difficulties with their harnesses, they will not be 'swept away' during the trial of water. As such, the agency of the digital elements in driving these relationships is also only an illusion and reflects an intentional creative choice made by McBurney in his capacity as stage director. Just as William Kentridge elected to employ digital scenography in a way that would instil his live performers with the illusion of agency over their digital surroundings in La Monnaie's production, McBurney elected to do the opposite, framing the technology as the driving force in the relationship between the digital and the live.

Victorian Opera, *Four Saints in Three Acts* (2016)—partial-synthesis

Victorian Opera's 2016 production of Virgil Thomson and Gertrude Stein's *Four Saints in Three Acts* is another example of a partial-synthesis production that prioritises the agency of its digital components during causal interplay. Co-directed by Nancy Black and Kim Vincs and designed by the Deakin Motion.Lab in Melbourne, Australia, the digital scenography for *Four Saints in Three Acts* centres on a number of surreal scenic environments that are projected onto a screen at the back of the stage (Vincs et al. 2016). Each environment is populated with animated animals and objects, including a lion, a serpent, a lamb, a goblet, and pigeons. The production is also notable for its use of 3D stereoscopic scenography, which assumes additional depth when viewed by the audience through polarised glasses.

While Dutch National Opera's *The Magic Flute* focuses on causal interplay between individual performers and specific digital components, the majority of the interplay in *Four Saints in Three Acts* is based on a broader relationship between the digital environments and the approximately 50 singers who remain on stage throughout the performance. The key to this overarching interplay is the use of a video game engine, which enables the computer programmers to 'drive' the projected digital environments in real time. This technique creates an ongoing sense of forward motion within the projected scenery that suggests the live performers and audience members are collectively travelling through a surrealist dynamic universe.

During the opera, the live performers and audience members are visually pulled into each subsequent environment by means of a virtual portal built into the projected imagery (Vincs et al. 2016). In the first act, for example, the scenic perspective begins in a digital walled garden, advances through a portal in the digital wall, and emerges from a digital sea of grass into the new environment of the second act. Shortly after, a digital staircase materialises from the grass, and the scenic perspective follows the staircase as it builds itself into space, eventually reaching another virtual portal (Vincs et al. 2016) (see Figure 2.2).

Because the digital environments are dynamic rather than fixed and remain in a near constant state of forward motion, the scenographic design establishes an implicit causal interplay between the live performers and the digital elements. The performers are not positioned in front of a static digital backdrop but appear to be travelling in tandem with the advancing scenographic perspective. This technique recalls the effect used in William Kentridge's production of *The Magic Flute* for La Monnaie, in which the digital jungle environment was linked to the physical moving walkway built into the stage floor. While Kentridge's environment appeared to move in response to Pamina and Papageno's physical movement, the dynamic environments in *Four Saints in Three Acts*, controlled by the computer programmers of the Deakin Motion.Lab, maintain implicit agency in driving the relationship with the live performers.

This sense of agency can be partially attributed to the visual perspective of the scenography, which is designed from the audience's viewpoint and

Figure 2.2 The stairway to heaven in Victorian Opera's *Four Saints in Three Acts*. Photograph © Charlie Kinross.

maintains a forward momentum independent of the performers' behaviour. Aspects of the staging reinforce this passive role, with the performers re-acting to changing elements in their environment in real time. When the scenography travels through the portal in the first act, the live performers look around in awe as the 3D stereoscopy makes it appear to the audience that the performers have been engulfed in giant stalks of digital grass. Later, as the digital staircase advances through the sky, the live performers duck to 'avoid' one of the staircase landings that suddenly protrudes into the audi-ence's spatial realm. In both cases, the performers' activity is designed to re-spond to the behaviour of the digital elements as perceived by the audience through their polarised glasses. The staging not only supports the illusion of causal interplay with the digital elements but perpetuates the passive role of the performers within the relationship.

At other points in the production, the live performers engage in instances of causal interplay with specific digital characters. As with the dynamic en-vironments, these relationships are generally driven by the digital elements rather than by the performers themselves. During the first act, the digital lion appears to nod to the performers standing in the foreground, and the live performer playing St Ignatius bows in response. While only a brief mo-ment, the combination of digital animation and choreography creates the illusion of a causal relationship prompted by the behaviour of the digital lion. At other points in the opera, the live performers react in fear to a dig-ital serpent, jump in surprise as a digital magpie drops dead, and duck to avoid a flock of digital pigeons (Vincs et al. 2016). Each time, the physical behaviour of the live performers is conceived in response to the digital ele-ments and perpetuates the illusion of digital agency.

Four Saints in Three Acts features a greater number of causal interactions than Dutch National Opera's *The Magic Flute*, but both productions explic-itly prioritise the agency of the digital elements in driving the relationship between the digital and the live. Yet, neither the live performers nor the dig-ital elements have any real agency in the relationship in either production. Instead, the relationship itself is an illusion, created for the benefit of the audience.

Augmentation: extension and transformation through digitalisation

A second variant of causal interplay that can be used to compare digitally enhanced productions centres on the potential for live performers to be ex-tended, transformed, and even replaced by digital technology. As discussed earlier, many instances of causal interplay are tied to explicit physical move-ment, such as Tamino recoiling from the digital snakes in Dutch National Opera's *The Magic Flute* and the live performers ducking and jumping in concert with the dynamic digital environment in Victorian Opera's *Four Saints in Three Acts*. However, the kinds of causal interplay that augment and transform the live performer are located and contained within the performing body itself. Rather than the live performer altering an external digital element through physical behaviour or vice versa, the live performer becomes a hybrid form within the theatrical space.[1]

In Komische Oper Berlin's full-synthesis *The Magic Flute* (2012), the variant of augmentation is demonstrated a number of times through the partial digitalisation of principal characters, including Tamino and the Queen of the Night. Tamino's legs are replaced with digital running ones when he flees from the digital dragon in the opening scene, while the Queen of the Night's physical body is transformed into a more menacing digital version. In both cases, the live performers are augmented through the use of visual superimposition, in which digital body parts are projected directly onto the performers via devices like Tamino's curved set piece and the Queen's white costume.

The Cleveland Orchestra's production of Janáček's *The Cunning Little Vixen* (2014) uses a similar technique to transform the physical bodies of its live performers into animated versions of the forest creatures they portray (Montgomery 2014). Unlike in *The Magic Flute*, director Yuval Sharon's staging for *The Cunning Little Vixen* does not rely on visual superimposition. Instead, his singers are positioned behind a physical set and insert their heads through designated portals that align to the location of their animated digital bodies (Woolfe 2014) (see Figure 2.3). Sharon explains, 'For the singers that sing the animals, it's a highly choreographed flow chart

Figure 2.3 The Vixen and the Fox in The Cleveland Orchestra's *The Cunning Little Vixen*. Photograph © Roger Mastroianni.

for them as to which portal they need to arrive at any given moment. And they'[re] moving around a lot. They're animals after all' (McClung 2017).

None of the performers in either *The Magic Flute* or *The Cunning Little Vixen* consciously drive the interactive relationship with the digital elements in these instances. Yet, each is augmented and transformed by the technology from the perspective of the audience. In addition to relying on the audience's suspension of disbelief, this variant of causal interplay also requires the characters themselves to suspend disbelief within the context of the narrative. Tamino shows no concern at the sudden appearance of his digital legs as he flees from the dragon, just as the Vixen is unperturbed by her animated animal body.

The variant of augmentation can also manifest in more extreme iterations that completely replace the live performer with a digitalised version. In many cases, this technique is used as a way to address staging challenges, particularly in operas that involve non-human characters. In Wagner's opera *Siegfried*, for example, the character of the Forest Bird is difficult to realise in a convincing way for the audience. Accordingly, in The Metropolitan Opera's 2011 production, the character appears as a digital bird projected onto the set, while the live performer sings from off stage (D'Aoust 2015). The audience recognises the causal relationship between the digital bird and the voice of the live performer even though only one of the two elements is visible within the scenic setting. Similarly, in Komische Oper Berlin's *L'Enfant et les Sortilèges* (2017), another collaboration with 1927, the performers who play the roles of the Black Cat and White Cat are never seen on stage. Instead, they sing from the wings, while giant digitalised versions of their characters play a game of cat and mouse with the live performer playing the Child (Komische Oper Berlin 2017).

Regardless of the extent of augmentation, the illusion of causal interplay between the live performer and digital components relies on the audience acknowledging and accepting the intended amalgam of the two elements within the theatrical space. When Tamino's legs are replaced with speedier digital versions and the virtual Forest Bird moves its beak in time with Wagner's music, the interplay is grounded in an overt theatricality that requires the audience members to mentally synthesise the causal relationship. Aronson (2008) explains the appeal of this conceit: 'the mechanics once exposed … serve to reinforce the illusion while seemingly admitting the spectator into the world of the manipulator. Everyone acknowledges the illusion; everyone knows that everyone knows' (20).

A closer examination of productions that employ augmentation yields a more detailed understanding of how these effects can be employed in different ways. The Royal Opera, Covent Garden's *Don Giovanni* (2014) and Victorian Opera's *The Flying Dutchman* (2015) are two examples of productions that specifically extend, transform, or replace the live performer through causal interplay. The staging in *Don Giovanni* involves both the extension and transformation of its live performers, while *The Flying Dutchman* uses an avatar-based approach to replace its live performers at certain points in the narrative. In each case, the causal interplay between the live and the digital—and the resulting hybrid form—is designed for the perspective of the audience, who alone comprehend the visual synthesis linked to the live performing body.

The Royal Opera, Covent Garden, *Don Giovanni* (2014)—partial-synthesis

In 2014, The Royal Opera, Covent Garden premiered a new production of Mozart's *Don Giovanni* in collaboration with Houston Grand Opera. Directed by Kasper Holten, the production features a multi-level, rotating set of Escher-like staircases and doors, designed by Es Devlin, along with expansive video designs by filmmaker Luke Halls. Mutter (2014) notes that the production constituted The Royal Opera's most extensive use of digital projections in its history of programming.

Holten's concept for *Don Giovanni* was inspired by the titular character's inner psyche and 'themes of reality and imagination' (Holten 2014). Luke Halls notes that, as Don Giovanni's state of mind devolves over the course of the opera, the digital projections are designed to become increasingly frenzied and chaotic (personal communication, August 29, 2017). The scenic design also incorporates references to Leporello's catalogue, with the names of Don Giovanni's past conquests projected onto the physical set at various points in the opera. Coinciding with Don Giovanni's descent into mental instability, the calligraphic script of the early scenes is gradually replaced with ink blots, scratched-out names, and sketches of a demonic all-seeing eye. When Don Giovanni is dragged down to hell by the Commendatore in the final scene, the projected handwriting slowly erases itself, and Don Giovanni is left cowering alone on an empty stage, presumably driven mad (Holten 2014).

Holten's production features several instances of causal interplay that specifically extend or transform the live performing body through augmentation. During the catalogue aria in the first act, Leporello lists Don Giovanni's numerous lovers to a distraught Donna Elvira, while Don Giovanni loiters against a digital doorway. At a key moment in Leporello's aria, Don Giovanni breaks from his fixed position and moves to the centre of the stage, leaving a 'living' digital shadow behind. This shadow mirrors the live performer's original position and is gradually replicated in various sizes on other digital doorways that appear on the physical set (see Figure 2.4). The implication is that each shadow and doorway represents a different romantic encounter recorded in Leporello's catalogue. While some iterations of Don Giovanni's digital shadow remain frozen in his original pose, others are fully animated and appear to stride towards the audience through the opening of their designated doorway.

This scenographic technique fundamentally redefines the physical presence of the live performer. Although the performer playing Don Giovanni

Figure 2.4 Don Giovanni's shadow avatars in The Royal Opera, Covent Garden's *Don Giovanni*. Photograph © Es Devlin.

remains on stage, his body is extended by dozens of digital avatars that are seemingly spawned from his physical body. These digital shadows evoke Dixon's (2007) concept of the 'digital double,' or a projected image that manifests as the seeming 'shadow self' of the live performer (241). Don Giovanni's avatars have a limited repertoire of movement, but their animation implies a certain physical independence that sets them apart from their originating source.

The live performer playing Don Giovanni never explicitly acknowledges the digital extensions of his own body. Even the seeming creation of the initial shadow, an example of causal interplay stemming from a physical prompt (i.e., Don Giovanni's move away from the digital doorway), does not appear to be an intentional decision made by Don Giovanni in the context of the narrative. Instead, the causal relationship between the live performer and his digital extensions is perceived only by the audience, who can trace the cause and effect between Don Giovanni's physical behaviour and the resulting digitalised shadows.

In the second act, Holten's staging again utilises a variant of causal interplay that augments the live performer. In this case, the augmentation manifests as the partial transformation of a live performer through visual superimposition. During the trio 'Ah taci, ingiusto core,' Leporello is tasked with wooing Donna Elvira in the guise of Don Giovanni while the real Don seduces Donna Elvira's maid. Stagings of this scene often err on the side of farce, with Leporello donning Don Giovanni's cape and mouthing words as Don Giovanni lingers out of sight. In Holten's production, Leporello steps into a fixed position against the physical set and raises his left arm in a gesture of courtship. Then, a digital version of Don Giovanni's costume is superimposed onto Leporello's physical body (Holten 2014).

This illusion of causal interplay—specifically the implication that Leporello is now dressed in Don Giovanni's clothing—relies on pre-determined choreography. The digital suit of clothes is inflexible, and Leporello must maintain his designated position against the set or risk destroying the illusion. Because the illusion is based on superimposition, the effect also requires certain lighting that only illuminates the live performer's head. This not only helps to obscure Leporello's physical body and existing costume beneath the digital suit of clothes but also ensures that the projected image is not dispersed by the stage lighting.

The transformation of Leporello with a digital suit of clothes, like Don Giovanni and his digital extensions, is based on an overt theatricality designed for the benefit of the audience. Beyond the initial prompts of causal interplay, both of which prioritise the agency of the live performer—Don Giovanni moving away from the doorway and Leporello assuming his stance of courtship—neither performer interacts with the digital elements through any additional physical behaviour or even acknowledges their integration within the scenographic design. Instead, the augmentation is initiated through their physical prompts and then maintained through the continued synthesis of the two components as perceived by the audience.

Victorian Opera, *The Flying Dutchman* (2015)—partial-synthesis

Victorian Opera's 2015 production of Wagner's *The Flying Dutchman* demonstrates a more extreme form of augmentation. While Kasper Holten's *Don Giovanni* transforms Leporello with Don Giovanni's digital clothing and extends Don Giovanni with dozens of digital shadows, *The Flying Dutchman* takes the process of augmentation a step further by completely replacing live performers with digital avatars. Directed by Roger Hodgman, *The Flying Dutchman* is relatively conventional in its scenic design, with its digital scenography aligning to the kinds of scenic projections often used in non-synthesis productions. The settings consist primarily of scenic vistas, including an ocean, a village, the lower deck of a ship, and a dock with mountains in the distance, all of which are projected onto a triptych of screens behind a multi-level physical platform.

Like the projection designs for *Four Saints in Three Acts*, which were also created by the Deakin Motion.Lab in Melbourne, Australia, the designs for *The Flying Dutchman* were built using 3D stereoscopy, which requires the audience to wear polarised glasses for the duration of the performance. The scenography was also built in a video game engine, which allows the computer programmers to 'drive' the visual perspective for each scene in real time, rather than as a pre-recorded and pre-rendered video. In contrast to *Four Saints in Three Acts*, however, the live performers in *The Flying Dutchman* never move in tandem with the moving digital environments. Instead, the only instances of causal interplay in the production are those that specifically augment the live performing body (Vincs et al. 2015).

In the opening scene, the Dutchman's digital vessel appears in the distance of the digital ocean, projected onto the three screens behind the physical set. As the vessel moves towards the apex of the set, a digital figure in red is barely visible at the ship's helm. This digital figure walks along the digital deck towards the audience and is briefly obscured by a cloud of digital mist before suddenly 'appearing' on the physical set, transformed into the live performer playing the Dutchman (Vincs et al. 2015) (see Figure 2.5).

This moment requires careful coordination to ensure that the live performer playing the Dutchman appears on stage just after the digital mist has obscured his digital avatar. The illusion also demands that the live and digital versions of the Dutchman are visually similar, with both characters costumed in red coats. With these requirements met, the audience can accept the premise that the digital avatar represents a virtual replacement of the live performer and that the live and the digital function as performative equivalents within the theatrical space.

In the final scene of the opera, Hodgman employs a similar technique to achieve the supernatural effect of Senta and the Dutchman rising up to heaven. The live performers are staged to disappear from the view of the

Figure 2.5 The Dutchman appears in Victorian Opera's *The Flying Dutchman*. Photograph © Jeff Busby 2015.

audience: the live performer playing Senta jumps off the back of the physical set, while the live performer playing the Dutchman vanishes through a side exit as his digital ship sinks in the distance. As soon as the stage is empty, digital versions of both characters suddenly emerge from the depths of the digital ocean and float up towards the stars (Vincs et al. 2015).

As in the opening scene, the costuming of the digital avatars approximates the costumes of the live performers playing Senta and the Dutchman. The behaviour of the live performers is also carefully choreographed. After the live Senta jumps off the set, for example, her digital replacement emerges from approximately the same location in order to ensure visual continuity for the audience. The live and the digital components do not have any specific interaction with one another nor are they present in the theatrical space at the same time. Yet, as with the Dutchman's opening entrance, the causal relationship is apparent to the audience members, who accept the implied synthesis of the two Sentas and two Dutchmans.

Digital avatars also feature extensively in the third act, when the live sailors from Daland's crew confront the Dutchman's ghost sailors in a duelling chorus. According to Wagner's stage directions, the live performers of Daland's crew are meant to sing on stage, while the Dutchman's ghostly crew remains unseen (Grey 2000). This scene often presents a challenge for stage directors, who must address issues of acoustics and sightlines for the off-stage chorus while also providing a visual manifestation of the ghost sailors for the audience. Hodgman places the live performers offstage as per Wagner's instructions and replaces their physical bodies with digital versions that can be seen by the audience. While the digital avatars for Senta and the Dutchman are clearly associated with the live performers through corresponding clothing and behaviours, the digital ghost sailors do not have any identifiable traits that could link them to actual performers. Instead, the sailors are characterised as dark silhouettes on the deck of the digital ship and are animated to move and gesture in response to the taunts of Daland's crew. In this instance, the augmentation of the live performers and their transformation into digital avatars occurs in real time: achieved through the synthesis of the 'live' voices heard from the wings and the digital bodies seen on stage.

In these scenes, the use of causal interplay to transform and replace the live performers functions as a way to resolve some of the staging difficulties inherent to Wagner's opera, such as ghost sailors and the lovers' final rise to heaven. In each case, rather than having the live and the digital share the same theatrical space, Hodgman's staging relies on coordination and narrative context to ensure that the audience makes the necessary connection between the live performers and their digital replacements.

In this, Hodgman was also constrained by the technological logistics of 3D stereoscopy. 3D stereoscopy is difficult to integrate with live performers on stage, as their physical presence can disrupt the dual images of the 3D effect, particularly when the two elements are in close proximity

(Beckwith and Vincs 2013). It would be impossible to use 3D stereoscopy to partially digitalise the live performing body in the way used in Komische Oper Berlin's *The Magic Flute* or even The Royal Opera's *Don Giovanni*. As such, the extreme form of augmentation employed in *The Flying Dutchman* was Hodgman's only option for causal interplay between the live and the digital.

Full-synthesis extremes of agency and augmentation

Each of the four productions discussed in detail above can be categorised as partial-synthesis. In order to understand the full scope of causal interplay in practice, it is also useful to consider a full-synthesis case study. Full-synthesis productions employ causal interplay as the underlying basis for their scenographic designs and therefore draw on extremes of agency and augmentation as a way of maintaining multiple modes of connection between their live performers and digital elements. Opéra de Lyon's *L'Enfant et les Sortilèges* (2016) maintains the illusion of constant causal interplay through a combination of all-encompassing digital environments, action-based interactions with digital entities, and the digital augmentation of its live performers (Pont and Bonas 2016).

Opéra de Lyon, L'Enfant et les Sortilèges *(2016)—full-synthesis*

Premiered in 2016, Opéra de Lyon's production of Ravel's *L'Enfant et les Sortilèges* was commissioned in association with L'Auditori de Barcelona and Maestro Arts. The production was led by animator Grégoire Pont and stage director James Bonas, with Pont credited for both concept and video, and Bonas credited for 'spatial installation' (Opéra de Lyon 2019). In an interview, Pont notes that he personally conceived the premise for the production after attending a different performance of *L'Enfant et les Sortilèges* and being disappointed with the scenographic design. 'I heard the princess sing, "See these broken rings, see these branches, see these fruits," and there was nothing to see! I imagined the magic branches coming out of her hands because the music expressed this emotion, but nothing on stage conveyed it,' he recalls (personal communication, August 13, 2020). In conceiving his own fully animated version of Ravel's opera, Pont explains, 'I wanted to bring to the opera what cinema has been doing for a century' (personal communication, August 13, 2020).

Opéra de Lyon's production is dominated by Pont's hand-drawn animations, which are used to establish all-encompassing scenic environments, including a playroom and a forest, as well as augmenting and transforming the live performers (Pont and Bonas 2016). The physical set itself is spare and consists primarily of a silver gauze screen that spans the width of the stage and functions as the primary projection surface. The performers are garbed in nearly identical grey costumes, which allow them to assume multiple roles in the narrative as well as visually blend into the background of the scrim when the projections are superimposed on and around them.

Pont explains his underlying objectives for the scenographic design in the production playbill, noting: 'My wish is to use animation as a living matter. Not to project video sequences on a screen as so often happens in concert, but that the animation turns up where one least expects it' (Opéra de Lyon 2019). 'For instance,' he confirms in a later interview,

> a character is sad, then the rain spreads all around the scene. Or they fall in love, and then hundreds of flowers come out of their mouth exploding in joyful colours. Or a shiny armour is being drawn on another one, whilst dreaming of being a knight.
>
> (personal communication, August 13, 2020)

As suggested by Pont's description, both the variants of agency and augmentation are prominent techniques used in the production to create the illusion of a shared theatrical realm. The technique of augmentation is particularly critical because of the fantastical elements of the opera, in which both inanimate household objects and forest animals interact with the live performer playing the Child. Pont most frequently draws on digital scenography in order to partially digitalise and transform live performing bodies through visual superimposition. The live performers playing the Dragonfly and the Squirrel, for example, are transformed with projected dragonfly wings and a tail, respectively.

Pont uses a similar technique for the performers playing the Armchairs, the Grandfather Clock, and the Fire. Each performer is superimposed with projected characteristics of their designated role: the Armchairs are surrounded with a silhouette of their chair frames, the Clock is presented as a digital clockface that pulses in time with the rhythm of his aria, and the Fire is superimposed with flickering flames (Pont and Bonas 2016). The majority of the time, the digital elements are projected onto the scrim while the live performers are positioned behind it, creating a visual synthesis from the audience perspective and an illusory live–digital hybrid within the narrative. In the case of the Fire, Pont also employs projection mapping techniques, projecting digital flames onto the live performer's physical body, as well as on the screen around her.

Pont also uses digital elements to create physical extensions of his live performers, as well as completely replacing them with digital avatars. The live performers playing the Black Cat and White Cat, for example, are not superimposed with digital imagery but are framed as human extensions of digital versions. As each performer enters the stage, they are accompanied by a digital silhouette, which begins in human form and then transforms into the silhouette of a cat. The Cat duet is then sung as a seeming quartet, with both the live performers and their silhouette cat extensions physically interacting with one another. At the extreme, the character of Maman, or the Child's mother, is replaced entirely by various digital avatars. While the live performer sings from off stage, the character first manifests as a giant digital hand that interacts with the Child in the first scene of the opera. At the end of the opera, Maman's digital avatar again appears, this time manifesting as a giant red skirt who comforts the Child after his adventure.

Because nearly all of the live performers are augmented in some way, Pont's production design enables frequent instances of causal interplay that readily shift between the agency of the live performer and the digital elements. The Child is the only character that is not augmented over the course of the opera and thus functions as the primary point of connection for the majority of these moments. During the Child's tantrum in the opening scene, for example, the live performer punches and kicks the air around them, each time prompting a corresponding flash or digital stream of light on the projection surface (see Figure 2.6). Later, the Child engages in a digital 'boxing' match with the digital teapot and teacup. The performer attempts to block their digital blows and eventually lashes out, 'smashing' the china into pieces that fall to the base of the projection screen. Throughout the opera, the seeming agency within these interactions is fairly evenly divided between the live and the digital. Each component is framed as an equal performer, and the live performer never assumes primacy as an innate 'user' within the scenographic design.

As in Komische Oper Berlin's *The Magic Flute*, the full-synthesis employed in *L'Enfant et les Sortilèges* establishes a shared theatrical realm in which the live and the digital not only function as equivalents but are

Figure 2.6 L'Enfant throws a tantrum in Opéra de Lyon's *L'Enfant et les Sortilèges*. Photograph © Jean-Pierre Maurin.

perceived by the audience as being interchangeable. This is achieved by establishing multiple modes of connection between the live performers and their digital counterparts, from physically driven interactions with digital environments and digital characters to the partial transformation and complete replacement of the live performing body itself.

Like *The Magic Flute*, the scenographic design for *L'Enfant et les Sortilèges* also places certain restrictions on the live performers, who must adhere to pre-determined choreography in order to maintain the visual illusion. Pont explains, 'It's a tough job for them to learn all the precise positions so that the interaction works.' Recalling the necessity of at least four weeks of dedicated staging rehearsals with director James Bonas before the production premiered, Pont notes that the performers needed to learn 'how to play with the animations to get a perfect relationship' from the audience perspective (personal communication, August 13, 2020).

Autonomy: faux-interactivity versus functional interactivity

In each of the productions discussed so far, the causal interplay between the live performers and digital elements is an illusion. This illusion is the reflection of what Vincent et al. (2016) term 'faux-interactivity,' or the appearance of an interactive relationship which is created through the combination of pre-determined choreography and pre-set digital animations. In contrast, 'functional interactivity' reflects the *reality* of interplay between the live and the digital, in which the behaviour of the digital elements is physically triggered by the performers in some way.

Faux-interactive scenography cannot change in real time but is fixed in advance. As a result, the burden of maintaining the illusion of causal interplay rests entirely with the performers. Tamino must change positions according to the location of Pamina's digital portrait in Dutch National Opera's *The Magic Flute*, just as Leporello must assume a precise physical position in order to step into Don Giovanni's digital costume in The Royal Opera's *Don Giovanni*. Otherwise, the illusion of interactivity is destroyed.

Even productions that prioritise the agency of the live performer, such as William Kentridge's *The Magic Flute* for La Monnaie, rely on the live performer adhering to specific choreography that has been determined in advance. If the Queen of the Night fails to gesture at the appropriate time, the illusion of causal interplay with the cosmic projections behind her is destroyed, regardless of her seeming agency in the relationship. 'The reality is that performers are more agile than the projector, so once the idea has been worked out, it is ... the performer who must always hit a certain mark and never deviate. Video, sadly, will never breathe differently,' notes projection designer Wendall K. Harrington (personal communication, June 27, 2018).

Meanwhile, functional interactivity 'privileges the performer as a conscious driver and/or respondent within a networked loop' (Vincent et al.

2016, 48). While faux-interactivity requires the performer to prioritise the technology within their own behaviour, functional interactivity allows the performer to maintain physical independence in these interactions and 'drive' the reality of the live–digital relationship. Live performers can 'find their own movement pathways with the expectation that the digital entities will respond accordingly' (50).

The dichotomy between faux-interactivity and functional interactivity has a direct impact on the autonomy of live performers within the theatrical space. Depending on which form of interactivity is employed, their behaviour may or may not be fundamentally controlled by the requirements of the technology. We can see how this possibility reinforces longstanding anxieties that technology threatens the integrity of live performance (Auslander 1999). Giesekam (2007), for example, notes concerns that performers in digitally enhanced productions may become the modern-day equivalent of Edward Gordon Craig's *Übermarionetten*, 'with hitting their marks and lines exactly preventing them from investing their performance with an in-the-moment vitality and spontaneity' (15). Causey (2006) cites similar fears that the logistics involved in maintaining a visual illusion through faux-interactivity ensure that 'the slave machine dominates the master human subject' (16).

The degree to which a performer's autonomy is actually 'dominated' by faux-interactive scenography varies by production and is particularly informed by the mode of synthesis. Consider the extensive causal interplay in Komische Oper Berlin's full-synthesis *The Magic Flute*. In order to maintain the constant illusion of interactivity with the digital elements, the performers must adhere to precise choreography for the entirety of the performance and, in so doing, surrender most of their physical autonomy (Vincent and Vincent 2018). Similarly, in Opéra de Lyon's *L'Enfant et les Sortilèges*, the success of the illusion relies on the performers hitting their marks at designated moments in the score. Otherwise, the seeming causality built into scenes like the Child's boxing match with the digital teapot and teacup is unsustainable.

In contrast, consider Florida Grand Opera's partial-synthesis *Florencia en el Amazonas* (2018). For the majority of the production, the performers simply stand on the physical set of the river boat while the digital scenery moves behind them. At certain points in the narrative, the captain of the vessel 'steers' the physical boat, prompting the perspective of the digital scene to shift in response. In these few instances, the performer must adhere to pre-set timing and choreography in order to maintain the illusion of causal interplay (Condemi 2018). However, for the majority of the production, the performers can enjoy relative physical autonomy and maintain the illusion of causal interplay with minimal effort.

Given the range of extremes for causal interplay in practice, faux-interactivity alone does not provide a useful benchmark for assessing digital enhancement. However, as part of a dichotomy with functional interactivity, the technique comprises a key variant of causal interplay that can be used to compare different digitally enhanced productions.

The Metropolitan Opera, Das Rheingold *(2010)—partial-synthesis*

Robert Lepage's production of Wagner's *Der Ring des Nibelungen* (the *Ring* cycle) for The Metropolitan Opera (2010–2012) uses functional, real-time interactivity to achieve instances of causal interplay between its performers and digital elements. Designed under the auspices of Lepage's Montreal-based production company Ex Machina, the production features a 45-ton set and extensive video imagery—designed by Boris Firquet (*Das Rheingold* and *Die Walküre*), Pedro Pires (*Siegfried*), and Lionel Arnould (*Die Götterdämmerung*) (Stewart 2015). The high-tech production was touted by The Metropolitan Opera's general manager Peter Gelb as 'revolutionary' and a representation of 'what Wagner actually wanted to see on stage' (Tommasini 2012).[2]

The most striking element of the design is the physical set, which was conceived by Lepage's frequent collaborator Carl Fillion and dubbed 'the Machine' in a nod to the stage machinery of Baroque opera (Wakin 2010). Comprised of 24 nine-metre planks mounted on a mechanical axis, the Machine rotates into different configurations to convey particular scenic settings during the production (Wakin 2010). Video projections then provide the aluminium planks with a 'hyper-realistic skin' that reflects the dramaturgical needs of each scene (Smith 2012). Many of these projections are pre-rendered videos of conventional scenic effects, such as shifting clouds, water, and flames. However, the scenographic design also incorporates functionally interactive video content that responds in real time to the movement and sound of the performers on stage (Barbour 2011).

Lepage's interpretation of *Das Rheingold*, the first opera in the cycle, features a number of instances of causal interplay that stem from this use of functional real-time interactivity. When the opera begins, the Rhinemaidens dangle from wire harnesses in front of the vertical expanse of the Machine, which is superimposed with digital projections of watery currents (Lepage 2012). When the Rhinemaidens begin to sing, the digital background is punctuated with air bubbles that appear to emanate from the performers' mouths (see Figure 2.7). Later in the scene, the Rhinemaidens perch on the upper ledge of the Machine, which, representing the banks of the Rhine River, is strewn with digital pebbles. These pebbles shift and cascade whenever the Rhinemaidens shift positions, as well as later in the scene, when Alberich attempts to 'climb' up the planks to reach them.

The causal interplay in these instances is undeniable. With both the bubbles and the pebbles, the physical behaviour of the live performers is linked to a corresponding response in the digital elements. While this kind of relationship is illusory in the other digitally enhanced productions discussed in this chapter, Lepage's staging here reflects the reality of an interactive

Figure 2.7 The Rhinemaidens blow digital bubbles in The Metropolitan Opera's
        Das Rheingold. Photograph © Ken Howard for The Metropolitan Opera.

relationship between the live and the digital. Roger Parent, president of
Réalisations.net, which designed the infrared network for the real-time ef-
fects, explains: 'We're not playing a video of pebbles' (Barbour 2011, 57).
Instead, the pebbles are

> computer generated particles that are waiting to be triggered by per-
> formers on stage … [with] behaviors that are waiting to be activated.
> Because they're triggered by motion detection devices, they're ready to
> be influenced by an actor's voice or gestures.
>
>   (Barbour 2011, 57)

The approximate staging for the Rhinemaidens and Alberich is roughly
pre-determined—for example, the Rhinemaidens are meant to be seated on
the banks of the Rhine by a certain musical cue. The precise details of their
behaviour, however, remain flexible and potentially variable from performance to performance (Lepage 2012). Because the projected imagery responds to both movement and sound in real time, the Rhinemaidens even
retain a certain flexibility in their vocal quality. 'Whoever sings the loudest
gets the most bubbles' explains Lepage (2012).

   Later in the production, the live performers playing the gods Loge and
Donner are also staged to work in concert with functionally interactive digital components. In each of Loge's appearances, the performer is accompanied by a digital fiery glow that follows wherever he moves on stage (Barbour

2011). Like the bubbles and pebbles in the opening scene, the particle images that comprise the fiery glow are pre-programmed with specific behaviours, which are triggered by the performer during the live performance (Barbour 2011). The performer playing Donner enjoys a similar autonomy when he summons the digital storm in the penultimate scene of the opera. As Donner brandishes his prop hammer and slowly turns on stage, a digital storm gradually forms behind him. The performer then strikes the planks of the Machine and a bolt of digital lightning cracks across the projection surface.

These real-time effects are achieved by means of motion sensors and LED units built into each performer's costume (Barbour 2011). Once equipped, the performers can move through the stage space without threatening the visual cohesion of the digital scenography. No matter where Loge steps, his fiery glow will follow. Similarly, Donner is able to set his own pace as he summons the digital storm, confident that it will respond accordingly.

The functional nature of this causal interplay provides the performers with the opportunity for true agency in their relationship with digital components. Donner is not simply pretending to summon the revolving digital storm; he is actually controlling its behaviour with his own movement. Unlike the performers in Dutch National Opera's *The Magic Flute* or Victorian Opera's *Four Saints in Three Acts*, the performers in *Das Rheingold* actively control their relationship with the digital elements, or as Lepage explains, 'drive the electronic play' (Barbour 2011, 70).

Implications for performers and audiences

Of the three variants of causal interplay, agency and augmentation have the greatest impact on the audience perspective, as they direct and frame the spectator's understanding of the relationship between the live and the digital within the theatrical space. Yet, the question of autonomy—whether the effects being realised are the result of faux-interactivity or functional interactivity—speaks more closely to the experience of the performers themselves in relation to the technology.

There is no question that faux-interactivity places significant pressure on live performers who must adhere to pre-determined choreography in order to maintain the visual illusion of causal interplay. Full-synthesis productions, like Komische Oper Berlin's *The Magic Flute*, Opéra de Lyon's *L'Enfant et les Sortilèges*, and The Cleveland Orchestra's *The Cunning Little Vixen*, each rely on faux-interactive scenography, and in each case, the performers' adherence to pre-determined choreography directly impacts the success of the scenographic design.

Yet, even at these extremes, there is still a certain flexibility and even 'liveness' within faux-interactive scenography. In most cases, faux-interactive elements are individually cued, triggered by the stage manager in the course of a live performance. This is a necessary consideration in order to enable real-time adjustments of animations depending on the particular nuances and timings of each night's live performance. Soprano Martina Janková, who performed the role of the Vixen in The Cleveland Orchestra's *The Cunning Little Vixen*, describes the importance of this flexibility: 'They are able to move the figures on your own tempo. Because I am not a machine, and I will not sing every day the same' (McClung 2017).

Moreover, while functional interactivity imbues live performers with greater physical autonomy onstage, even this freedom has certain limitations. The performers in The Metropolitan Opera's *Das Rheingold* must continue to make their pre-set entrances and adhere to Lepage's staging instructions within the conventions of the operatic genre. They must also adhere to the text, rhythms, and notes of Wagner's score, as well as the musical tempo selected by the musical conductor. Performers are further restricted by the production's physical set, which shifts through pre-programmed configurations and dominates the majority of the stage space (Froemke 2012).

A comparison of functional interactivity and faux-interactivity must also take the audience into account. In The Metropolitan Opera's *Das Rheingold*, the Rhinemaidens are prompting their digital bubbles in real time, just as Donner is controlling the digital storm live. However, the visual effect is not substantially different from that of a faux-interactive production. As long as the relationship between the live and the digital appears to be causal, it is difficult for any spectator to discern whether the interplay is actually 'real' or merely an illusion. Given that the visual result is potentially the same, opera companies have to consider whether the use of functional interactivity is ultimately practical.

Projection designer Sven Ortel suggests that functional interactivity can be a major risk for companies that want a predictable outcome because the end result hinges on so many different factors.

> It's really hard to predict that a person will do exactly the right thing to generate a specific visual. If it's interactive, there's a pretty high chance it will not look exactly right. With pre-produced content that *looks* live, I can tell you exactly what it will be.
>
> (personal communication, May 21, 2020)

Ortel notes that, in his professional experience, functional interactivity is often discussed during conceptual meetings, but the effect is frequently cut and replaced with faux-interactivity at some point during the production design process.

Stage director Katie Mitchell cites cost as another major deterrent for using functional interactivity, both in terms of budget and in terms of staff resourcing. Mitchell frequently uses a technique called 'live cinema' in her theatrical productions, which involves real-time film footage that is cut and assembled during the live performance. However, she notes that the technique is rarely viable for opera productions. 'Inside normal opera budgets, staffing, and schedules, it's not possible to do that kind of work.

It's expensive and time-consuming, requiring very labor-intensive rehearsals with full technical equipment and staff—and a lot of technical time on stage' (personal communication, March 10, 2018). Except in exceptional circumstances, she suggests, pre-rendered illusions are simply more practical for opera companies than functionally interactive designs.

Given these considerations, it is perhaps not surprising that The Metropolitan Opera's *Ring* cycle is one of the only productions discussed in this book that explicitly employs real-time functional interactivity in order to achieve causal interplay. The overwhelming majority of digitally enhanced productions that were reviewed for this book instead rely on faux-interactive techniques, which create only the illusion of causal interplay between the live and the digital.

As we have seen, agency, augmentation, and autonomy are strategic dramaturgical techniques that can be used to create a visual synthesis between the live and the digital from the perspective of the audience. In each case, the variant suggests possibilities for the kind of causal interplay that will emerge during a partial- or full-synthesis production. From questions of which entity drives an interactive relationship to the nature of the interactivity itself, each form provides additional nuance for a consideration and comparison of digital scenography in opera production. The discussion also begins to highlight the degree to which digital scenography can potentially disrupt opera production, both on and off the stage, depending on the mode of synthesis and the variants of causal interplay employed. The next section of the book will explore this potential disruption, beginning with an examination of how digital technology fits into opera's scenographic lineage and longstanding production conventions.

Notes

1 There is extensive literature on hybrid figures in theatrical performance, particularly the concept of the cyborg. See Segel (1995), Giannachi (2004), Dixon (2007), Parker-Starbuck (2011), and Eckersall (2015).

2 Wagner's epic scenographic visions have long been at odds with the reality of theatrical resources. 'The quest to produce a perfect Ring remains opera's greatest challenge,' notes the opening to Susan Froemke's documentary about Lepage's production, *Wagner's Dream* (Froemke 2012). Even the premiere production of the *Ring* cycle in 1876—for which Wagner assumed the roles of both conductor and stage director—was fraught with complications due to the clash between Wagner's vision and the scenographic reality he was able to achieve on stage (Williams 2004; Kreuzer 2018).

References

Aleu, Franc, dir. 2019. *Turandot*, by Giacomo Puccini, Giuseppe Adami, and Renato Simoni. Streaming video. Gran Teatre del Liceu, Spain. https://www.youtube.com/watch?v=ltRdiafP0Us.

Aronson, Arnold. 2008. *Looking Into the Abyss: Essays on Scenography*. Ann Arbor: University of Michigan Press.

Auslander, Philip. 1999. *Liveness: Performance in a Mediatized Culture*. New York: Routledge.

Barbour, David. 2011. "The Road to Valhalla." *Lighting and Sound America*, January 2011. http://www.lightingandsoundamerica.com/metoperaringcycle.pdf.

Beckwith, Megan, and Kim Vincs. 2013. "Stereoscopic Theatre: The Impact of Gestalt Perceptual Organization in the Stereoscopic Theatre Environment." In *Proceedings of the 19th International Symposium on Electronic Art, ISEA2013*, edited by Kathy Cleland, Laura Fisher, and Ross Harley, 1–5. Sydney: University of Sydney.

Cassiers, Guy, dir. 2013. *Das Rheingold*, by Richard Wagner. DVD. Teatro alla Scala, Milan. Arthaus Musik.

Causey, Matthew. 2006. *Theatre and Performance in Digital Culture: From Simulation to Embeddedness*. London: Routledge.

Condemi, Jose Maria, dir. 2018. *Florencia en al Amazonas*, by Daniel Catán and Marcela Fuentes-Berain. Streaming video. Florida Grand Opera, USA.

D'Aoust, Jason R. 2015. "Digital Scenography and the Mimetic Aporia of Richard Wagner's *Ring Cycle*." *Journal of Aesthetics & Culture* 7, no. 1: 1–11. https://doi.org/10.3402/jac.v7.28238

Dixon, Steve. 2007. *Digital Performance: A History of New Media in Theater, Dance, Performance Art, and Installation*. Cambridge: MIT Press.

Eckersall, Peter. 2015. "Towards a Dramaturgy of Robots and Object-Figures." *The Drama Review* 59, no. 3: 123–131. https://doi.org/10.1162/DRAM_a_00474

Froemke, Susan, dir. 2012. *Wagner's Dream: The Making of The Metropolitan Opera's New Der Ring Des Nibelungen*. DVD. Deutsche Grammophon.

Giannachi, Gabriella. 2004. *Virtual Theatres: An Introduction*. New York: Routledge.

Giesekam, Greg. 2007. *Staging the Screen: The Use of Film and Video in Theatre*. Basingstoke: Palgrave Macmillan.

Grey, Thomas, ed. 2000. *Richard Wagner: Der Fliegender Holländer*. Cambridge: Cambridge University Press.

Holten, Kasper, dir. 2014. *Don Giovanni*, by Wolfgang A. Mozart and Lorenzo da Ponte. DVD. Royal Opera House, London. Opus Arte.

Kentridge, William. 2007. "Drawing the Stage." In *William Kentridge: Flute*, edited by Bronwyn Law-Viljoen, 66–78. Johannesburg: David Krut Publishing.

Kentridge, William, dir. 2012. *Die Zauberflöte*, by Wolfgang A. Mozart and Emanuel Schikaneder. DVD. Teatro alla Scala, Milan. Opus Arte.

Komische Oper Berlin. 2017. "Petruschka/L'Enfant et les Sortilèges | Trailer | Komische Oper Berlin." Youtube video, 1:15. https://www.youtube.com/watch?v=SJpjHR5-Ki0.

Kreuzer, Gundula. 2018. *Curtain, Gong, Steam: Wagnerian Technologies of Nineteenth-Century Opera*. Oakland: University of California Press.

Lepage, Robert, dir. 2012. *Das Rheingold*, by Richard Wagner. DVD. The Metropolitan Opera. Deutsche Grammophon.

McBurney, Simon, dir. 2015. *Die Zauberflöte*, by Wolfgang A. Mozart and Emanuel Schikaneder. DVD. Dutch National Opera, Amsterdam. Opus Arte.

McClung, Don, dir. 2017. *Opera Reimagined: Animating the Cunning Little Vixen*. Documentary, 26:47. WVIZ/PBS Ideastream.

Montgomery, Alan. 2014. "In Review: *The Cunning Little Vixen*." *Opera News*, May 17, 2014. https://www.operanews.com/Opera_News_Magazine/2014/5/Reviews/CLEVELAND__Vixen.html.

Mutter, Zoe. 2014. "Case Study: Ambitious Opera Pushes the Visual Bounda-
ries." *AV Magazine*, April 28, 2014. https://www.avinteractive.com/features/
case-studies/case-study-ambitious-opera-pushes-visual-boundaries-28-04-2014/.

Opéra de Lyon. 2019. *Program for L'Enfant et les Sortilèges*. November 2019. https://
fr.calameo.com/read/0009046824044f51db97f.

Packer, Randall, and Ken Jordan, eds. 2001. *Multimedia: From Wagner to Virtual
Reality*. New York: W.W. Norton & Company.

Parker-Starbuck, Jennifer. 2011. *Cyborg Theatre: Corporeal/Technological Intersec-
tions in Multimedia Performance*. Basingstoke: Palgrave Macmillan.

Pont, Grégoire, and James Bonas, dir. 2016. *L'Enfant et les Sortilèges*, by Maurice
Ravel and Colette. Streaming video. Opéra de Lyon, France. https://www.france.
tv/france-5/passage-des-arts/1385465-l-enfant-et-les-sortileges.html.

Segel, Harold B. 1995. *Pinocchio's Progeny: Puppets, Marionettes, Automatons, and
Robots in Modernist and Avant-Garde Drama*. Baltimore: Johns Hopkins University Press.

Smith, Roberta. 2012. "Video's Shifting 'Ring' Roles." *New York Times*, May 13, 2012.
http://www.nytimes.com/2012/05/14/arts/music/video-as-art-in-lepages-ring-
at-the-metropolitan-opera.html.

Smuts, Aaron. 2009. "What Is Interactivity?" *The Journal of Aesthetic Education* 43,
no. 4: 53–73.

Stewart, James B. 2015. "A Fight at the Opera." *The New Yorker*, March 23, 2015.
https://www.newyorker.com/magazine/2015/03/23/a-fight-at-the-opera.

Tommasini, Anthony. 2012. "The Met, the 'Ring' and the Rage against the Machine." *New York Times*, April 4, 2012. https://www.nytimes.com/2012/04/04/arts/
music/peter-gelb-on-wagners-ring-cycle-at-met-opera.html.

Vincent, Caitlin, and Jordan Beth Vincent. 2018. "Notation by Context: Digital Scenography as Artifact of Authorial Intent." *Leonardo Music Journal* 28: 72–76.
https://doi.org/10.1162/lmj_a_01044.

Vincent, Jordan Beth, Caitlin Vincent, Kim Vincs, and John McCormick. 2016.
"Navigating Control and Illusion: Interactivity Versus 'Faux-Interactivity' in
Trans-Media Dance Performance." *International Journal of Performance Arts and
Digital Media* 12, no. 1: 44–60. https://doi.org/10.1080/14794713.2016.1161955.

Vincs, Kim, Nancy Black, Jordan Beth Vincent, John McCormick, Daniel Skovli,
Peter Divers, Simeon Taylor, Kieren Wallace, Thom Ingram, Stephen Jeal, and
Casey Dalbo. 2016. *Four Saints in Three Acts (3D Stereoscopic Scenographic Vis-
ualisations) for Victorian Opera*. Melbourne: Victorian Opera.

Vincs, Kim, John McCormick, Daniel Skovli, Simeon Taylor, and Kieren Wallace.
2015. *The Flying Dutchman (3D Stereoscopic Scenographic Visualisations) for Victorian Opera*. Melbourne: Victorian Opera.

Wakin, Daniel J. 2010. "The Valhalla Machine." *New York Times*, September 15,
2010. http://www.nytimes.com/2010/09/19/arts/music/19ring.html.

Williams, Simon. 2004. *Wagner and the Romantic Hero*. Cambridge: Cambridge
University Press.

Woolfe, Zachary. 2014. "Adding Technology to Animal Instincts: 'The Cunning
Little Vixen' Uses Projections in Cleveland." *New York Times*, May 23, 2014.
https://www.nytimes.com/2014/05/24/arts/music/the-cunning-little-vixen-uses-
projections-in-cleveland.html.

3 The lineage of digital scenography in opera

Baroque origins to the twentieth century

Chapters 1 and 2 establish a framework for identifying and assessing trends in digital scenography in opera production. The modes of synthesis and, in particular, the variants of causal interplay outline the ways in which live performers can be integrated with digital elements from the audience perspective. What remains unclear from the discussion is the degree to which these forms of digital scenography are disruptive to operatic conventions, both on and off the stage.

This chapter will explore whether digital scenography represents a deviation from opera's longstanding scenic conventions or merely a high-tech continuation of them. This analysis continues to draw on the premise of 'scenography,' or the three-way interplay between the performer, the stage setting, and the spectator, to trace the artistic lineage of opera production from its Baroque origins to the turn of the twentieth century. The discussion considers the ways in which opera scenography historically engaged with the same interplay that informs dramaturgical possibilities for digital scenography in the present day. The analysis will also consider pre-digital parallels to the modes of synthesis in practice.

As Giesekam (2007) argues, the use of recorded media in theatre is generally perceived as a recent development. Part of this 'historical amnesia,' according to Giesekam, stems from a misunderstanding of the difference between the physical technology that enables digital projections on stage and the scenographic effects that are produced (1). While many of the techniques and technologies currently being employed in digitally enhanced production are indeed 'new,' the scenographic objectives that drive their use are not.

Technological developments have long provided the means for scenic innovation in theatre (McKinney and Butterworth 2009; Baugh 2013). The introduction of technologies such as Giovan Battista Aleotti's rolling chariots in the seventeenth century and Émile Argand's stage lamps in the eighteenth century allowed for new kinds of stage settings to emerge. Baugh (2013) cites nineteenth-century inventions like limelight, aniline dye, and hydraulic power as equally influential for the advancement of theatrical design.[1] In each of these cases, the underlying catalyst for scenographic development

DOI: 10.4324/9781003093305-3

was not solely the technology, but the technology in concert with a practitioner who was attempting to shift existing production conventions.

In this context, the historical development of scenography is best understood as a self-perpetuating cycle in which new innovations were both the result of, and catalyst for, further developments. As innovations were gradually accepted and integrated into production conventions, the new scenographic status quo inspired subsequent innovations among the next generation of practitioners. We can see examples of this dating back to the theatre of the Renaissance, with prominent stage practitioners like Bernardo Buontalenti, Inigo Jones, and Philippe de Loutherbourg[2] establishing new standards for sets and scenery, only to be, as Baugh (2013) notes, 'radically questioned and overthrown' by subsequent artists and practitioners (11).

Here, the concept of 'artistic spawning' is useful in considering the development of digital scenography in opera. Outlined by Vincent et al. (2018), the concept describes a dual existence for any 'spawn' within the artistic lineage of a performance art form. A spawn is firstly 'an autonomous and self-contained work that may benefit from, but does not rely on, an understanding of its unique lineage.' At the same time, a spawn is also 'the embodiment of a specific history, origin, and inspiration that can *only* be defined by its "parent" source' (285). Extrapolating from this premise, every scenographic innovation over the course of opera's history can be classified as an artistic 'spawn,' or part of a continuous artistic lineage that extends back to an original paradigm or 'parent' source. This original paradigm stems from the production standards that were established when the operatic genre first emerged as a commercial art form in seventeenth-century Italy. While digital scenography may seem far removed from the antiquated conventions of the Baroque opera stage, the premise of artistic spawning suggests that digital elements in modern-day production can be seen as the latest 'spawn' in a lineage of scenic conventions that stems from this early paradigm.

This chapter begins with an outline of the original Baroque paradigm, or 'parent' source, for opera scenography and the resulting relationship between the performer, the scenic setting, and the spectator. The chapter then examines three innovations that occurred over subsequent centuries with major impacts on the trajectory of operatic design: Ferdinando Galli-Bibiena's theory of angled perspective, Richard Wagner's designs for the Bayreuth Festspielhaus, and Adolphe Appia's concept of dynamic light.

No attempt is made to outline a complete artistic lineage of operatic scenography or trace every facet of the genre's evolution up to the turn of the twentieth century. Instead, the discussion focuses on the work of Galli-Bibiena, Wagner, and Appia as representative of larger shifts that occurred in the genre, as well as in theatre production more generally. Each of the scenographic innovations can be linked to advances in technology, as McKinney and Butterworth (2009) and Baugh (2013) suggest. They can also be recognised as artistic reactions to the production conventions that preceded them. In each case, the underlying source of this reaction—and the subsequent innovation—centred on a dissatisfaction with the relationship between the performer, stage setting, and spectator within the theatrical space.

In the course of the discussion, we will find parallels to current trends in digital scenography in opera, centuries before film and media technologies existed. Of course, these early developments were limited by the technological capabilities of their time. Yet, each innovation can still be framed in the context of the modes of synthesis and recognised as part of an effort to address a perceived imbalance in the three-way interplay of scenography.

The origins of the Baroque opera paradigm

In *Opera in Seventeenth-Century Venice: The Creation of the Genre,* Rosand (1991) provides a detailed overview of the origins of opera in Italy, beginning with the courtly musical entertainments of Venice and Florence. Works such as Jacopo Peri's *Euridice* (1600), Giulio Caccini's *Il rapimento di Cefalo* (1600), and Claudio Monteverdi's *L'Orfeo* (1607) were commissioned to honour specific political and social events, and production logistics were determined by both space considerations and the whims of noble patrons. According to *Il Corago*, a theatrical treatise published in the 1620s, nearly any space could be converted into a theatrical setting for a courtly performance (Baker 2013). The anonymous author boasts, 'in the same room in which a prince was received with public ceremony ... within the space of four hours, while the prince lunched elsewhere, a stage with its scenery could be made to appear' (Ossi 1998, 16).

While *L'Orfeo* and other early works established a model of private, courtly performance, the genre of opera as a commercial entertainment emerged in the late 1630s (Rosand 1991; Glixon and Glixon 2006; Johnson 2018). Baker (2013) identifies the 1637 premiere of Benedetto Ferrari and Francesco Manelli's *Andromeda* at the Teatro San Cassiano in Venice as the first instance of an opera audience paying for admission. From this point on, opera was no longer limited to aristocrats and scholars in royal courts but was 'a public and for-profit enterprise' (11) in which 'anyone who could afford the price of a ticket now had the opportunity to witness the scenic marvels' (16). The new model of public opera quickly spread to other European countries via travelling opera troupes, published theatrical treatises, and Italian scenic designers hired by various royal courts (Baker 2013; Johnson 2018).

A paying audience that included both aristocrats and the bourgeoisie had a substantial impact on the scenographic model for opera during this early period. Given the necessity of funding productions solely from admission costs, theatre owners and impresarios had an active interest in enticing audience members to attend their theatres over those of their competitors (Baker 2013).[3] Public opera productions adopted spectacular settings and impressive visual effects in order to appeal to the audience of 'patricians and *cittadini,* tourists and travelers, Venetians and foreigners, all of whom paid for the privilege of being entertained' (Rosand 1991, 14).[4]

It became clear that existing venues were ill-equipped to meet the scenic needs of commercial opera. Opera productions required permanent theatrical venues with built-in technical capacity rather than the temporary arrangements used for courtly performances or the small-scale theatres that hosted *commedia dell'arte*[5] (Johnson 2018). Following the premiere of *Andromeda*, the standard for newly constructed opera houses was a horseshoe-shaped auditorium with benches and either raised galleries or tiered boxes that extended into the proscenium arch outlining the stage (Ferrero 2002). These galleries and boxes reflected the social hierarchy of the time, with the lowest two rows—and the best views of the stage—reserved for the most important audience members and the royal box (Rosand 1991; Izenour 1992). The stage itself extended into the auditorium, and this deep 'forestage' was primarily used by the performers, who entered and exited on either side (Baker 2013, 15).

The sets for these early operas were modelled after the theatrical concepts of the Renaissance, many of which, in turn, revived concepts from classical antiquity. The primary basis for all sets was the perspective stage (see Figure 3.1). Architect Sebastian Serlio (1475–c. 1554) served as a key figure in this development due to his use of *periaktoi*, three-dimensional wings that were placed symmetrically at receding points along the stage (Johnson 2018).[6] These set pieces had scenery painted on each side and could be rotated to allow for quick set changes over the course of a performance. The painted imagery adhered to the laws of linear perspective and created the illusion of depth when combined with the painted backdrop and raked stage (Kuritz 1988).

Baroque opera productions also typically featured a number of set changes achieved through a complex system of ropes, pulleys, and levers. Machinery was operated by stagehands who, under the command of a chief machinist, would either walk elements of the scenery on and off the stage or raise and lower set pieces via pulleys and winches (Izenour 1992). Particularly complex stage machinery was fitted above, behind, and beneath the stage in order to enable 'supernatural interventions, sudden apparitions and magical transformations' (Kreuzer 2018, 8). The most common effects involved 'descents and ascents of gods, often in or on clouds, which not only moved, but could expand or contract, open up to reveal persons or things inside, or even transform into words or figures' (Glixon and Glixon 2006, 246).

Even in the early decades of opera production, scenic innovations were in a state of constant refinement. Soon after the turn of the seventeenth century, architect Giovan Battista Aleotti (1546–1636) redesigned Serlio's three-dimensional wings as flat panels and mounted them on rolling chariots, or *carozze*, that could be moved in and out of the audience's line of sight (Baker 2013; Baker 2018). Inigo Jones (1573–1652) improved on Aleotti's innovation in his designs for the court masques of Charles I, in which he ran the wings through wooden grooves in the floor to allow for more efficient set changes (Radice 1998). Jones also introduced a set of shutters that could be used to change the scenic backdrop (Crabtree and Beudert 2005).

Figure 3.1 Design for a theatre set by Giacomo Torelli for the ballet *Les Noces de Thétis*. Engraved by Israel Silvestre, 1654. Metropolitan Museum of Art: The Elisha Whittelsey Collection, The Elisha Whittelsey Fund, 1951. Creative Commons Public Domain.

The emphasis on refinement extended to the stage machinery used to achieve special effects. The majority of these devices were not new inventions designed for commercial opera production but had been developed for other theatrical genres in previous decades (Baker 2018). The dissemination of several seventeenth-century theatrical treatises, including those by Nicola Sabbatini (1574–1654) and Giacomo Torelli (1608–1678), popularised their use in opera by providing clear instructions on the varying effects that could be achieved (Baker 2013).

Torelli's treatise, in particular, outlined a new method for the logistical operation of existing stage machinery. Moving stage settings generally required a number of stagehands to physically push or pull chariots into position, but Torelli's invention allowed a stagehand to operate a single winch, 'which pulled the ropes attached to one set of chariots onto the stage while simultaneously pulling the other set of chariots into the wings and out of view' (Baker 2013, 22). Torelli's method for moving set pieces became known as the 'chariot and pole system' and led to his emergence as the first real celebrity of the operatic genre (Crabtree and Beudert 2005). Deemed *grand sorcier*, or the Great Wizard, Torelli and his stage machinery would set the standard for spectacle in opera throughout Europe (Baker 2013).

The Baroque paradigm and the interplay between performer, stage setting, and spectator

The significance of stage machinery and spectacle as part of the early Baroque paradigm is critical for understanding the resulting relationship between the performer and the scenic setting from the audience perspective. 'Audiences went to the theatre to be stunned by the cleverness of the illusions the scene designers had created,' notes Johnson (2018, 221). Ossi (1998) argues that stage machinery was particularly crucial for the establishment of what Italian musicologist Nino Pirrotta termed the 'theatrical game' (Pirrotta and Povoledo 1975, 237). 'Central to the aesthetics of early opera,' Ossi (1998) explains, 'was a kind of competition between the audience and the architecture in which the former tried to figure out the means by which the stage effects were carried out, while the latter endeavored to hide them' (16).

Ossi (1998) cites Bernardo Buontalenti's stage designs for Giulio Caccini's *Il Rapimento di Cefalo* (1600) as an example of this kind of active engagement between the stage design and the spectator. According to the production notes, the curtain opened on an 11-metre recreation of Mount Helicon, which deflated into a woodland setting, morphed into a seascape featuring an eight-metre whale with a moveable tail, and then transformed into a giant pyramid of Tuscan cities. These spectacular settings were meant to dazzle the audience with both their obvious artificiality and the mystery of how they were achieved. Ossi notes, 'That one could see the transformation and yet not divine its workings was integral to the success of the "theatrical game"' (33).

The premise of the theatrical game was enhanced by the physical layout of the Baroque opera theatre. The protruding forestage, as well as the gallery boxes that extended into the proscenium arch, prevented a clear delineation between the illusion of the stage and the reality of the spectator (Howard 2002; Baugh 2013). 'The forestage effectively placed the actors in the same room as the audience,' note McKinney and Butterworth (2009), as well as the orchestral musicians, who were seated on the same level (107). The presentational style of Baroque opera also blurred the realms between the stage and the audience, with performers often addressing spectators directly (Kelly 2004). In addition, while a curtain separated the stage from the audience before the start of each performance, all subsequent scene changes were presented in full view. These exposed scene changes were considered an integral element of the 'theatrical game,' as well as the overall operatic experience.

The primary objective for the use of stage machinery was to impress the audience by highlighting the overtly theatrical nature of the performance. Technology functioned as 'an artistic miracle in and of itself' (Kreuzer 2018, 8). In this, we can see parallels to the suspension of disbelief built into instances of causal interplay between live performers and digital elements in digitally enhanced opera production. In both cases, while the audience members are cognisant of the 'smoke and mirrors' at play, the mystery of how the effects are achieved contributes to the enjoyment of the experience.

While fantastical visual effects allowed for active engagement between the stage setting and the spectator via the theatrical game, the conventions of Baroque opera were highly restrictive for the performer. Performers were primarily limited to the forestage area as this ensured they would not ruin the illusion of the painted perspective scenery (Ossi 1998). As long as they remained on the forestage, they cohered with the dimensions of the background setting (Baker 2013). However, any 'full-size humans toward the rear of the scene would expose the tricks of perspective in the diminishing rear wing flats and drops' (Stahura 1998, 101). The only exception to this detachment was when performers entered or exited through the traps in the stage floor or were physically transported by stage machinery (Ossi 1998).

The potential threat posed by the performer to the visual cohesion of the set is one that we can also trace to modern-day concerns about faux-interactivity and causal interplay. Although the scenic materials are different in the two periods, in both cases efforts to maintain the illusion of the stage setting are prioritised over the performers' physical independence.

As a result, Baroque opera scenography was largely defined by a layered visual experience. Stage machinery, visual effects, and painted perspective scenery were used upstage and comprised the majority of the stage space. Meanwhile, performers had limited interaction with their scenic surroundings and remained largely restricted to the forestage where they interacted with the audience (Ossi 1998). In essence, 'two very different scenic approaches were employed simultaneously, giving audiences two contrasting modes of presentation' (McKinney and Butterworth 2009, 106). This layered effect can be seen as a precursor to non-synthesis and the use of visual correlation, with performers operating almost completely independently from the scenery behind them.

While modern-day manifestations of non-synthesis reflect a dramaturgical choice, Baroque conventions were driven by necessity. Scenography was constrained by the limitations of technology at the time, which, in turn, informed the relationship between performer, stage setting, and spectator. Performers could not be physically integrated into the stage space because they interfered with the visual illusion of the painted scenery and threatened the theatrical game. With the relationship between the stage setting and the spectator prioritised, the Baroque performer remained disconnected from the visual world of the narrative.

New perspectives: the scenic reforms of Ferdinando Galli-Bibiena (1657–1743)

Through the first two decades of the eighteenth century, the Baroque paradigm dominated operatic design. Scenic painters endeavoured to impress their audiences with the illusion of size and depth in their perspective scenery. Meanwhile, 'gods constantly intervened in human affairs, providing a pretext for ... displays of theatrical machinery' (Baker 2013, 39). Distaste for these visual excesses led to the first major operatic reform, led by Gian Vincenzo Gravina (1664–1718) and other members of the Arcadian academy in Rome. Aspiring for a return to the Aristotelian model of Greek tragedy (van Baest 2000), these literati reformers objected to opera's excessive spectacle and emphasised historical events over myths and legends in their opera libretti (Littlejohn 1994; Heartz 2004).[7] Dissatisfaction with existing scenic conventions also led to a major innovation in scenographic design: Ferdinando Galli-Bibiena's new principles of perspective.

Painted scenery within the Baroque paradigm relied on traditional linear perspective, in which a single vanishing point was positioned at the exact centre of the stage (Baker 2018; Brejzek 2018). This placement emphasised the importance of the ruling noble or patron who was guaranteed to have the best view of the visual illusion from the central box of the auditorium (Baker 2013). In his 1711 treatise *L'Architettura Civile,* however, Galli-Bibiena proposed a new method for skewing the lines of painted perspective at 45-degree angles, a concept which he termed '*scena veduta per angolo,*' or 'scenes viewed through angles' (Baker 2013). Through this technique, the vanishing point in painted scenery was no longer restricted to a central location but could be placed anywhere within the stage setting (see Figure 3.2).

Other theatre designers, such as Nicola Sabbatini, had theorised using angled lines of perspective, but Galli-Bibiena was the first to outline the technique in practice, a shift which 'revolutionized theatrical production' (Baker 2013, 49). In addition to providing instructions on how to build a variety of perspectives into a painted setting, Galli-Bibiena included detailed illustrations in his treatise that helped others recreate his methods in their own work. Designers could now incorporate multiple perspectives into a single stage setting (Camp 2014) and create 'the illusion of seemingly limitless stage depth for larger, and even more critically, for smaller stages' (Baker 2013, 51).

Galli-Bibiena's innovation had a major impact on the relationship between the performer, the stage setting, and the spectator. Because lines of perspective could now be placed anywhere within the painted scenery, everyone in the audience could appreciate the visual illusion, regardless of social station (Pérez-Gómez and Pelletier 2000). This democratisation of the audience reflected the changing social hierarchy of the time but also helped to create a more immersive theatrical experience (Baker 2013). Pelletier (2006) explains,

> the perspective illusion of the *scena per angolo* projected the walls of virtual cities forward, to embrace the audience. The eye of the spectator was intentionally pulled in various directions to create the illusion of an endless extension to the stage.

(26)

Figure 3.2 Angled lines of perspective in a stage setting by Ferdinando Galli-
Bibiena ('Varie opere di Prospettive'). Drawn and engraved by Pietro
Giovanni Abbati, 1703. Metropolitan Museum of Art: Harris Brisbane
Dick Fund, 1926. Creative Commons Public Domain.

Rather than highlighting the mystery of machinery as the forefront of a
theatre production, Galli-Bibiena endeavoured to create an experience that
would draw the spectator into the reality of the narrative world.

Galli-Bibiena's scenographic innovation was particularly significant for
the performer. No longer limited to the forestage, performers could now

move freely up to the first set of wings (Baker 2013). They could still potentially disrupt the illusion of the perspective scenery—for example, if they moved too close to the backdrop or did not travel in a diagonal pattern that aligned with the angle of the painted flats—but performers enjoyed far greater flexibility of movement than in the Baroque paradigm (Baker 2018).

With Galli-Bibiena's development, scenic design was no longer defined in terms of two detached visual layers. Instead, performers could be partially integrated into the visual illusion of the stage setting. While this partial integration is a far reach from the examples of causal interplay seen in digitally enhanced opera production in the present day, we can see how this integration was designed to create a more synthesised theatrical experience. Rather than functioning as a separate visual effect, performers were increasingly framed within the visual context of their scenic surroundings.

Galli-Bibiena's techniques spread throughout Europe, and angled perspective soon became an integral element of opera and theatre production worldwide.[8] Crabtree and Beudert (2005) describe the innovation as 'the most pervasive force in scenic design in the seventeenth and eighteenth century' (382). Along with Aleotti's rolling chariots and Torelli's scenery winches, Galli-Bibiena's new principles for perspective fundamentally reshaped the principles of stage design in opera for the next two centuries.

The increasingly immersive relationship between the stage setting and the spectator signalled a withdrawal from the established conventions of the Baroque. More crucially, Galli-Bibiena's innovation led to a new understanding of the potential role of the performer. No longer a disconnected figure in competition with the scenic design, the performer could now be partially integrated into the overall setting. Both of these adjustments would inform and influence subsequent generations of designers and impresarios in opera and beyond, all while leading to another key scenographic innovation: Richard Wagner's (1813–1883) designs for the Bayreuth Festspielhaus.

The scenographic transition to 'grand opera'

By the 1820s, Baroque scenographic conventions as modified by Galli-Bibiena remained largely unchanged. Opera theatres continued to feature the standard arrangement of a horseshoe auditorium, a proscenium arch and protruding forestage, galleries of boxes, and a designated orchestral area on the same level as the audience (Baker 1998). The combination of painted scenery and complex stage machinery continued to dominate scenic designs, while set changes also generally remained on full display.

The style of operatic repertoire being presented on stage, however, began to shift towards Romanticism, with an emphasis on historical accuracy and the 'architectural grandeur suggested by distant places and eras' (Pendle and Wilkins 1998, 173). This shift was led by the Opéra de Paris[9]—the pinnacle of operatic innovation at the time—through the company's development of an archetype that would become known as 'grand opera.'[10] Pendle and Wilkins (1998) identify the 1828 premiere of Daniel-Francois-Esprit

Auber's *La Muette de Portici* as the first opera in this new style, which was defined by its five-act structure, 'historical plots, local color, a dramaturgy based on the concept of the musico-visual tableau, modern dancing styles, masses of people on stage, and scenic wonders' (171).

In order to achieve the large-scale scenic effects required for grand opera, productions made certain adjustments to existing scenographic techniques, including the adoption of panoramic backdrops, irregularly shaped flats, and three-dimensional set pieces (Baker 1998). However, the fundamental principles of set design still aligned to those of previous centuries. Scene changes at the Opéra de Paris, for example, relied on the same mechanical methods established by Torelli and Aleotti in the seventeenth century but simply drew on more manpower to support the increased scale of their productions.[11]

Concerns about maintaining the illusion of painted perspective scenery also continued to inform production logistics. The Opéra's *Comité de Mise en Scène,* which was founded in 1827 to maintain set and costume standards, specifically prohibited any painted figures in backdrops or flats. The argument was that 'whenever actual performers stood next to that scenery, the settings, due to a skewed perspective, invited ridicule' (Baker 2013, 141). As in previous centuries, performers were still at odds with their scenic surroundings as their physical presence threatened to destroy the illusion of the painted perspective.

The rise of grand opera notably corresponds to the earliest use of projected imagery in opera. Abbate and Parker (2015) cite a production of Carl Maria von Weber's *Der Freischütz* at Berlin Schauspielhaus in 1821 as the first example, noting that projections were used to realise the supernatural effects required for the midnight scene in the Wolf's Glen. The production relied on a variation of a magic lantern optical device, which projected images onto the stage through a combination of lenses, hand-painted glass slides, and an internal light source (Mannoni 2000).[12] Invented in 1659, the device was popular among travelling showmen but had been somewhat impractical for theatrical venues until the invention of limelight in the early 1820s. This innovation allowed for brighter and larger projections and led to a marked increase in the use of magic lantern effects in both opera and theatre production (Walne 1995).

Magic lantern devices were subsequently used to project clouds and apparitions in Arrigo Boito's *Mefistofele* in 1868, realise the supernatural ride of the Valkyries for the premiere of Richard Wagner's *Die Walküre* in 1870, and enhance the painted moon for the premiere of Jules Massenet's *Esclarmonde* in 1888, among other examples (Huebner 1999; Wilson Smith 2007; Campana 2015). Then as now, we can see how projected elements often solved staging challenges built into opera narratives, particularly those requiring supernatural or fantastical effects.

The shift to Romanticism also led to an exploration of projecting 'ghostly' performers on stage, again anticipating present-day digital performers. The popular effect of 'Pepper's Ghost'[13] involved reflecting light from a hidden object or person onto a pane of glass on stage. A projected image of the original object would then appear to be floating in mid-air, much to the delight of the audience (Luckhurst and Morin 2014). Burdekin (2015) cites a number of opera productions that experimented with the technique as a way of realising ghosts, demons, and other supernatural apparitions in works such as Richard Wagner's *The Flying Dutchman,* Carl Maria von Weber's *Der Freischütz,* and John Barnett's *The Mountain Sylph.*[14]

Yet, as the form of grand opera assumed primacy in the repertoire, the overall experience was still defined by overt theatricality, much as in the Baroque paradigm. This was due in part to opera's continued emphasis on spectacle and dazzling special effects as a way of attracting audience members (Kreuzer 2018). Audience members were also still acutely aware of their own presence within the theatrical space and attended the opera not only to witness the illusions on stage but to become part of the spectacle themselves (Lacombe 2003). This seeming imbalance within existing production conventions had a significant effect on composer Richard Wagner, who was driven to respond with new scenic innovations.

The 'mystic chasm': Richard Wagner (1813–1883) and the Bayreuth Festspielhaus

Wagner moved to Paris in 1839 with the intention of launching his career as an opera composer. He attended at least ten different productions at the Opéra de Paris and even befriended one of the theatre's chief scenic designers, Éduoard Despléchin (Baker 1998; Carnegy 2006). Wagner was initially eager to emulate the marvels of the Opéra in his own productions. His early opera *Rienzi*, which premiered at the Dresden Court Theatre in 1843, was specifically designed around the model of grand opera and featured 'massive choruses, processions, public prayers, ballets, riots, off-stage battles, and a conflagration to conclude it all' (Carnegy 2006, 33).

While Wagner admired the technical capabilities of the Opéra, he became dissatisfied with productions that seemed designed solely to entertain the audience (Williams 2004). In his opinion, the use of technology for technology's sake, or what Wagner derided as 'effect without cause,' undermined the integrity of the work and dissolved 'the whole of Art into its mechanical integers' (Wagner 1851, 95–99). Wagner was also appalled by the social aspect of opera performance, in which audience members openly talked, ate, and moved through the auditorium. Because of the distractions perpetuated by both the spectacle on stage and the spectators themselves, Wagner believed that audiences were prevented from experiencing opera as a cohesive artistic work (Baker 1998).

In 1849, Wagner published *The Artwork of the Future*, one of several theoretical essays that outlined his proposed changes to existing production conventions. He would later embed many of these changes in the physical structure of the Bayreuth Festspielhaus, built between 1872 and 1876. Wagner began by arguing for a redesign of the opera house itself, replacing the traditional Baroque horseshoe with an undecorated auditorium (Baker 1998). The auditorium was modelled after Greek amphitheatres, with a single expanse of seating that extended the full width of the space rather than any galleries or boxes (Carnegy 2006). Each audience member would have an unrestricted view of the stage, while the forward-facing direction of each seat would hinder any social interaction (McKinney and Butterworth 2009).

Wagner also argued for removing the orchestra from the audience's view and hiding all elements of stage machinery. The combined sight of 'the mechanical movement of the musicians and their conductor' and the 'technical evolutions' of set changes, Wagner claimed, 'destroys all vestige of illusion' (Barth, Mack, and Voss 1975, 199–200). He intended to remove any distractions that might prevent the audience's immersion into the illusion of the stage. In this, Wagner essentially proposed stripping any remnants of the Baroque theatrical game from the operatic experience (Baker 1998).

Just as Galli-Bibiena was not the first to theorise the use of angled perspective, so too was Wagner not the first to propose reforms redefining the relationship between the stage setting and the spectator. In the early nineteenth century, Prussian architect Karl Friedrich Schinkel (1781–1841) had similarly advocated for removing gallery boxes, lowering the orchestra pit, and redesigning the forestage in order to better focus the audience's attention (Bomberger 1998). Schinkel was unable to implement most of his reforms in practice and instead published illustrations of his proposed designs. These later inspired architect Gottfried Semper, whose unrealised designs for an opera house in Munich were adopted by Wagner for the Bayreuth Festspielhaus (Carnegy 2006).

Wagner's driving principle for his reformed theatrical space was to create a world of total illusion on stage (Carnegy 2006). While Schinkel had suggested a slightly lowered level for the orchestra, Wagner built a fully sunken orchestra pit in the Festspielhaus that extended six levels beneath the stage (Baker 2013). He also positioned a second proscenium arch between the audience and the orchestra pit to create a *'mystiches Abgrund,'* or 'mystic chasm.' This 'chasm' removed any visual points of reference that could reveal the true depth of the stage, as well as obscuring the technical workings of the production (Carnegy 2006). As Wagner (1983) explained, 'Between him [the spectator] and the picture to be looked at there is nothing plainly visible, merely a floating atmosphere of distance ... whereby the scene is removed as it were to the unapproachable world of dreams' (366) (see Figure 3.3).

Wagner broke from a number of other onstage conventions. He refused to showcase set changes and either dropped a curtain or employed more inventive means for obscuring technical inner workings. For the premiere of *Das Rheingold* in 1876, for example, Wagner and his technical director, Carl Brandt, used two locomotive steam boilers to pump 'rising mists' onto the stage and obscure the production's scenic transition out of Nibelheim (Kreuzer 2018, 170). Wagner also introduced dimmed lights in his auditorium

Figure 3.3 Interior of the Bayreuth Festspielhaus with the 'Grail Temple' stage design for Wagner's *Parsifal*. Postcard from Ramme & Ulrich, Hoffotograf, Bayreuth, ca. 1910. Creative Commons Public Domain.

as a way of focusing his audience's attention on the action of the stage (Baker 1998; Carnegy 2006). Through each modification, Wagner attempted to reinforce and maintain the illusion of the theatre.

Kreuzer (2018) notes that many of Wagner's innovations drew on existing practices from contemporary theatre production. Curtains, steam, a darkened auditorium—each had precedence in theatre and opera from earlier decades (Carnegy 2006; Kreuzer 2012; Burdekin 2018). However, Wagner combined these varying techniques in extreme ways, using them in concert with the physical design of the Festspielhaus to 'sustain both the theatrical illusion and the gaze fixed upon it, without a splinter from the stage-practical machinery hitting the audience's eye' (Kreuzer 2018, 91).

The scenic innovations realised in the Bayreuth Festspielhaus had a significant effect on the three-way interplay of scenography. Galli-Bibiena's angled perspective had democratised the audience by removing the symbolic gaze of the royal box, but Wagner's Greek-inspired amphitheatre allowed for a truly egalitarian experience. In addition, his spectators were no longer privy to the artificiality of the performance and the theatrical game. Instead, they were both physically and metaphorically separated from the realm of the stage and could only witness the action of the narrative through the mystic chasm of the double proscenia. By hiding the mechanical means used to construct the settings, creating a soundscape that emanated from invisible instrumentalists, and focusing the audience's complete attention on the framed portal of the stage, Wagner hoped to persuade his spectators of the reality of the imaginary world in front of them (Carnegy 2006).

The impact of Wagner's scenographic innovation on the performer was more limited, but still reflected a shift from existing production conventions. Like Galli-Bibiena, Wagner's goal was to increase the degree to which his performers could be visually integrated into the stage setting (McKinney and Butterworth 2009). This was partially achieved through Wagner's adjustments to the spectator–stage relationship. Contained within the framed portal of the double proscenia, his performers were fundamentally separated from the audience and visually linked to the scenic setting. Wagner emphasised this disconnect by instructing his performers to forgo any remnants of the presentational acting style of the Baroque paradigm (Kelly 2004). By removing any direct interaction between the performers and the spectators, Wagner hoped to maintain the spectator's immersion in his fictional world.

However, the performer still posed a threat to Wagner's visual illusion. Wagner's stage designs continued to rely on painted perspective scenery and stage devices drawn from 'the arsenal of nineteenth-century scenic illusion' (Wilson Smith 2007, 33). Even with the use of Galli-Bibiena's angled perspective, these scenic elements limited the scope of the performers' movement on stage, as their physical presence could disrupt the visual cohesion of the scene. As in the Baroque paradigm, one exception was the use of stage machinery that transported performers. In *Das Rheingold*, for example, the three Rhinemaidens were suspended on 'swimming apparatus,' which created the illusion of their 'swimming' in the Rhine (Fricke 1998, 64). The effect clearly evokes the modern-day variant of causal interplay, in which technology assumes agency in driving the physical movement of the performer.

Through his scenic innovations, Wagner endeavoured to delineate between the worlds of the stage and the audience to create a more immersive theatrical experience. Instead of engaging with the theatrical game, Wagner's spectators were expected to invest in the shared illusion of the performer and scenic setting. 'The spectator never entertains the thought that he is confronted with a machinery guided by technical devices ... the onlooker sees in front of him the real nature,' explains Heinrich Porges in his rehearsal report for Wagner's premiere production of the *Ring* cycle (Kreuzer 2018, 183). In this way, Wagner established the audience's gaze as the primary means of engagement with his fictional worlds. The resulting scenographic experience still aligns to non-synthesis in terms of the functional relationship between the performers and the scenic setting. Yet, Wagner's objectives were based on the larger goal of total integration between his performers and the narrative world of the stage.

In practice, Wagner's designs fell short of his goals, largely due to the limitations of existing technology. Even the scope and scale of innovations implemented at the Festspielhaus were unable to support the total scenic illusion that was Wagner's objective. 'Costumes, scenery, everything must be done anew for the repeat performances. R. is very sad, says he wishes he could die!' wrote his wife Cosima Wagner in her diary following the premiere of the *Ring* cycle (quoted in Williams 2004, 149).

Nonetheless, Wagner's scenographic reforms had a far-reaching influence on opera production, as demonstrated by the continued use of dimmed auditoriums, lowered orchestra pits, and hidden set changes in the present day. Within his lifetime, his innovations were slower to disseminate. Baker (2013) suggests that the full range of Wagner's changes were not realised in the operatic landscape until after World War II, when theatres throughout Europe had to be rebuilt and could implement his designs. However, only a few years after his death, Wagner's reforms inspired another seminal practitioner who impacted the lineage of operatic scenography: Adolphe Appia.

Adolphe Appia (1862–1928) and dynamic light

Less than six years after Wagner reshaped production conventions with his first opera in the Bayreuth Festspielhaus in 1876, the theatrical world was stunned by the introduction of electric lighting (Wiens 2010). Baker (2013) identifies an industrial exposition in Munich in 1882 as the first demonstration of electric lighting as the new standard for theatrical illumination. Less than a year later, the Teatro alla Scala in Milan transitioned to the new system, followed by the Munich Nationaltheater in 1885, the Vienna Hofopera in 1887, and both the Opéra de Paris and the Bayreuth Festspielhaus in 1888 (Baker 2013). By 1900, the majority of European opera houses had transitioned from gas to electric lighting for their productions.

Prior to this time, electricity had only been used for occasional scenic effects in large-scale opera production due to its unreliability (Campana 2015). With the expansion to full theatrical lighting, however, electricity suddenly offered a solution to issues that had plagued opera production for decades. Gas lighting produced toxic fumes, and its open flames posed a danger to both performers and instrumentalists, who could easily set their costumes or sheet music alight during a performance (Baker 2013). Gas lighting had previously caused fires that destroyed a number of opera theatres, including the Opéra de Paris in 1873, the Opéra-Comique in 1887, the Dresden Hofttheater in 1869, and the Vienna Ringtheater in 1881 (Baker 2013).

The new ability to darken an auditorium and illuminate the stage space via electrical lighting helped to perpetuate Wagner's scenographic innovations (Greenwald 1998) but also highlighted 'fatal flaws' in existing scenic conventions, particularly the use of perspective painting (Baugh 2013, 34). The garish light of the early incandescent bulbs flattened two-dimensional painted images, highlighting the stage setting's artificiality. Any sense of spatial depth and visual illusion was rendered effectively moot, resulting in an artistic catch-22: 'the brighter the stage lighting, the more the painted scene looked false, and the more the theatre responded by ever more intricately carpentered architectural detail' (Baugh 2013, 25). Galli-Bibiena's angled perspective and Wagner's mystic chasm had allowed for the performer's increased integration into the stage setting, but the transition to electric lighting reinforced the disconnect between the two elements. Performers were still only layered in front of background scenery, not truly integrated with their surroundings.

Even before the advance of electrical lighting, Swiss designer Adolphe Appia identified the relationship between three-dimensional performers and two-dimensional stage settings as problematic. Appia attended a production of Wagner's *Parsifal* at the Bayreuth Festspielhaus in 1882 and was deeply disappointed with its use of conventional stage settings, which he believed undermined Wagner's artistic achievements (Salter 2010). 'The master,' Appia wrote, 'set his work into the conventional framework of the period; and if everything in the auditorium at Bayreuth expresses his genius, on the other side of the footlights everything contradicts it' (Bablet and Bablet 1982, 67).

After attending *Parsifal*, Appia attempted to articulate a number of scenographic reforms to combat the failings he had witnessed at the Festspielhaus. In two seminal texts, *The Staging of Wagnerian Drama* (1895) and *Music and Stage Setting* (1899), he outlined a new approach to set design that would address and resolve this disconnect between performer and stage. Painted scenery, he wrote, 'pretends to create for us the illusion of reality. But this illusion is in itself an illusion, for the presence of the actor contradicts it' (Beacham 2013, 115). To resolve this contradiction, Appia argued for replacing two-dimensional painted scenery with geometrical pieces, such as staircases, ramps, platforms, and screens (Salter 2010). These abstract pieces would help to establish a scenic atmosphere that aligned with the performers, rather than competing with them. A key element of this approach was the use of electric lighting as a self-contained artistic tool', one that could function both as 'an expressive element and a "co-player"' within the scenographic design (Wiens 2010, 26). Through the combination of abstract set pieces and dynamic light, Appia hoped to achieve the true integration of performers within the scenic setting (Baugh 2013).

We can consider Appia's efforts in terms of the modes of synthesis and a theatrical experience in which all elements share the same spatial realm. Appia's dynamic light is not merely a tool for production but, as Wiens (2010) suggests, a co-player that can perform in concert with the actor on stage. In Appia's vision, the performer is not a disconnected visual element or constrained by the limitations of painted perspective scenery. Instead, Appia's performer is both basis and impetus for the stage design, unified with the scenic surroundings through atmospheric electric light (Aronson 2008). Consider his description of the ideal staging for Wagner's *Siegfried*:

> We shall no longer try to give the illusion of a forest, but the illusion of a man in the atmosphere of a forest. Man is the reality, and nothing else counts. Whatever this man touches must be intended for him— everything else must contribute to the creation of a suitable atmosphere around him. And if, leaving Siegfried for a moment, we lift our eyes,

the scenic picture need not give a complete illusion. It is composed for Siegfried alone.

(Beacham 2013, 66)

Here, the character of Siegfried is innately connected to the surrounding set design and not only provides context for the setting but completes the illusion of the stage.

By redefining the relationship between the performer and the stage setting as one of integration, Appia also intended to change the spectator experience from that of a 'passive onlooker to active participant' (Salter 2010, 7). Appia considered both the conventional proscenium arch and Wagner's 'mystic chasm' to be obstacles to this transformation. He derided the idea that immersion could be achieved with spectators watching a brightly lit portal from a fixed distance (McKinney and Butterworth 2009). Instead, Appia argued that total immersion required a shared space for performer, stage setting, and spectator (Bablet and Bablet 1982; Salter 2010). In this idealised theatrical space, the role of the spectator would eventually vanish (Salter 2010).[15]

Even though Wagner was the impetus for his scenographic innovations, Appia's reforms were far from welcome at the Bayreuth Festspielhaus. In fact, his proposed production designs for Wagner's operas were soundly rejected by Wagner's widow, Cosima, in the 1890s (Burian 1983). It was not until 1911 that Appia was able to put his theories into practice through his work with Swiss composer and educator Émile Jacques-Dalcroze (1865–1950). Together, they developed a workshop space in Dresden-Hellerau to experiment with both Dalcroze's theory of eurythmics[16] and Appia's theories of a dynamic theatrical space (Beacham 2013).

One highlight of this artistic partnership was a production of Christoph Willibald Gluck's *Orfeo ed Euridice* performed in 1912 and 1913. The production design demonstrated the potential for Appia's innovations with its combination of abstract set pieces and dynamic light (Salter 2010). According to Wiens (2010), 'the performers' bodies and the material elements onstage were transformed (and almost virtualized) by the atmospheres and movements of an ever-changing "performing" light' (26). The performative nature of Appia's lighting design reached its pinnacle through the figure of Amor, who was characterised as a beam of light while the live performer sang from offstage (Levitz 2001). While the technology driving these effects was electric, the parallels with modern-day digital scenography are unmistakable. Not only were Appia's performers augmented by the use of the light, but one of the characters in the opera was entirely replaced with the technology.

Appia was not as prolific a designer as Galli-Bibiena. His experiments at Dresden-Hellerau were cut short by the start of World War I, and two of his later design commissions for the Teatro alla Scala in the 1920s never came to fruition.[17] Still, Appia's scenographic innovations were at the forefront of a stylistic movement that extended to all genres of theatrical performance (Aronson 2008; Wiens 2010). By freeing the performer from the confines of two-dimensional pictorial scenery and theorising an immersive audience experience, Appia highlighted new artistic possibilities for exploring the atmospheric and psychological underpinnings of performance. Most significantly, Appia's work directly prefigured the multimedia developments of opera and theatre in the twentieth century.

Looking towards the twentieth century

Since the earliest public performances of opera in seventeenth-century Venice, opera design has been shaped by the efforts of those who believed that existing production conventions were inadequate. Many scenic innovations were conceived in an attempt to refine existing technologies, such as Giovan Battista Aleotti's rolling chariots, Inigo Jones' grooved stage floors, and Giacomo Torelli's scenery winches. Other developments stemmed from a desire not to refine existing infrastructures but to fundamentally *redefine* them, and change the balance of the interplay between the performer, the stage setting, and the spectator.

Galli-Bibiena, Wagner, and Appia each endeavoured to address elements of this three-way relationship in their scenographic contributions to opera. In response to the limitations of Baroque painted scenery, Galli-Bibiena's angled perspective democratised the spectator experience and helped to integrate the performer into the scenic setting. Wagner designed his Festspielhaus as a theatre of total illusion that would immerse his spectators in the drama of the stage and resolve the technological distractions of grand opera. Citing an irrevocable contradiction between two-dimensional stage scenery and three-dimensional performers, Appia proposed a model of abstract stage design that integrated performers with their surroundings through the use of dynamic light. Each practitioner was reacting to the work of their predecessors and attempting to shift opera's production conventions through their own innovations.

These developments helped to establish some of the most fundamental onstage conventions of the operatic genre. We can also recognise the early origins of digital scenography and elements of the modes of synthesis in their achievements. Most often, the relationship between the performer and the set was defined by its detachment, a layered effect that enabled the visual coherence of the scene. In this, we can see traces of non-synthesis in its most detached and traditional permutation. Even then, however, technology was being used to shift this relationship and achieve a better synthesis of the various components of the theatrical experience. Whether physically transporting performers with stage machinery, integrating them into scenery through new perspective techniques, or replacing their physical forms with beams of light, we see glimpses of causal interplay in practice throughout opera's first three centuries.

Galli-Bibiena, Wagner, and Appia were limited by the technology and conventions of their time. Nonetheless, their innovations can be recognised as part of a larger artistic lineage of opera scenography, one that connects the earliest paradigm of Baroque opera to its modern-day digital manifestations. The next chapter continues this analysis by mapping the further development of opera scenography through the twentieth century and examining key innovations drawing on film and computer technologies. These innovations actively consider the synthesis of the performer, the stage setting, and the spectator, and function as a scenographic bridge between the present day and the past.

Notes

1 Aleotti's rolling chariots allowed painted scenery to be rolled on and off the stage, while Argand's 'Argand burner' could produce ten times more light than standard theatrical illumination at the time (Baker 2013). Thomas Drummond's 'limelight' in the 1820s similarly produced better and brighter lighting (Walne 1995). Developed in the 1830s through distilling coal products, aniline dye was used to brighten colours in stage costumes (Baugh 2013). Hydraulic lifts were first introduced on Paris stages in the 1860s and allowed stagehands to move extensive scenery (Baugh 2013).

2 Italian architect Bernardo Buontalenti (1531–1608) was renowned for his technical wizardry in theatrical productions in Florence at the turn of the seventeenth century (Ossi 1998). Inigo Jones (1573–1652) was an architect and designer at the court of Charles I in England and one of the earliest practitioners to use stock theatrical scenery (Radice 1998). Philippe de Loutherbourg (1740–1812) was a painter at the Drury Lane Theatre who promoted scenographic realism in his stage designs (Baugh 2007; Baugh 2013).

3 Between 1637 and 1678, more than 150 operas were produced by nine different theatres in Venice (Rosand 1991).

4 Economic considerations still drive both programming decisions and production designs at opera companies in the present day. See Chapter 6.

5 Translated as 'comedy of the profession,' *commedia dell'arte* was a popular form of professional theatre in Europe from the sixteenth through the eighteenth century, commonly characterised by stock characters in masks (Balme, Vescovo, and Vianello 2018).

6 Also called 'telari,' *periaktoi* were first outlined in Vitruvius' *Ten Books on Architecture* in the first century BC (Temple, Czcibor-Piotrowski, and Heredia 2019).

7 The resulting form, *opera seria,* was defined by its historical subject matter.

8 Both Ferdinando and his brother, Francesco (1659–1739), worked as stage designers throughout Italy, France, Spain, and Austria. They implemented the new perspective techniques in their designs for theatre, opera, and ballet for the Habsburgs, the Holy Roman Empire, the Austrian Imperial Court, and the Viennese Court (Baker 2013). Ferdinando's four sons—in particular, Giuseppe (1696–1757) and Antonio (1697–1774)—continued the family tradition, employing angled perspective in their theatrical designs at major European courts throughout the second half of the eighteenth century (Biermann et al. 2003). Baker (2013) cites Giovanni-Niccolo Servandoni (1695–1766) as a key inheritor of Galli-Bibiena's artistic legacy and notes that Servandoni personally imported angled perspective to the Opéra de Paris with his production of Jean-Féry Rebel's *Pirame et Thisbé* in 1726 (see also Camp 2014). Servandoni was appointed

chief designer for the company less than two years later and continued to use Galli-Bibiena's methods at the Opéra for nearly two decades (Baker 2013).

9 Founded in 1669 as the Académie d'Opéra and colloquially known as the Opéra or Opéra de Paris, the company is currently known as the Opéra National de Paris.

10 While the Opéra was the primary model of 'grand opera,' similar large-scale scenographic techniques were simultaneously developing in theatre and ballet across Europe (Snowman 2009).

11 According to Pendle and Wilkins (1998), the Opéra employed as many as 'sixty machinists and a crew of at least forty men to produce a single work on the stage' (189–190).

12 Like other devices that stemmed from the seventeenth century and earlier, the history of the magic lantern is one marked by refinement, rather than new invention. In the eighteenth century, an improved version featured multiple lenses that allowed for quick dissolving effects between various images. Another improvement came in the form of the phantasmagoria, which could project imagery from behind a projection surface (Dixon 2007; Baker 2013). Further refinements included the phenakistiscope in 1833, the zoetrope in 1834, and the zoopraxiscope in 1879 (Callas and Watson 1996; Mannoni 2000).

13 The effect was first devised by Henry Dircks in 1858 and later refined for practical use by Professor John Henry Pepper in 1862 (thus the moniker 'Pepper's Ghost') (Luckhurst and Morin 2014).

14 Burdekin (2015) notes that these productions were generally presented as part of fairground tours by so-called spectral opera companies, which used the cutting-edge effect as a marketing strategy.

15 Appia's concept preceded the development of experimental theatre spaces, such as the modern-day 'black box' theatre.

16 Dalcroze developed a number of pedagogical techniques. His theory of eurythmics particularly examined the relationship between movement and music. See Spector (1991).

17 Appia designed abstract productions of Wagner's *Das Rheingold* and *Die Walküre* for the Teatro alla Scala that were so controversial that the remaining two operas of the *Ring* cycle were never staged (Burian 1983).

References

Abbate, Carolyn, and Roger Parker. 2015. *A History of Opera: The Last Four Hundred Years.* New York: W.W. Norton & Company.

Aronson, Arnold. 2008. *Looking Into the Abyss: Essays on Scenography.* Ann Arbor: University of Michigan Press.

Bablet, Denis, and Marie-Louise Bablet. 1982. *Adolphe Appia 1862–1928: Actor–Space–Light.* Translated by Burton Melnick. London: John Calder.

Baker, Evan. 1998. "Richard Wagner and His Search for the Ideal Theatrical Space." In *Opera in Context: Essays on Historical Staging from the Late Renaissance to the Time of Puccini*, edited by Mark A. Radice, 241–278. Portland: Amadeus Press.

Baker, Evan. 2013. *From the Score to the Stage: An Illustrated History of Continental Opera Production and Staging.* Chicago: University of Chicago Press.

Baker, Evan. 2018. "Scenography in the First Decades of Opera." In *The Routledge Companion to Scenography*, edited by Arnold Aronson, 315–337. Abingdon: Taylor & Francis.

Balme, Christopher B., Piermario Vescovo, and Daniele Vianello, eds. 2018. *Commedia dell'Arte in Context.* Cambridge: Cambridge University Press.

Barth, Herbert, Dietrich Mack, and Egon Voss, eds. 1975. *Wagner: A Documentary Study*. New York: Oxford University Press.

Baugh, Christopher. 2007. "Philippe de Loutherbourg: Technology-Driven Entertainment and Spectacle in the Late-Eighteenth Century." *Huntington Library Quarterly* 70, no. 2 (June): 251–268. https://doi.org/10.1525/hlq.2007.70.2.251.

Baugh, Christopher. 2013. *Theatre, Performance and Technology: The Development of Scenography in the Twentieth Century*. New York: Palgrave Macmillan.

Beacham, Richard C. 2013. *Adolphe Appia: Texts on Theatre*. London: Routledge.

Biermann, Veronica, Alexander Grönert, Christoph Jobst, and Roswitha Stewering. 2003. "Giuseppe Galli Bibiena." In *Architectural Theory: From the Renaissance to the Present*, edited by Bernd Evers, Veronica Biermann, and Christof Thoenes, 156–163. Köln: Taschen.

Bomberger, E. Douglas. 1998. "The Neues Schauspielhaus in Berlin and the Premiere of Carl Maria von Weber's *Der Freischütz*." In *Opera in Context: Essays on Historical Staging from the Late Renaissance to the Time of Puccini*, edited by Mark A. Radice, 147–170. Portland: Amadeus Press.

Brejzek, Thea. 2018. "Physicality and Virtuality: Memory, Space and Actor on the Mediated Stage." In *The Potentials of Space: The Theory and Practice of Scenography and Performance*, edited by Alison Oddey and Christine White, 157–172. Bristol: Intellect.

Burdekin, Russell. 2015. "Pepper's Ghost at the Opera." *Theatre Notebook* 69, no. 3: 152–164.

Burdekin, Russell. 2018. "Darkening the Auditorium in the Nineteenth Century British Theatre." *Theatre Notebook* 72, no. 1: 40–57.

Burian, Jarka. 1983. *Svoboda, Wagner: Josef Svoboda's Scenography for Richard Wagner's Operas*. Middletown: Wesleyan University Press.

Callas, Peter, and David Watson, eds. 1996. *Phantasmagoria: Pre-Cinema to Virtuality*. Sydney: Museum of Contemporary Art.

Camp, Pannill. 2014. *The First Frame: Theatre Space in Enlightenment France*. Cambridge: Cambridge University Press.

Campana, Alessandra. 2015. *Opera and Modern Spectatorship in Late Nineteenth-Century Italy*. Cambridge: Cambridge University Press.

Carnegy, Patrick. 2006. *Wagner and the Art of the Theatre*. New Haven: Yale University Press.

Crabtree, Susan, and Peter Beudert. 2005. *Scenic Art for the Theatre: History, Tools, and Techniques*. Burlington: Focal Press.

Dixon, Steve. 2007. *Digital Performance: A History of New Media in Theater, Dance, Performance Art, and Installation*. Cambridge: MIT Press.

Ferrero, Mercedes Viale. 2002. "Stage and Set." In *Opera on Stage: The History of Italian Opera, Part II: Systems*, edited by Lorenzo Bianconi and Giorgio Pestelli, 1–116. Translated by Kate Singleton. Chicago: University of Chicago Press.

Fricke, Richard. 1998. *Wagner in Rehearsal, 1875–1876: The Diaries of Richard Fricke*. Translated by George R. Fricke. Edited by James Deaville with Evan Baker. Stuyvesant: Pendragon Press.

Giesekam, Greg. 2007. *Staging the Screen: The Use of Film and Video in Theatre*. Basingstoke: Palgrave Macmillan.

Glixon, Beth L., and Jonathan E. Glixon. 2006. *Inventing the Business of Opera: The Impresario and His World in Seventeenth-Century Venice*. Oxford: Oxford University Press.

Greenwald, Helen M. 1998. "Realism on the Opera Stage: Belasco, Puccini, and the California Sunset." In *Opera in Context: Essays on Historical Staging from the Late Renaissance to the Time of Puccini*, edited by Mark A. Radice, 279–298. Portland: Amadeus Press.

Heartz, Daniel. 2004. *From Garrick to Gluck: Essays on Opera in the Age of Enlightenment*. Edited by John A. Rice. Hillsdale: Pendragon Press.

Howard, Pamela. 2002. *What Is Scenography?* New York: Routledge.

Huebner, Stephen. 1999. *French Opera at the Fin de Siècle: Wagnerism, Nationalism, and Style*. Oxford: Oxford University Press.

Izenour, George C. 1992. *Roofed Theaters of Classical Antiquity*. New Haven: Yale University Press.

Johnson, Eugene J. 2018. *Inventing the Opera House: Theater Architecture in Renaissance and Baroque Italy*. Cambridge: Cambridge University Press.

Kelly, Thomas Forrest. 2004. *First Nights at the Opera*. New Haven: Yale University Press.

Kreuzer, Gundula. 2012. "*Wagner-Dampf*: Steam in Der Ring des Nibelungen and Opera Production." *The Opera Quarterly* 27, no. 2–3: 179–218. https://doi.org/10.1093/oq/kbr024.

Kreuzer, Gundula. 2018. *Curtain, Gong, Steam: Wagnerian Technologies of Nineteenth-Century Opera*. Oakland: University of California Press.

Kuritz, Paul. 1988. *The Making of Theatre History*. Englewood Cliffs: Prentice-Hall.

Lacombe, Hervé. 2003. "The 'Machine' and the State." In *The Cambridge Companion to Grand Opera*, edited by David Charlton, 21–42. Cambridge: Cambridge University Press.

Levitz, Tamara. 2001. "In the Footsteps of Eurydice: Gluck's *Orpheus und Eurydice* in Hellerau 1913." *ECHO: A Music-Centered Journal* 3, no. 2. http://www.echo.ucla.edu/Volume3-issue2/levitz/levitz1.html.

Littlejohn, David. 1994. *The Ultimate Art: Essays Around and About Opera*. Berkeley: University of California Press.

Luckhurst, Mary, and Emilie Morin, eds. 2014. *Theatre and Ghosts: Materiality, Performance and Modernity*. Basingstoke: Palgrave Macmillan.

Mannoni, Laurent. 2000. *The Great Art of Light and Shadow: Archaeology of the Cinema*. Translated and edited by Richard Crangle. Exeter: University of Exeter Press.

McKinney, Joslin, and Philip Butterworth. 2009. *The Cambridge Introduction to Scenography*. Cambridge: Cambridge University Press.

Ossi, Massimo. 1998. "*Dalle machine…la meraviglia*: Bernardo Buontalenti's *Il rapimento di Cefalo* at the Medici Theater in 1600." In *Opera in Context: Essays on Historical Staging from the Late Renaissance to the Time of Puccini*, edited by Mark A. Radice, 15–36. Portland: Amadeus Press.

Pelletier, Louise. 2006. *Architecture in Words: Theatre, Language and the Sensuous Space of Architecture*. London: Routledge.

Pendle, Karin, and Stephen Wilkins. 1998. "Paradise Found: The *Salle le Peletier* and French Grand Opera." In *Opera in Context: Essays on Historical Staging from the Late Renaissance to the Time of Puccini*, edited by Mark A. Radice, 171–208. Portland: Amadeus Press.

Pérez-Gómez, Alberto, and Louise Pelletier. 2000. *Architectural Representation and the Perspective Hinge*. Cambridge: MIT Press.

Pirrotta, Nino, and Elena Povoledo. 1975. *Music and Theatre from Poliziano to Monteverdi*. Translated by Karen Eales. Cambridge: Cambridge University Press.

Radice, Mark A. 1998. "Theater Architecture at the Time of Henry Purcell and Its Influence on His 'Dramatick Operas.'" In *Opera in Context: Essays on Historical Staging from the Late Renaissance to the Time of Puccini*, edited by Mark A. Radice, 73–94. Portland: Amadeus Press.

Rosand, Ellen. 1991. *Opera in Seventeenth-Century Venice: The Creation of a Genre*. Berkeley: University of California Press.

Salter, Chris. 2010. *Entangled: Technology and the Transformation of Performance*. Cambridge: MIT Press.

Snowman, Daniel. 2009. *The Gilded Stage: A Social History of Opera*. London: Atlantic Books.

Spector, Irwin. 1991. *Rhythm and Life: The Work of Émile Jacques-Dalcroze*. New York: Pendragon Press.

Stahura, Mark. 1998. "Handel's Haymarket Theatre." In *Opera in Context: Essays on Historical Staging from the Late Renaissance to the Time of Puccini*, edited by Mark A. Radice, 95–110. Portland: Amadeus Press.

Temple, Nicholas, Andrzej Czcibor-Piotrowski, and Juan Manuel Heredia, eds. 2019. *The Routledge Handbook on the Reception of Classical Architecture*. London: Routledge.

van Baest, Arjan. 2000. *A Semiotics of Opera*. Delft: Eburon.

Vincent, Jordan, Caitlin Vincent, Scott deLahunta, John McCormick, and Kim Vincs. 2018. "Artwork Spawning Artwork: Trans-Disciplinary Approaches to Artistic Spin-Offs and Evolution in the Digital Context." In *Digital Echoes: Spaces for Intangible and Performance-Based Cultural Heritage*, edited by Sarah Whatley, 283–299. London: Routledge.

Wagner, Richard. 1851. *Opera and Drama*. Translated by William Ashton Ellis. London.

Wagner, Richard. 1983. *My Life*. Translated by Andrew Gray. Cambridge: Cambridge University Press.

Walne, Graham. 1995. *Projection for the Performing Arts*. Waltham: Focal Press.

Wiens, Birgit. 2010. "Modular Settings and 'Creative Light': The Legacy of Adolphe Appia in the Digital Age." *International Journal of Performance Arts and Digital Media* 6, no. 1: 25–39.

Williams, Simon. 2004. *Wagner and the Romantic Hero*. Cambridge: Cambridge University Press.

Wilson Smith, Matthew. 2007. *The Total Work of Art: From Bayreuth to Cyberspace*. Abingdon: Routledge.

4 The lineage of digital scenography in opera

Multimedia developments in the twentieth century

The scenic developments discussed in the previous chapter suggest that digital scenography is not a disruptive force in terms of onstage conventions. In the innovations driven by Ferdinando Galli-Bibiena, Richard Wagner, and Adolphe Appia, among others, we can identify early forms of the modes of synthesis in practice, as well as an ongoing preoccupation with the relationship between performer, scenic setting, and spectator. Yet, this artistic lineage is incomplete without consideration of the theatrical experiments that followed. With the turn of the twentieth century and the rise of multimedia performance,[1] we find the most immediate precursors to modern-day digital scenography in opera production. This chapter continues the historical analysis of the previous chapter, bridging the analogue technologies of pre-twentieth-century opera production and the cutting-edge technologies of the present day.

The theatrical theories of the modernist and avant-garde periods of the early twentieth century have long been tied to the development of multimedia performance. Practitioners and theorists like Edward Gordon Craig, Sergei Eisenstein, Walter Gropius, László Moholy-Nagy, Frederik Kiesler, and Erwin Piscator are widely recognised as crucial forerunners in the development of multimedia and digitally enhanced theatre (Giannachi 2004; Hagebolling 2004; Chapple and Kattenbelt 2007; Dixon 2007). 'These avant-garde movements and their passionate belief in technology were inspirational to experimental art and performance in the 1960s and 1970s,' notes Giannachi (2004, 2). She touts these early theories as 'laying the groundwork' for the later work of Merce Cunningham, The Wooster Group, Dumb Type, Robert Lepage, and The Builders Association in the 1980s and 1990s (3). Dixon (2007) and Hagebolling (2004) outline a similar timeline of development, with the avant-garde theories of the 1910s and 1920s directly inspiring the multimedia experiments of the 1960s and 1970s, which, in turn, led to the computer-based innovations of the 1980s and 1990s.

These early theories can also be identified as catalysts in the artistic lineage of digitally enhanced opera production in the twentieth century. Unlike other theatrical forms, however, opera was more limited in its ability to leverage experimental techniques due to its embedded production conventions.

DOI: 10.4324/9781003093305-4

Consider the mixed-media theatrical performances of the 1960s, which both Dixon (2007) and Giannachi (2004) identify as direct descendants of the avant-garde theories of the early twentieth century. Allan Kaprow's *18 Happenings in 6 Parts* (1959) and Nam June Paik's *Participation TV I* (1966) are both touted as groundbreaking moments in multimedia performance during this period, with each inspiring subsequent developments in the field (Giannachi 2004; Dixon 2007). Both works, like others of the time, were predicated on two scenographic innovations: first, the rejection of the traditional theatrical space, and second, the reinterpretation of the spectator as a co-performer who engages with and even modifies the work.[2]

Neither of these shifts was tenable for opera production at the time. Then as now, large-scale opera is generally presented in traditional, proscenium-based venues that incorporate a designated stage, auditorium, and orchestra pit (Ille 2018). This 'genteel, fenced off zone where opera is supposed to reside' is reinforced by the physical infrastructure of existing opera houses, many of which were built in previous centuries (Ross 2015).

Opera also continues to maintain clearly delineated and non-participatory roles for its audience members. This stems from the conventions established by Richard Wagner at the Bayreuth Festspielhaus and can also be attributed to the genre's emphasis on historical repertoire in the twentieth century (Till 2012). It would be taboo for audience members to engage with or modify canonical works like W.A. Mozart's *The Marriage of Figaro* or *Don Giovanni* in the same way as the audiences at Kaprow's *Happenings* or Paik's *Participation TV I*. Even the avant-garde sensibilities associated with *Regietheater*, or 'director's theatre,' and the work of innovative stage directors like Wieland Wagner, Patrice Chéreau, and Hans Neuenfels still typically reinforce these standard production conventions, as well as the traditional relationship between performer, stage setting, and spectator.[3]

There are certainly exceptions to these conventions, particularly in the present day. Ille (2018) points to a number of what she terms 'Alt Op' opera companies that are operating in non-traditional venues and attempting to shift the role of the spectator, including Los Angeles' The Industry, Toronto's Against the Grain Theatre, Opera Philadelphia, and Fort Worth Opera, among others (4). Yet, across the broader sector, the conventions of the traditional proscenium-based venue and the observational role of the spectator remain standard for most opera productions.

Accordingly, while drawing on the general timeframe of scenic innovations proposed by Giannachi and echoed by Dixon (2007) and Hagebolling (2004)—the 1910s–1920s, the 1960s–1970s, and the 1980s–1990s—it is impossible to analyse multimedia opera and its practitioners in the same way as avant-garde theatre practitioners like The Wooster Group or The Builders Association. Instead, this chapter focuses on scenographic innovations that can be applied to an opera-specific context.

The chapter begins with an exploration of the works of two practitioners active during the early avant-garde period. Of the many theatrical practitioners who engaged with ideas around the integration of technology and performance in the 1910s and 1920s, Edward Gordon Craig and Enrico Prampolini each proposed scenographic innovations that directly anticipated aspects of digital scenography in opera. While neither was able to realise their theories in practice, Craig's 'thousand scenes in one' and Prampolini's 'luminous forms' both explore the potential for causal interplay to be realised and driven by technology-based scenic innovation.

The chapter then examines the work of twentieth-century opera scenographers Josef Svoboda and Günther Schneider-Siemssen. Each drew inspiration from the theories of the early avant-garde and experimented with new ways of integrating projected elements into opera production. Each can also be seen as directly realising pre-digital forms of causal interplay in their operatic designs in the 1960s and 1980s, respectively. Svoboda's 1962 production of *The Tales of Hoffmann* with Laterna Magika uses projected film footage to create a dynamic setting that appears to interact with its live performers. More than two decades later, Schneider-Siemssen experimented with holography in his 1985 production of *The Tales of Hoffmann* at the Salzburg Marionette Theatre, which replaced and augmented puppet performers with virtual avatars.

Like the theatrical practitioners discussed in Chapter 3, Craig, Prampolini, Svoboda, and Schneider-Siemssen were limited by the available technologies of their times. Yet, their experiments function as crucial stepping-stones linking the theatrical ideas of the early twentieth century to the current use of digital scenography in opera production. Their work also codifies the premise that was suggested in the previous chapter's analysis of opera's early scenic innovations. Current trends in digital scenography do not ultimately constitute a 'disruption' in terms of opera's onstage conventions. Instead, the modern-day modes of synthesis are best understood as merely the latest iteration, or artistic 'spawn,' in a long lineage of scenographic evolution.

Avant-garde origins

As noted in the previous chapter, projection-based effects were first used in opera production in the 1820s. Following the development of the *cinématographe* by the Lumière brothers in 1895, however, the magic lantern and its various iterations were no longer the only means for projecting imagery on stage (Elsaesser and Barker 1990; Mannoni 2000). Within a decade of the *cinématographe's* first public exhibition in Paris, theatrical practitioners throughout Europe were incorporating elements of film into their scenic designs in lieu of conventional projections (Walne 1995; Giesekam 2007; Baugh 2013).

In these early years, many theatre and opera productions used film footage in largely conventional ways: to provide background scenery, enable transitions between scenes, or realise supernatural effects. Giesekam (2007) cites Franz Kranich's extensive text *Bühnetechnik der Gegenwart* (Contemporary Theatre Technology) from 1928, which details a number of opera productions in Germany that used film footage, including a 1913 production of E.T.A. Hoffmann's *Undine* that incorporated footage of waves and waterfalls. Among the many productions detailed in Kranich's two-volume treatise, generic film footage of waves, clouds, landscapes, and railway trains is most commonly mentioned, as this footage could be easily incorporated into multiple productions at low expense (Giesekam 2007). Although film was undoubtedly a technological innovation, its early use served roughly the same aesthetic function as the perspective scenery, stage machinery, and magic lantern projections employed in previous decades.

The modernist and avant-garde movements of the early twentieth century led to a shift in thinking about the ways that film and other new technologies could be integrated with live performance. Outside of opera, we can find numerous examples of practitioners leveraging new technologies in order to change the relationship between the performer, the scenic setting, and the spectator. In a number of cases, these shifts explicitly manifest as pre-digital forms of causal interplay.

In 1914, for example, American cartoonist Winsor McCay embarked on a national tour of the United States with his production, *Gertie the Dinosaur* (Canemaker 2005). In the performance, McCay relied on a combination of choreography and timing to create the illusion of interactivity with Gertie, an animated dinosaur projected on a screen behind him. An early example of 'faux-interactivity' in practice, Gertie nodded, rolled over, and 'caught' an apple, all in seeming response to McCay's physical prompts. Dixon (2007) describes the performance as one of the first to 'use ideas of close timing to "cheat" a sense of "liveness" … prefiguring numerous digital theater performances that utilize essentially the same technique' (74).

Giesekam (2007) describes a 1911 musical revue in Hamburg that used a similar method to create the illusion of interactivity. The performance began with film footage of the two main characters running through the streets of Hamburg towards the entrance of the theatre. Just as the film ended, the live performers 'burst out of the orchestra pit onto the stage' (33). This example recalls the technique used in Victorian Opera's *The Flying Dutchman,* with coordinated timing establishing the live performers and their digital avatars as equivalents in the theatrical space. Both Gertie the Dinosaur and the Hamburg revue clearly evoke the kinds of causal interplay being employed in digitally enhanced opera in the present day, in which the live and the digital not only appear to interact but are framed as interchangeable components.

Dancer Loie Fuller was another early twentieth-century innovator who leveraged projection technology in a way that explicitly evoked causal interplay. In a technique patented in 1895, Fuller would project imagery onto her own body and then appear to animate the images by 'manipulating her voluminous robes into swirling shapes above her head' (Garelick 2007, 4).

Donger (2018) cites works such as *Fire Dance* (1895), *Firmament* (1896), *Night* (1896), and *Ballet of Light* (1908), in which 'Fuller used her body as a screen to force the two-dimensionality of the projected image into a three-dimensional and physical phenomenon' (130). This technique of augmenting and extending her own performing body through projections evokes the extreme causal interplay of Komische Oper Berlin's *The Magic Flute* and Opéra de Lyon's *L'Enfant et les Sortilèges*, in which the live performers are partially digitalised from the audience perspective.

Bauhaus artists, including Walter Gropius, Oskar Schlemmer, László Moholy-Nagy, and Farkas Molnár, also actively engaged with film and projected imagery throughout the 1920s (Baugh 2013). Director Erwin Piscator was a particularly seminal figure in scenographic efforts involving film (see Willett 1986). His vision for the Total Theatre, designed by Gropius, aimed to create an immersive experience for the audience using a combination of film clips, projected images, newsreels, and stage machinery. Echoing the three-way interplay inherent to scenography, Piscator (1980) described his 'proletarian theatre' as one 'based on a relationship of complete equality between the actors, stage designers ... and the theatre goers' (43).

Of the many avant-garde practitioners experimenting with new forms of technology during the 1910s and 1920s, the work of Edward Gordon Craig and Enrico Prampolini align most closely to the modes of synthesis currently being used on operatic stages. Both practitioners explored the potential for a kind of theatrical scenography that would break from the conventions of painted scenery and 'synthesise' with the live performer.[4] Craig was fascinated by the possibilities of the stage setting itself and questioned whether scenery could play an expressive and dynamic role equal to that of the performer. Prampolini was intrigued by the role of the performer and whether technology could be used to replace the performer entirely. Despite the growing popularity of film at the time, neither Craig nor Prampolini considered film technology as a means for achieving their scenic visions. Instead, both framed their concepts in terms of electric light.

Edward Gordon Craig (1872–1966) and Enrico Prampolini (1894–1956): 'a thousand scenes in one' and 'luminous forms'

Craig outlined a number of significant theatrical theories during his career (Bablet 1981; Innes 1998; McKinney and Butterworth 2009), but one of his early concepts, 'Screens,' proposed a kind of scenic dynamism that directly anticipated current aspects of digital scenography. Submitted for a patent in 1910 under the title 'Stage-scenery,' Craig's concept consisted of a series of canvas flats made from wooden frames of varying widths and uniform height (Baugh 2013). The screens were double-hinged, self-supporting, and mounted on retractable castors that allowed for efficient movement within the stage space (Craig 1915; Innes 1998).[5] In his patent application, Craig noted that theatrical producers were limited to either painted scenery or plain curtains for their scenic backgrounds (Craig 1912). His invention, he argued, combined the best of both elements, merging 'the artistic variety and mechanical advantages of painted scenery with the portable nature of the curtain' (Craig 1912, 1).

Craig believed his concept would have its greatest impact by enabling what he termed 'a thousand scenes in one' (Craig 1915, 139). Because of their ability to shift and move on stage, the screens would be 'infinitely flexible and capable of different expressions and moods—as mobile and responsive as a human face' (Bablet 1981, 155). This emotive flexibility, he argued, would allow for a range of scenographic possibilities.[6] The functionality of the screens would also enable smooth transitions over the course of a performance, far superior to the intrusive mechanics of moving painted flats or backdrops. Craig (1915) explains, 'we pass from one scene to another without a break of any kind, and when the change has come we are not conscious of any disharmony between the new scene and that which is past' (148).

In addition to establishing scenic configurations that could move of their own accord, Craig's screens were intended to reflect the drama unfolding onstage. This, he argued, would allow for an artistic cohesion between performer and stage setting, in which the scenery would function as a kind of co-performer. Describing Craig's design in a 1910 letter to Jacques Rouché, painter René Piot notes:

> Up until now the scenery designed by painters, or self-styled painters, has consisted of motionless rags, dangling round the moving figures on the stage. Craig wants his scenery to move like sound, to refine certain moments in the play just as music follows and heightens all its movements; he wants it to advance with the play.
>
> (quoted in Bablet 1981, 122)

Craig's goal was to create a stage setting that would be dynamic, autonomous, and, most importantly, work in concert with both the performer and the narrative: portraying the scene 'imaginatively whilst simultaneously responding to the movements of the actor' (Baugh 2013, 50). Breaking from the tradition of fixed painted backgrounds, Craig envisioned a scenographic design in which the set and the live performers were fully integrated and even interdependent. As Baugh (2013) explains, Craig wanted 'to define the stage setting as a *place* for performance rather than a *scene*' (46). In this, we can see allusions to causal interplay. Craig's screens were meant to have the capacity to respond to the narrative, as well as the physical prompts of the performer within a shared theatrical realm. The innate dynamism of the scenery, both 'advancing' with the play and appearing to interact directly with the performers, suggests the premise of partial-synthesis within Craig's idealised scenographic vision.

Five years after Craig patented his design for 'Screens,' Enrico Prampolini made his own contribution to theatrical theory with the publication of his 1915 manifesto, *Futurist Stage Design* (Rainey, Poggie, and Wittman 2009). Like Craig, Prampolini envisioned a theatrical scenography that could evolve and advance with the action of the narrative (Dixon 2007). Prampolini (1969) explains, 'The stage must live the theatrical action in its dynamic synthesis; it must express the essence of the character conceived by the author just as an actor at once expresses and lives it within himself' (95). Prampolini believed the stage setting should express the artistic vision of the playwright and 'synthesise' with the narrative action of the work, functioning as an 'actor' in its own right.

Prampolini saw painted scenery as the primary obstacle to this artistic 'synthesis.' Deriding conventional set designers as 'sterile whitewashers' who 'prowl around the dusty and stinking corners of classical architecture,' he argued for a complete rejection of pictorial scenery in favour of architectural set pieces and electricity (96). He notes:

> The stage will no longer be a colored backdrop, but an *uncolored electromechanical architecture, powerfully vitalized by chromatic emanations from a luminous source* ... Instead of the illuminated state, let's create the *illuminant stage: luminous expression which will irradiate the colors demanded by the theatrical action with all its emotional power.*
>
> (Prampolini 1969, 97)

Through the use of electric 'luminosity,' Prampolini's proposed theatre would abandon the painted realism of traditional flats and backdrops and establish a visual world that matched the 'emotional power' of the narrative. Craig posed a similar idea with his architecturally abstract screens, but Prampolini went further, suggesting technology as the specific means for achieving this effect. Rather than fixed or pictorial, his 'illuminant' stage would 'emanate,' 'express,' and 'irradiate,' changing and evolving by means of an electric force.

Prampolini also expanded on Craig's vision in terms of the status of the performer within this dynamic setting. Craig proposed a scenography that could be integrated with performers and both evolve in concert with and react to their physical behaviour on stage, However, Prampolini (1969) argued for redefining the role of the live performer itself. He proposed the use of 'luminous forms,' created by 'electric currents and colored gases,' that would 'wriggle and writhe dynamically' within the stage setting (98). Instead of existing alongside the live performers as part of the scenic background, 'these authentic actor-gases of an unknown theatre' could be used to replace live performers entirely (98).

Prampolini's focus on the role of the performer anticipates similar practices around the augmentation, extension, and replacement of live performers in modern-day digital scenography. Interestingly, however, Prampolini does not suggest integrating his luminous forms with the physical presence of live performers or creating a hybrid form in the theatrical space. Instead, he proposes the performer's total replacement, aligning to the kinds of digital transformations and wholly digitalised performers employed in Komische Oper Berlin's *The Magic Flute* (e.g., Monostatos' digital dogs, the digital personification of the magic flute) and The Metropolitan Opera's *Siegfried* (e.g., the digital forest bird).

Neither Craig nor Prampolini was able to realise their scenographic visions in practice. Craig was stymied by a lack of opportunity and the burden of his controversial reputation, while Prampolini was limited by available technology and the challenge of using electric currents to somehow create 'illuminant stages' and 'actor-gases.' Technology continued to advance into the 1920s and might eventually have provided a platform for both Craig and Prampolini to realise their concepts. Unfortunately, avant-garde experimentation underwent a hiatus shortly after they proposed their theories, due in part to the onset of World War I (Dixon 2007). Instead, decades later, Craig's vision for a 'thousand scenes in one' and Prampolini's 'luminous forms' would spawn further artistic innovations in the work of two operatic practitioners: scenographers Josef Svoboda and Günther Schneider-Siemssen.

Josef Svoboda (1920–2002) and the dynamic setting of the Laterna Magika

Josef Svoboda straddled the realms of experimental avant-garde theatre and traditional opera in his work as a scenographer. Principal designer at the Czech National Theatre from 1948 to 1992, Svoboda designed more than 700 theatrical productions over the course of his career (Jones 2002; Martin 2002). He was known for his 'radical assaults on the limitations of the still dominant proscenium theatre' (Burian 2002, 105) and is widely acknowledged as the scenographic heir of Adolphe Appia and the avant-garde practitioners of the Bauhaus (Giesekam 2007). At the same time, Svoboda was also commissioned and celebrated by some of the most prominent opera companies in the world. Accordingly, in highlighting Svoboda's role as a driving force of multimedia performance in the 1960s, Salter (2010) describes Svoboda as an artistic mediator who managed to 'carve the way for hybrid-media events' in both 'theaters and opera houses accustomed to more traditional performance forms' (152).

Svoboda co-founded the Laterna Magika theatre company in Czechoslovakia in 1958, prompting what Dixon (2007) identifies as a key turning point in the re-emergence of multimedia theatre after World War II.[7] Named as a nod to the traditional magic lantern device (Giesekam 2007), Laterna Magika launched with a multimedia performance at the Brussels World's Fair that integrated live performers with projected filmed material (Svoboda, Morris, and Munk 1966; Hagebolling 2004). A major technological feat for the time, the performance was received enthusiastically by audiences (Dixon 2007).

The production featured several instances of causal interplay between the performers and filmed elements, which relied on a combination of pre-determined choreography and pre-recorded content. As Vincent et al. (2016) explain, the 'filmed portions of the performance had to be prepared months in advance, and artistic decisions, once made, were largely inflexible ... the dancers were forced to adapt their movement to the projections or the sequence would be cut' (51). Svoboda acknowledged that his production 'virtually enslaved the live performer' and ultimately stripped the performance of its liveness (quoted in Burian 1974, 86). This aligns with modern-day concerns surrounding the integration of the live and the digital through faux-interactive techniques. Svoboda's comment particularly recalls 1927 animator Paul Barritt's acknowledgement that the performers in Komische Oper Berlin's *The Magic Flute* function as 'puppets within the animated world' (Babbs 2012).

Despite these challenges, Laterna Magika gave Svoboda an opportunity to explore the possibilities of a 'kinetic stage,' an idealised theatrical experience in which live performers would be fully integrated with their scenic surroundings (Burian 2002, 105). Svoboda explains: 'One thing is not the background for the other; instead you have a simultaneity, a synthesis and fusion of actors and projections' (McKinney and Butterworth 2009, 134). Like Galli-Bibiena, Wagner, and Appia before him, Svoboda hoped to leverage technology in order to address a seeming imbalance in the relationship between performer, stage setting, and spectator. Moreover, he hoped to achieve what none of his predecessors had done: create a full-synthesis theatrical experience that successfully fused all elements on stage.

One year after the premiere of Laterna Magika in Brussels, Svoboda provided a further explanation of his goals for the relationship between the performer and the scenic setting:

> I don't want a static picture, but something that evolves, that has movement, not necessarily physical movement, of course, but a setting that is dynamic, capable of expressing changing relationships, feelings, moods, perhaps only by lighting, during the course of the action... The setting should evolve with the action, cooperate with it, be in harmony with it, and reinforce it, as the action itself evolves.
>
> (quoted in Burian 1974, 27–28)

Svoboda's explanation aligns with Craig's intentions for his 'Screens' nearly 40 years earlier. Both practitioners envisioned a scenographic design with the capacity to evolve in concert with the narrative action and behaviour of the live performers.

Like Craig and Prampolini, Svoboda also believed that scenography was limited by its reliance on existing production conventions. He reasoned, 'dramatic space ... cannot be expressed by stiff flats that stand behind the action and have no contact with it' (Burian 1970, 126). While Craig hypothesised a series of physical screens that would move independently on stage, Svoboda explored a number of different methods for establishing his 'kinetic stage,' including moving scenery, mirrors, and projections that evolved with the advancing narrative on stage (Burian 1970).

Svoboda was able to realise many of his theatrical concepts in practice (Svoboda 1993). Laterna Magika provided both the infrastructure and opportunity for Svoboda to experiment with projected imagery in works such as *Polyekran* (1958) and *Diapolyekran* (1967), both of which used projected slides and film excerpts in the absence of live performers (Burian 1970). Giesekam (2007) and Salter (2010) detail a number of Svoboda's other multimedia theatrical productions, including *The Last Ones* (1966) and *The Wonderful Circus* (1977). Baugh (2013) suggests that Svoboda deviated from many other avant-garde practitioners working at the time as he chose to maintain the traditional theatrical space and proscenium arch, viewing both as a means to 'absorb and emotionally involve the spectator' (88).

In addition to his theatrical work, Svoboda applied his scenographic vision to the framework of large-scale opera production. Not surprisingly, when working in canonical repertoire for prominent companies such as The Metropolitan Opera and Teatro alla Scala, Svoboda's designs were more conservative than in his theatrical work and generally erred on the side of abstract minimalism.[8] Productions that featured extensive projection design include Wagner's *Tristan und Isolde* (1974) for Bayreuth Festspielhaus, Tchaikovsky's *The Queen of Spades* (1982) for Houston Grand Opera, and Dvořák's *Rusalka* (1991) for the National Theatre of Prague, among others (Metropolitan Opera Archives n.d.; Burian 1983; Sutcliffe 1998; Cheek 2013; DiGaetani 2016). In each of these productions, projection technology served as a tool to support Svoboda's larger scenographic goal of a kinetic stage that could adapt, evolve, and synthesise with his performers.

The Tales of Hoffmann (1962)

One of Svoboda's earliest attempts to synthesise projections with live performers in opera was his 1962 production of Jacques Offenbach's *The Tales of Hoffmann* with Laterna Magika. According to its playbill, the production was intended as an experiment to determine whether the company was actually 'capable of tackling the technical and artistic problems of a large-scale dramatic work' (Svoboda, Morris, and Munk 1966, 142). *The Tales of Hoffmann* was the first opera designed by Laterna Magika, as well as the company's first production of any pre-existing dramatic work (Burian 2002). There are limited secondary sources that describe Svoboda's design for the production, but the Laterna Magika playbill provides a description of the various scenic elements employed (Svoboda, Morris, and Munk 1966).

The physical set for the production consisted of projection screens, and a combination of projected images and film sequences featured significantly in each of the opera's three episodes.[9] In the first episode with the dancing doll Olympia, the inventor Spalanzani is characterised in various demonic forms that are projected onto the screens. In the second episode with Antonia, Hoffmann's dream about Doctor Miracle 'blends stage and back projections' with film sequences showing the rooms of Councillor Crespel, 'filled with caged songbirds, moldy wreaths, old trophies, dusty tables, collections of beetles and butterflies' (Svoboda, Morris, and Munk 1966, 144). The end of the episode also features a video projection of Antonia's impending death, while the live performer playing Antonia lies on a chaise in the foreground. In the third episode of the opera, when Hoffmann travels to Venice and falls in love with Giulietta, the film sequences portray an expanse of water 'from which rise the symbols of Venice—buildings and mirrors, gondolas and scarlet boudoirs' (Svoboda, Morris, and Munk 1966, 144).

This overview provides an admittedly incomplete picture of Svoboda's scenographic designs. Yet, these few scenes still give a sense of the range of artistic potentials that Svoboda was exploring with his use of projections, including characterising Spalanzani as a virtual performer, establishing the background setting of Councillor Crespel's rooms, and portraying an abstract manifestation of Venice as a combination of water and symbols. In these differing ways, Svoboda used projections to create a dynamic setting that changed and evolved while still serving the needs of the narrative by communicating time and place to the audience. Svoboda's projection surfaces did not move, as Craig envisioned with his 'Screens,' but his 'kinetic stage' still served multiple roles over the course of the narrative.

We can also frame Svoboda's techniques in terms of the modes of synthesis. Svoboda's background environments suggest the use of visual correlation, with the performers layered with the scenic imagery behind them but not necessarily engaging with it. This is most evident in Svoboda's use of the technique to suggest Antonia's death in the second episode. Even though the consumptive Antonia is alive and interacting with Dr Miracle (another permutation of Spalanzani) in the foreground, the projected premonition highlights the reality of the situation for the audience members.

Svoboda also experiments with causal interplay, in particular, the variant of augmentation in his characterisation of Spalanzani. During the first episode with Olympia, Hoffmann watches Olympia play the harp, while a projection of Spalanzani's face looms behind them in the guise of Olympia's creator, Coppelius (see Figure 4.1). Hoffmann and Olympia are staged as if they are unaware of Spalanzani's presence, and Svoboda uses the projection to emphasise Spalanzani's role as an antagonist to the audience. As in digitally enhanced operas that feature virtual avatars, such as Senta and the Dutchman in Victorian Opera's *The Flying Dutchman* and Maman in Opéra de Lyon's *L'Enfant et les Sortilèges,* this technique relies on the audience drawing a causal connection between the live performer and its filmic manifestation.

Burian (2002) notes that *The Tales of Hoffmann* received mixed reviews, particularly compared to the enthusiastic reception of other Laterna Magika

Figure 4.1 Spalanzani watches Olympia and Hoffmann in Josef Svoboda's *The Tales of Hoffmann*. Production premiered by Laterna Magika, Prague (1962). Set design: Josef Svoboda. Photograph © The National Theatre Archive, Prague, Czech Republic.

productions. Negative criticism largely centred on the integration of projected elements with live performers, with critics describing the production as 'insufficiently unified or adequately balanced in its combining of stage and film' (Burian 2002, 116). These responses echo the critical reception to the non-synthesis and partial-synthesis productions of *The Magic Flute* discussed in Chapter 1, in which both Jun Kaneko and William Kentridge were criticised for the uneven integration of the performers and digital elements. Interestingly, Burian suggests the lack of integration in Svoboda's production was due to the limiting conventions of the operatic genre, rather than the scenographic design itself. In particular, Burian suggests the work's emphasis on singing restricted the scope of Svoboda's creative possibilities.

The Tales of Hoffmann was only one of Svoboda's earliest forays into projection design in opera. Following this experiment, Svoboda continued to explore film and projection techniques in canonical repertoire over the next five decades. Each time, he returned to the concept of a 'kinetic stage' and attempted to use technology to achieve an integrated relationship between the performer and the stage setting. Svoboda was unquestionably inspired and influenced by Edward Gordon Craig and other avant-garde theatrical theorists, as traces of this artistic lineage are clearly evident in his scenographic innovations. However, Svoboda endeavoured to achieve an even more cohesive scenographic design than his predecessors, using film as a means for wholly encompassing the performer, the stage setting, and the spectator.

Günther Schneider-Siemssen (1926–2015) and the holograms of the Salzburg Marionette Theatre

Günther Schneider-Siemssen designed more than 500 productions for opera and theatre in his career as a scenographer and has been recognised as one of the most important opera designers of the twentieth century (Davis 2001; Cooper 2015). Schneider-Siemssen also had a far-reaching influence on wider industry trends due to his high-level appointments at major companies, including the Vienna State Opera and other Austrian federal theatres ('Günther Schneider-Siemssen' 2015). Schneider-Siemssen became active as a scenic designer around the same time as Svoboda and other abstract heavyweights like Wieland Wagner, but his aesthetic was significantly more traditional (DiGaetani 2016). This dichotomy is evident in the performing archives of The Metropolitan Opera, a longstanding bastion of conservative taste in opera. While the more experimental Svoboda only designed two productions for the company, Schneider-Siemssen is credited on 20 individual productions between 1966 and 2017, all of which feature his trademark lush scenic realism (Metropolitan Opera Archives n.d.).

Davis (2001) highlights Schneider-Siemssen's appointment to the Salzburg Landestheater in 1952 as his first real opportunity to use projection technology on stage. Another artistic turning point came with his appointment to the Bremen Staatsoper in 1954, where he designed 90 productions over seven years, including a 1958 production of Paul Hindemith's *Die Harmonie der Welt* that featured extensive projections (Davis 2001). Schneider-Siemssen's collaboration with conductor Herbert von Karajan and appointment as Chief of Scenic Design at the Vienna State Opera in 1962 created an even higher profile for his designs, many of which included projected elements and were staged and revived internationally (Cooper 2015). Particularly seminal productions include Wagner's *The Flying Dutchman* (1983) for the Salzburg Festspielhaus; Wagner's *Tristan und Isolde* (1971), *Ring* cycle (1967–1974; 1986–1988), *Tannhäuser* (1982), and *Parsifal* (1991) for The Metropolitan Opera; von Weber's *Der Freischütz* (1977) for The Royal Opera, Covent Garden; and Janáček's *Katya Kabanova* (1977) for San Francisco Opera, among others (Metropolitan Opera Archives n.d.; San Francisco Opera Archives n.d.; Rockwell 1982; Davis 2001).

While Svoboda viewed film projection as a scenographic tool that could help to achieve his larger goal of a 'kinetic stage,' Schneider-Siemssen's designs were more focused on the technology's possibilities within a given scenic design. As he explained in 1977:

> Projection is an artistic means of expression that must be treated with respect ... It ... can be a style, a substitute for scenery; it can conjure up dreams, visions, changes of place and atmosphere; it can evoke symbolic

associations and illustrate the intermingling of the real world with the world of fantasy. It can also represent the stage as cosmic space, and even suggest the weightlessness of the players and the set.

(Schneider-Siemssen 1977a, 41)

At first glance, Schneider-Siemssen does not seem to propose an overarching vision for multimedia theatre in the same way as Svoboda. Instead, he simply emphasises the importance of viewing projection technology as its own 'means of expression' and rejects the premise of using it as a basic background that 'degenerate[s] into mere slideshows' (41).

As such, in his scenic designs, Schneider-Siemssen was primarily committed to illuminating the operatic work itself. 'When designing a new set,' he wrote in 1977, 'the first question must be: "How can I do justice to the work?"' (Schneider-Siemssen 1977b, 51). While Svoboda's designs were meant to advance his own vision of what theatre should be, Schneider-Siemssen's designs were conceived in service of the artistic vision of the original authors, rather than his own theatrical philosophy (Davis 2001). Accordingly, in Schneider-Siemssen's obituary in the *New York Times,* Cooper (2015) refers to conflicting opinions about Schneider-Siemssen's designs, viewed by opera traditionalists as 'sumptuous realizations of the visions of the composers and librettists' and by critics as 'old-fashioned and overly literal.'

However, aspects of Schneider-Siemssen's 1977 description of projection design run parallel to the objectives outlined by Craig, Prampolini, and Svoboda in their efforts to achieve an integrated theatrical space. In particular, Schneider-Siemssen suggests that projections should be used to achieve an 'intermingling' of the world of the live performer and the world of the narrative. This speaks to the same kind of synthesis that the other practitioners envisioned, one which would break from the traditional painted backgrounds and layered visual effects of previous centuries. Schneider-Siemssen also considered the role that projections could play in concert with narrative action, reflecting the inner workings of the characters, conjuring 'dreams,' and exposing psychological motivations.

Despite the traditionalist aesthetic of much of his work, Schneider-Siemssen must also be acknowledged as a major innovator in the artistic lineage of digital scenography. While Svoboda helped to advance and develop Craig's vision of a dynamic setting, Schneider-Siemssen played a seminal role in advancing the kinds of 'luminous forms' that Prampolini envisioned in 1915 through his experiments with holography as a means for augmenting and replacing live performers. The work of Schneider-Siemssen, as with Svoboda, actively links the avant-garde theories of the early twentieth century to contemporary digital scenography.

The Tales of Hoffmann *(1985)*

In 1952, Schneider-Siemssen was appointed set designer at the Salzburg Marionette Theatre, which produces miniaturised puppet productions of canonical opera repertoire. Over the following four decades, Schneider-Siemssen used the company as a means for testing new scenographic concepts before applying them to his large-scale productions ('Gunther Schneider-Siemssen' 2015).[10] Schneider-Siemssen explained in 1977: 'the smallest stage turns theatre into magic, into dreams. The puppet theatre has remained my laboratory for examining many aspects of artistic interpretation and dramatic communication' (Schneider-Siemssen 1977b, 50). Accordingly, the Salzburg Marionette Theatre provided the platform for one of Schneider-Siemssen's most groundbreaking experiments in operatic design: the use of projected holograms in a production of Offenbach's *The Tales of Hoffmann* in 1985 (Brockett, Mitchell, and Hardberger 2010).

Davis (2001) describes this production as the 'world premiere of on-stage scenic holography' (20). As with Svoboda's 1962 production with Laterna Magika, however, there is limited material discussing the details of Schneider-Siemssen's innovation. As a result, Davis' (2001) overview of the production and interview with Schneider-Siemssen serve as the primary sources of information about the design aspects of the work.

The holographic technology for the production was created in collaboration with Schneider-Siemssen and physicists Walter Kroy and Thorsteinn Halldorsson. Schneider-Siemssen designed the visual aspects of the holograms, which were then produced at a holographic laboratory in England. Describing the logistical means for using the technology onstage, Schneider-Siemssen notes: 'The small holograms were projected, using argon lasers, onto glass surfaces covered with a foil holographic coating' (Davis 2001, 19). As soon as the images were 'hit' by the lasers or by a standard theatrical light, they were revealed to the audience. This technique evokes the Pepper's Ghost trick of the nineteenth century but also aligns with Prampolini's technical description of dynamic forms created through a combination of projected light and 'colored gases.'

Schneider-Siemssen's scenographic design for *The Tales of Hoffmann* is most innovative for its use of holographic figures as independent performers within the narrative. Schneider-Siemssen incorporates several of these figures into the first scene with the dancing doll Olympia, as well as in the second scene with Antonia, in which holographic musicians appear to 'perform' in the background (Davis 2001). None of the holograms assume principal roles in the opera and, as such, they remain removed from the kinds of digitalised performers being used in modern-day digital scenography. Yet, the holograms still demonstrate a certain physical autonomy, much like Don Giovanni's shadow avatars in The Royal Opera's *Don Giovanni*. They move and shift in concert with the music and function as independent performers that co-exist alongside the three-dimensional 'live' puppets. By elevating his virtual figures to the level of autonomy within his design, Schneider-Siemssen essentially realises Prampolini's 'luminous forms' that can replace live performers.

In the third scene of the opera, Schneider-Siemssen explicitly experiments with causal interplay as a way of further synthesising the two elements. A set of holographic doors are projected onto the background and, at a key moment in the scene, the puppet performer playing Dr Miracle is staged to 'move ghost-like though the closed doors' (Davis 2001, 21). In this moment, Schneider-Siemssen endows his puppet performer with holographic characteristics, enabling his passage through a closed door from the perspective of the audience. Not only does Schneider-Siemssen augment his 'live' performer with the projection technology, his scenographic technique establishes a shared spatial realm in which Dr Miracle is able to 'cross the celluloid divide' (Forkbeard Fantasy n.d.). Whether in the form of a holographic performer or a holographic stage component, Schneider-Siemssen frames the technology as an equal partner within the scenographic design (see Figure 4.2).

As with his other experiments at the Marionette Theatre, Schneider-Siemssen intended for his holograms to be repurposed for large-scale opera production. *The Tales of Hoffmann* was conceived as the first stage of a larger experiment that would see the technology implemented in a production at the Bavarian State Opera House. Unfortunately, this second stage never came to fruition (Davis 2001). Like Craig and Prampolini, Schneider-Siemssen was restricted by the technological capabilities of the time. Building the holograms was prohibitively expensive, and the holograms themselves were

Figure 4.2 Holographic columns in Günther Schneider-Siemssen's *The Tales of Hoffmann*. Production premiered by Salzburg Marionette Theatre, Salzburg (1985). Photograph © Salzburg Marionette Theatre, Austria.

limited in aesthetic flexibility and could only be created in green or red-purple shades. Both factors made them impractical for use in a standard opera production (Davis 2001). Even so, Schneider-Siemssen's foray into onstage holography can be seen as an extension of Prampolini's vision for the 'Futurist theatre,' as well as a clear predecessor of the digital performers now appearing on operatic stages.

Looking towards the twenty-first century

Edward Gordon Craig and Enrico Prampolini were limited by the technological and theatrical capabilities of their time, and neither specifically envisioned their theatrical theories within the confines of opera. Nonetheless, both practitioners can be seen as anticipating the kinds of scenic dynamism and augmented performers now commonplace in modern-day digital scenography. Like Galli-Bibiena, Wagner, and Appia before them, Craig and Prampolini focused their scenographic innovations on the interplay between the performer, the stage setting, and the spectator. While Craig envisioned a dynamic and expressive stage setting that could advance with the narrative action, Prampolini imagined virtual performers that could replace live performers entirely.

These ideas were reframed and reimagined in the operatic experiments of practitioners like Josef Svoboda in the 1960s and Günther Schneider-Siemssen in the 1980s. In his production of *The Tales of Hoffmann*, Svoboda leveraged projection technologies to create his own version of Craig's dynamic setting: a partial-synthesis 'kinetic stage' that could provide additional layers of meaning for the audience. Using his miniature laboratory at the Salzburg Marionette Theatre, Schneider-Siemssen created his own version of Prampolini's 'luminous forms' and constructed autonomous holographic figures that co-existed with 'live' puppet performers.

Neither Svoboda nor Schneider-Siemssen was wholly successful at achieving their scenic visions. Each was similarly restricted by the limitations of technology, as well as the conventions of the operatic genre. Yet, their experiments shaped and directed the continued development of digital scenography in opera through the end of the twentieth century, informing and inspiring the next generation of computer-driven opera productions like Steve Reich and Beryl Korot's *The Cave* (1993), Philip Glass and Robert Wilson's *Monster of Grace* (1998), and Mark Reaney's *The Magic Flute* (2003), among others (Cheng 1998; Kirk 2001; Dixon 2007; Kuksa and Childs 2010).

These two chapters establish a loose lineage for the development of digital scenography over opera's four-century history. This lineage is not meant to address every aspect of opera production but rather to highlight particular innovations and innovators that not only impacted the progression of the genre but directly prefigured aspects of digital scenography in the modern day. Based on the analysis, it is clear that the issues surrounding the use of digital scenography and its integration with live performers are far from new. While the techniques and technologies are more advanced, sceno-graphic innovations have long been driven by similar objectives: to shift the relationship between the performer and the scenic setting to create a more powerful theatrical experience for the audience.

In this way, the use of digital scenography on stage cannot be framed as a 'disruption' to opera's existing scenographic conventions. Rather, digital scenography must be acknowledged as the latest iteration of scenographic practice that leverages new technologies to achieve certain effects. Yet, the question of digital disruption requires consideration beyond onstage practices. Opera is as much informed by its backstage production processes as by the product that is ultimately realised on stage. The next two chapters will explore this backstage aspect of digital scenography in opera and assess the scope of potential disruption to opera's production conventions off the stage.

Notes

1 In this context, the term 'multimedia opera' is used to describe productions that incorporated film or other non-digital projection technologies in the twentieth century, as opposed to Giesekam's (2007) definition of 'multimedial' as outlined in Chapter 1.
2 In Paik's work, the image on a television set responded to the sound of the viewer's voice. Kaprow's *Happenings,* while fairly low-tech, involved explicit instructions for its audience members to follow.
3 *Regietheater* is marked by its innovative staging techniques and what Burian (1983) describes as 'an extreme reinterpretation of the traditional themes and philosophic overtones of the operas, including explicit dislocations in the place and period of the settings' (20). This approach to stage interpretation, heavily championed at Wieland Wagner's New Bayreuth, effectively stripped the composer of all creative ownership in the performative space. Stage directions, even when documented in the material score, were considered optional and open to revision, reinterpretation, and deconstruction for the sake of the stage director's artistic vision. Germany became—and remains—the artistic epicentre of the *Regietheater* style of production. Payne (2005) attributes this to the legacy of Walter Felsenstein, who founded the Komische Oper Berlin in 1947 as a 'theatre in which the Director was the most powerful creative force, superior to the Music Director, the singers and the composers' (316). Another contributing factor is undoubtedly the impact of the European funding model and the extensive government support for state opera companies (see Chapter 6).
4 For more about Edward Gordon Craig's theatrical theories and controversial career, see Milling and Ley (2001), Oddey and White (2006), Dixon (2007), and McKinney and Butterworth (2009). For more about Enrico Prampolini and the Italian Futurists, see Segel (1995), Grau (2003), Dixon (2007), and Rainey, Poggey, and Wittman (2009).
5 Craig provides a detailed overview of the artistic impetus behind his design in 'Screens: The Thousand Scenes in One,' published in Craig's theatrical journal *The Mask* in May 1915.
6 Craig's proposed design runs parallel to a number of recent digitally enhanced productions, including Opera Australia's *Aida* with its moveable LED screens and Santa Fe Opera's *The (R)evolution of Steve Jobs* with its shifting monoliths (see Chapter 6).

7 Svoboda's earliest work using film in theatre actually pre-dates Laterna Magika and can be tied to an experimental production with director Alfréd Radok in 1950 (Burian 2000).
8 One exception to this conservative aesthetic was Svoboda's design for the Opera Company of Boston's production of Luigi Nono's *Intolleranza* (1965), which combined projected film footage and live television (Burian 2002).
9 *The Tales of Hoffmann* is divided into three parts by its three heroines: Olympia in Act 1, Antonia in Act 2, and Giulietta in Act 3. In the playbill for their production, Laterna Magika refers to these as 'episodes.'
10 Schneider-Siemssen's work with the Salzburg Marionette Theatre recalls Philippe de Loutherbourg's Eidophusikon, a miniature mechanical theatre that was first exhibited in 1781 (Baugh 2007).

References

Babbs, Helen. 2012. "The Theatre Film Hybrid—An Interview with Paul Barritt." *Animations Online*, December 19, 2012. http://www.puppetcentre.org.uk/animations-online/features/theatre-film-hybrid/.

Bablet, Denis. 1981. *The Theatre of Edward Gordon Craig*. Translated by Daphne Woodward. London: Heinemann.

Baugh, Christopher. 2007. "Philippe de Loutherbourg: Technology-Driven Entertainment and Spectacle in the Late-Eighteenth Century." *Huntington Library Quarterly* 70, no. 2 (June): 251–268. https://doi.org/10.1525/hlq.2007.70.2.251.

Baugh, Christopher. 2013. *Theatre, Performance and Technology: The Development of Scenography in the Twentieth Century*. New York: Palgrave Macmillan.

Brockett, Oscar G., Margaret A. Mitchell, and Linda Hardberger. 2010. *Making the Scene: A History of Stage Design and Technology in Europe and the United States*. San Antonio: Tobin Theatre Arts Fund, University of Texas Press.

Burian, Jarka. 1970. "Josef Svoboda: Theatre Artist in an Age of Science." *Educational Theatre Journal* 22, no. 2 (May): 123–145.

Burian, Jarka. 1974. *The Scenography of Josef Svoboda*. Middletown: Wesleyan University Press.

Burian, Jarka. 1983. *Svoboda, Wagner: Josef Svoboda's Scenography for Richard Wagner's Operas*. Middletown: Wesleyan University Press.

Burian, Jarka. 2000. *Modern Czech Theatre: Reflector and Conscience of a Nation*. Iowa City: University of Iowa Press.

Burian, Jarka. 2002. *Leading Creators of Twentieth-Century Czech Theatre*. London: Routledge.

Canemaker, John. 2005. *Winsor McCay: His Life and Art*. New York: Harry N. Abrams.

Chapple, Freda, and Chiel Kattenbelt, eds. 2007. *Intermediality in Theatre and Performance*. 3rd ed. Amsterdam: Editions Rodopi B.V.

Cheek, Timothy. 2013. *Rusalka: A Performance Guide with Translations and Pronunciation*. Lanham: Scarecrow Press.

Cheng, Meiling. 1998. "Review: *Monsters of Grace 1.0: A Digital Opera in Three Dimensions* by Philip Glass, Robert Wilson." *Theatre Journal* 50, no. 4 (December): 513–514.

Cooper, Michael. 2015. "Schneider-Siemssen Dies at 88; Envisioned Elaborate Opera Sets." *New York Times*, June 3, 2015. https://www.nytimes.com/2015/06/04/arts/music/gunther-schneider-siemssen-opera-stage-designer-dies-at-88.html?_r=0.

Craig, Edward Gordon. 1912. Stage-scenery. United States Patent Office, US Patent 1022020 A, Filed April 27, 1910, and Issued April 2, 1912. https://www.google.com/patents/US1022020.

Craig, Edward Gordon. 1915. "The Thousand Scenes in One Scene." *The Mask* 7, no. 2 (May): 139–158.

Davis, Tony, ed. 2001. *Stage Design.* East Sussex: RotoVision.

DiGaetani, John Louis. 2016. *An Invitation to the Opera, Revised Edition.* Jefferson: McFarland & Company.

Dixon, Steve. 2007. *Digital Performance: A History of New Media in Theater, Dance, Performance Art, and Installation.* Cambridge: MIT Press.

Donger, Simon. 2018. *Scenography.* Wiltshire: The Crowood Press.

Elsaesser, Thomas, and Adam Barker, eds. 1990. *Early Cinema: Space, Frame, Narrative.* London: BFI Publishing.

Forkbeard Fantasy. n.d. "Forkbeard's Use of Film." Accessed November 15, 2018. http://www.forkbeardfantasy.co.uk/useoffilm1.php.

Garelick, Rhonda K. 2007. *Electric Salome: Loie Fuller's Performance of Modernism.* Princeton: Princeton University Press.

Giannachi, Gabriella. 2004. *Virtual Theatres: An Introduction.* New York: Routledge.

Giesekam, Greg. 2007. *Staging the Screen: The Use of Film and Video in Theatre.* Basingstoke: Palgrave Macmillan.

Grau, Oliver. 2003. *Virtual Art: From Illusion to Immersion.* Translated by Gloria Custance. Cambridge: MIT Press.

"Günther Schneider-Siemssen, 88, Stage and Lighting Designer Who Made His Mark with Seven Different *Ring* Cycles, Has Died." 2015. *Opera News,* June 4, 2014. https://www.operanews.com/Opera_News_Magazine/2015/6/News/Gunther_Schneider-Siemssen.html.

Hagebolling, Heide. 2004. *Interactive Dramaturgies: New Approaches in Multimedia Content and Design.* Berlin: Springer.

Ille, Megan Steigerwald. 2018. "Bringing Down the House: Situating and Mediating Opera in the Twenty-First Century." PhD diss., Eastman School of Music.

Innes, Christopher. 1998. *Edward Gordon Craig: A Vision of Theatre.* Oxford: Routledge.

Jones, Kenneth. 2002. "Czech Scenographer Josef Svoboda Is Dead at 81." *Playbill,* April 23, 2002. http://www.playbill.com/article/czech-scenographer-josef-svoboda-is-dead-at-81-com-105278.

Kirk, Elise Kuhl. 2001. *American Opera.* Urbana. University of Illinois Press.

Kuksa, Iryna, and Mark Childs. 2010. "But a Walking Shadow: Designing, Performing and Learning on the Virtual Stage." *Learning Media and Technology* 35, no. 3: 275–291.

Mannoni, Laurent. 2000. *The Great Art of Light and Shadow: Archaeology of the Cinema.* Translated and edited by Richard Crangle. Exeter: University of Exeter Press.

Martin, Douglas. 2002. "Josef Svoboda, 81, Stage Designer for Hundreds of Productions." *New York Times,* April 22, 2002.

McKinney, Joslin, and Philip Butterworth. 2009. *The Cambridge Introduction to Scenography.* Cambridge: Cambridge University Press.

Metropolitan Opera Archives. n.d. Accessed April 2017. http://archives.metoperafamily.org.

Milling, Jane, and Graham Ley. 2001. *Modern Theories of Performance: From Stanislavski to Boal.* New York: Palgrave.
Oddey, Alison, and Christine White, eds. 2006. *The Potentials of Space: The Theory and Practice of Scenography and Performance.* Bristol: Intellect.
Payne, Nicholas. 2005. "Opera in the Marketplace." In *The Cambridge Companion to Twentieth-Century Opera*, edited by Mervyn Cooke, 306–320. Cambridge: Cambridge University Press.
Piscator, Erwin. 1980. *The Political Theatre.* London: Eyre Methuen.
Prampolini, Enrico. 1969. "Futurist Scenography (Manifesto)." In *Total Theatre: A Critical Anthology*, edited by Ernest Theodore Kirby, 95–98. New York: E.P. Dutton.
Rainey, Lawrence, Christine Poggie, and Laura Wittman, eds. 2009. *Futurism: An Anthology.* New Haven: Yale University Press.
Rockwell, John. 1982. "Critic's Choice." *New York Times*, November 21, 1982. http://www.nytimes.com/1982/11/21/arts/critic-s-choice-047805.html.
Ross, Alex. 2015. "Golden Oldies: An Onslaught of Italian Opera, at the Met." *New Yorker*, October 12, 2015. http://www.newyorker.com/magazine/2015/10/12/golden-oldies-musical-events-alex-ross.
Salter, Chris. 2010. *Entangled: Technology and the Transformation of Performance.* Cambridge: MIT Press.
San Francisco Opera Archives. n.d. Accessed April 2017. http://archive.sfopera.com.
Schneider-Siemssen, Günther. 1977a. "Lighting and Projection." In *Opera*, edited by Rudolf Hartmann, 38–42. New York: W. Morrow & Co.
Schneider-Siemssen, Günther. 1977b. "Coping with Very Large and Very Small Stages." In *Opera*, edited by Rudolf Hartmann, 49–51. New York: W. Morrow & Co.
Segel, Harold B. 1995. *Pinocchio's Progeny: Puppets, Marionettes, Automatons, and Robots in Modernist and Avant-Garde Drama.* Baltimore: Johns Hopkins University Press.
Sutcliffe, Thomas. 1998. *Believing in Opera.* London: Faber and Faber.
Svoboda, Josef. 1993. *The Secret of Theatrical Space: The Memoirs of Josef Svoboda.* Translated and edited by Jarka M. Burian. New York: Applause Theatre Books.
Svoboda, Josef, Kelly Morris, and Erika Munk. 1966. "Laterna Magika." *The Tulane Drama Review* 11, no. 1 (Autumn): 141–149.
Till, Nicholas, ed. 2012. *The Cambridge Companion to Opera Studies.* Cambridge: Cambridge University Press.
Vincent, Jordan Beth, Caitlin Vincent, Kim Vincs, and John McCormick. 2016. "Navigating Control and Illusion: Interactivity Versus 'Faux-Interactivity' in Trans-Media Dance Performance." *International Journal of Performance Arts and Digital Media* 12, no. 1: 44–60. https://doi.org/10.1080/14794713.2016.1161955.
Walne, Graham. 1995. *Projection for the Performing Arts.* Waltham: Focal Press.
Willett, John. 1986. *The Theatre of Erwin Piscator: Half a Century of Politics in the Theatre.* London: Methuen.

5 The projection designer and evolving creative hierarchies

The previous chapters establish some dramaturgical possibilities for integrating digital elements with live performers, as well as demonstrating the alignment of current trends with historical precedents. When considered as part of a broader lineage, digital scenography is not inherently disruptive to onstage conventions. But to gauge the full impact of digital scenography, one must also examine its impact offstage. The next two chapters explore two aspects of 'backstage' opera production, beginning in this chapter with creative hierarchies and the role of the projection designer.

As noted previously, projected imagery in performance has a well-established history that originated with technologies like the magic lantern. However, the role of the projection *designer* is much less understood. As the use of digital scenography continues to grow—in frequency, scale, and creative possibilities—the individuals creating and designing this work are becoming more important to the production workflow. With this increasing use, questions about the role and responsibilities of projection designers have become more pressing.

Integrating a single projection designer in itself interferes with the standard theatrical hierarchy, traditionally limited to a stage director, set designer, lighting designer, and costume designer. Yet, digital designs often now require large teams of computer programmers and animators, all of whom must be incorporated into the creative structure. This raises further complications around status, workflow, and reporting processes, as programmers and animators often lack the training and institutional knowledge of theatrical production and instead bring hierarchical expectations from the film and game industries.

To consider these developments, one must first understand the role of the projection designer and the ways in which the position functions as part of a creative team. This chapter begins by outlining the varying responsibilities of projection designers and the challenges such practitioners face in terms of creative collaboration and industry acknowledgement. Since much of what we know about creative hierarchies and projection design comes from the world of theatre, the discussion draws significantly from theatrical

DOI: 10.4324/9781003093305-5

sources to establish both historical context and current practice for projection designers.

Shifting to a consideration of projection designers within opera production, I outline two of the most common hierarchical models used in opera—the traditional vertical hierarchy and the more collaborative lateral hierarchy—and explore some of the tensions that emerge with the integration of projection designers. Next, I discuss examples of digitally enhanced opera productions that circumvent these hierarchies in fundamental ways. Drawing on interviews with major practitioners of projection, video, and set design, including S. Katy Tucker, Paul Barritt, Mark Grimmer, Luke Halls, Victoria 'Vita' Tzykun, Sven Ortel, and Finn Ross, I discuss the ways in which new models of creative collaboration are developing in concert with advancing digital technologies.

The roles and responsibilities of the projection designer

Despite the growing prevalence of digital scenography in theatre and opera production, projection designers are still seen as a fairly new phenomenon, or what Buntrock (2013) terms a once 'rare and peculiar breed.' As recently as 2010, the *New York Times* critic Anita Gates expressed surprise that projection designers were so frequently listed in theatrical credits (Gates 2010). Although this suggests that projection designers have only appeared in theatrical circles in the past few decades, practitioners of projection and video design have been active since the early part of the twentieth century.

Following the experiments of Erwin Piscator and Sergei Eisenstein in the 1920s, innovators such as Emil František Burian staged numerous productions that integrated film and projections prior to World War II (Giesekam 2007). Another early forerunner in projection design, American scenic designer Jo Mielziner incorporated projections in the musical *Allegro* in 1947, as did set designer Tony Walton and lighting designer Richard Pilbrow in the West End's *One Over the Eight* in 1961 and Broadway's *A Funny Thing Happened on the Way to the Forum* in 1962 (Barbour 2011). In the latter half of the twentieth century, projection designer Wendall K. Harrington used projected imagery in *They're Playing Our Song* in 1979 and *The Who's Tommy* in 1992 (Gendrich and Archer 2017). Now touted as the 'godmother of all modern projection design,' Harrington boasts a number of former assistants who have since become well-established in the field, including Elaine J. McCarthy, Michael Clark, and Zachary Borovay (Johnson 2003).

While major practitioners such as Harrington are individually lauded for their theatrical contributions, even now the exact duties of the role remain unclear. Writing in 2006, projection designer Zachary Borovay (2006) notes, 'To be honest, what exactly projection designers do … is a bit murky' (27). Fourteen years later, projection designer Sven Ortel echoes the same sentiment: 'It's just not a very well understood profession … As a newbie, I had to basically explain all the time what I would do, why, and how' (personal communication, May 21, 2020).

The inherent variability of theatrical productions hampers a clear understanding of what projection designers actually do. The specific status, duties, and reporting relationships of the projection designer shift depending on the needs of a production, the artistic vision of the stage director, and the creative hierarchy employed. 'It always depends what purpose the imagery fulfils as part of the production,' explains Ortel (personal communication, May 21, 2020). One director may expect a projection designer to conceive and design video imagery in close collaboration with the director and other designers. Another might expect the projection designer to function more as an independent contractor, providing content to particular specifications but not actively engaged in conceptual discussions.

Duties and responsibilities are further complicated by iterations that occur once the projection design is integrated with live performers. A non-synthesis production in which projected elements serve as background scenery may require minimal creative input from the projection designer, as the director or set designer may simply request a particular environmental setting. Alternatively, a partial-synthesis or full-synthesis production with extensive animations may require a more active role for the projection designer, including collaboration with the director at the earliest stages of the design process.

The sheer range of credits used by different practitioners demonstrates the variety of roles related to digital scenography. For the numerous digitally enhanced operas presented by The Metropolitan Opera between the 2005/6 and 2019/20 seasons, credit listings included 'projection designer,' 'video designer,' 'video projection designer,' 'projections and animation,' 'animation and projection design,' 'video compositor and editor,' 'video image artist,' 'interactive video designer,' and 'set and projection designer' (Metropolitan Opera Archives n.d.). Each designation suggests a different dramaturgical use of digital elements, as well as a different workflow and collaborative process alongside the other creative practitioners.

Even removed from the context of specific productions, the lack of uniformity across self-assigned titles is apparent from practitioners' websites. Designer S. Katy Tucker describes herself as a 'video and projection designer' (Tucker n.d.), while Finn Ross is explicitly a 'video designer' (Ross n.d.). Luke Halls describes himself as a 'filmmaker' who works at a 'multidisciplinary moving image design studio' (Luke Halls Studio n.d.), while Wendall K. Harrington is a 'designer of projections for performance' (Harrington n.d.). Sven Ortel refers to himself as a 'projection designer' but then acknowledges that neither projection design nor video design 'fully describes what I really do' (Ortel n.d.).

Projection designer Zachary Borovay (2006) argues that such discrepancies must be resolved to promote a better understanding of the field: 'We need to come up with a title for our vocation and stick with it' (26). However,

Oliszewski and Fine (2018) suggest that a single title is incapable of capturing the scope of content and technologies that might be employed. 'Titles ... will change depending on exactly what kind of digital or analog media you are using and how it is integrated into the performance,' they explain (xviii). They propose the term 'media designer' as a possible catch-all for the field but simultaneously admit that the title is still 'too broad and confusing,' since 'media can be inclusive of so many mediums' (xviii). I encountered similar difficulties in crediting different designers for this book and ultimately resorted to a compromise: using each practitioner's preferred title when referenced individually but defaulting to the traditional 'projection designer' in general.

Without a fixed standard for responsibilities, let alone a consistent title, projection designers can have an uneasy relationship with other creative practitioners, particularly set and lighting designers, with whom they have traditionally been competitors. Consider this backstage anecdote about the projections used in the musical *A Funny Thing Happened on the Way to the Forum* in 1962. According to lighting designer Richard Pilbrow, a box of glass projection slides fell off the lighting tower and were destroyed a few days before the production's premiere (Pilbrow 2011). Pilbrow recreated the slides in time for the performance but later learnt that the so-called accident had been intentional. 'Under enormous stress, the projector operator had been instructed by his union to "nudge" the box off the edge—the success of such scenic projections might put all of his "brother" scene painters out of work,' Pilbrow recalls (2011, 72). In this case, the use of projections for a high-profile Broadway-bound production was seen as a direct threat to set designers, so much so that, if this anecdote is to be believed, a theatrical union resorted to sabotage to ensure its failure.

With the wider acceptance of digital technologies in recent years, the number of 'projection designers' has increased, and the role is now generally acknowledged as a key part of the creative team. Nonetheless, the notion that projection designers may be intruding on other artistic areas remains commonplace. Interviewed about his work for a 2004 production of *Measure for Measure*, projection designer Sven Ortel recalls that he felt his work was 'trespassing' into the domains of the other designers. He acknowledges that much of his discomfort was self-driven, stemming from his status as 'the new kid on the block' (Newman 2004, 3). In particular, by choosing to project content onto the stage floor, Ortel was keenly aware that he was 'stepping into traditional set design and lighting design territory' (3).

In his 2020 interview for this book, Ortel notes that this sense of competition with other design practitioners has faded somewhat. However, he admits that the dynamic of a production always depends on the practitioners who are involved. 'Some [designers] are in their siloes and trying to protect their respective disciplines from what they ... perceive as some sort of encroachment. Then it's not necessarily productive, and it takes some time to learn what each of us can and cannot do,' he notes (personal communication, May 21, 2020).

This tension is particularly heightened when working with lighting designers, for whom the introduction of video or projections has the greatest impact. The design work of the projection designer can potentially undermine the work of the lighting designer and vice versa, as both practitioners are working with light. Too much light in the lighting design can wash out any projected video imagery, for example, while the contrast used in a video can interfere with the nuance of certain lighting cues. Both practitioners are also tasked with realising their designs on stage at the same time during technical rehearsals. 'That's when the lighting designer is traditionally used to having their time,' explains projection designer Elaine J. McCarthy. 'It takes a collaborative spirit on behalf of the lighting designer to recognise that this is when I get my job done too' (personal communication, May 23, 2020).

Industry recognition and acknowledgement

Uncertainty about the role and responsibilities of projection designers extends to their recognition within the industry. Critical reviews often struggle to define the creative contribution of projection designers and, in many cases, their work is attributed to other designers or omitted entirely from acknowledgement. Napoleon (2017a) wryly explains: 'Suppose a music critic understood the symphonic form, but just couldn't hear the difference between a trumpet and a sax, and regularly credited the saxophonist for marvelous trumpet work ... welcome to the world of the projection designer.'

Part of the challenge is the way that projection design—whether digital imagery, video, animation, or some other form of media—potentially overlaps with the established realms of set and lighting. Sven Ortel suggests that 'reviewers feel like they have to credit somebody for what they've seen, and that is most often the people whose profession they understand' (personal communication, May 21, 2020). Accordingly, video designer Andrzej Goulding notes, 'every show I do has my video work credited to either the lighting designer or the set designer, or both sometimes' (quoted in Napoleon 2017b).

Both Ortel and lighting designer Japhy Weideman suggest that this confusion is ultimately a sign of a strong scenographic design. 'The really successful stuff is when you almost can't tell where the lighting ends and the video begins or vice versa,' explains Weideman (personal communication, July 29, 2020). Ortel agrees, noting,

> Some of the work I pride myself most on is not really visible to the uneducated eye [and] behaves like lighting and scenery ... I cannot fault the reviewer or the general public for not understanding what I've done, if the object of my work is to integrate with the other elements.
> (personal communication, May 21, 2020)

While arguably irritating for individual practitioners, misattribution in critical reviews reflects a larger issue in how projection designers are formally acknowledged in the industry. Projection design was only recognised as an independent design field by the American-based labour union, United Scenic Artists, in 2008 (McElroy 2008). In the same year, the United States Drama Desk established its first award in recognition of 'Outstanding Projection and Video Design' as distinct from either set or lighting design (McElroy 2008). As of August 2020, however, projection design was still not acknowledged by the United States Tony Awards or the Society of London Theatre's Laurence Olivier Awards, both of which only grant honours for scenic design, costume design, lighting design, and sound design (Pesner 2009; Official London Theatre n.d.). These omissions speak to the continued lack of formal recognition for the dramaturgical potential of digital scenography, as well as the designer who drives it.

Projection designers are also held to largely outdated industry standards in terms of work conditions and employment expectations. Consider the United Scenic Artists, the largest theatrical design union in the United States, which currently represents nearly 4,000 design practitioners across film, theatre, opera, ballet, and television. In its 2019–2022 Collective Bargaining Agreement with the Broadway League,[1] the union omits any definition of services specific to projection designers. Set designers, costume designers, and lighting designers are each designated certain duties for theatrical productions, such as to 'complete a working model of the setting to scale' (set or scenic designer), 'provide color sketches of all costumes' (costume designer), and 'provide a full equipment list and light plot drawn to scale' (lighting designer) (USA 829 2019, 1–3). Yet, the projection designer has no standard responsibilities of any kind listed. The design fees for projection designers are similarly noted as 'subject to negotiation,' even though standard fees are explicitly outlined for all other design practitioners (USA 829 2019, 5).

In addition to reinforcing the industry-wide vagueness about the duties and responsibilities of projection designers, the United Scenic Artists' agreement establishes a hierarchy for where projection designers sit in relation to the other designers. The agreement explicitly credits the set or scenic designer with complete creative authority over the projection design, noting in its definition of services that the set designer will 'design and/or supervise special scenic effects for the production, including projections' (USA 829 2019, 1). By attributing projections to the set designer by default, the union agreement directly undermines the creative autonomy of projection designers. The agreement further implies that projection designers are not required to be credited for their work (USA 829 2019, 4). Instead, the producer of a show 'retains the exclusive discretion to designate an individual as a Projection Designer on any production, or to not designate such an individual, *regardless of the use of projections* in a production' (4; italics mine). Under these standards, the theatrical producer has the authority to decide whether or not to formally recognise the artistic contribution of the projection designer.

Video and projection designer S. Katy Tucker notes that industry practice also allocates the intellectual property rights of a scenographic design entirely to the set designer, regardless of the role played by any projections, video, or animation. The projection designer only owns the intellectual property for the specific imagery they create, as well as any projection design system built for its use, Tucker explains (personal communication, September 5, 2018). Video designer Finn Ross recalls a musical theatre production in which his video designs constituted almost the entirety of the set, but the set designer still retained complete intellectual property rights for the scenographic design and was allotted twice the amount of royalties for subsequent productions (personal communication, September 25, 2018). Tucker acknowledges that intellectual property can potentially be shared between the set and projection designer in the event that the video 'is so integrated one can't exist without the other.' However, this is not guaranteed and is subject to negotiation (personal communication, September 5, 2018).

These ambiguities place the onus on individual practitioners to negotiate the conditions of their work for every digitally enhanced production. This, in turn, perpetuates the lack of a consistent standard for projection designers across the industry. As Tucker explains, there is not so much an 'industry standard' as numerous 'industry standards' that vary by show and producer (personal communication, September 5, 2018). Sven Ortel agrees, noting he has received design contracts that are 40 pages long and others that are only a single page. 'There are standards that every designer has for themselves. It basically boils down to a conversation and a handshake at some point,' he notes (personal communication, May 21, 2020). This poses yet another challenge to establishing a consistent framework for digitally enhanced production, as industry standards have not evolved alongside the shifting role of the projection designer.

The traditional theatrical hierarchy: director as ultimate authority

The United Scenic Artists' agreement outlines a hierarchy for design practitioners, in which the set designer is in a position of greater creative authority than the projection designer, while the director or producer sits above both (USA 829 2019). This expectation adheres to the vertical creative hierarchy that was traditionally used in theatrical production throughout the twentieth century. In his practical guide for theatre practitioners, *Working Together in Theatre: Collaboration & Leadership*, Cohen (2011) describes the standard for this hierarchy, in which the stage director serves as the primary authority for every aspect of the production. 'The director … gives aim, shape, and focus to his or her enterprise,' he explains, but 'also directs its *players*: which includes not just the theatre's actors, but its designers, stage managers, stage technicians, and crews' (55). Swain (2011) makes a similar claim in his handbook for emerging theatre directors, remarking that the theatre 'only functions successfully under a dictatorship—a director' (10). Each designer may take the lead over their individual contributions at some point in the process, but final oversight and authority rests with the stage director.

Historically, the shift towards directorial dominance in theatrical production began in the 1890s, when the 'retheatricalization of the theatre' led to a fundamental shift in perceptions of the genre (Williams 2012, 152). Productions were no longer the 'mere transmission of a dramatic text' but rather, a reflection of the 'fundamental concept that theatre represents an art *sui generis*' (Williams 2012, 152). Stage directors such as Vsevolod Meyerhold and Konstantin Stanislavski rose to prominence within this new environment, as did specialised design practitioners who created unique set designs for individual productions rather than stock scenery for generic use (Howard 2006). With the stage director cast as the primary authority in this new framework, designers were automatically relegated to a subservient position within the creative structure (Henderson 2001). Accordingly, designer Jo Mielziner did not mince words during a 1972 lecture at Yale University when he remarked, 'Designers never precede the dauphin in the theatre. They are hardworking worms' (quoted in Henderson 2001, 30).

Within the traditional vertical hierarchy, each designer assumes a different position beneath the leadership of the stage director. Cohen (2011) describes a second creative tier, or the 'Big Four,' which includes the set designer, costume designer, lighting designer, and sound designer (101). In the words of Tony Award-winning costume designer William Ivey Long, 'the set designer creates the world, the costume designer peoples the world, the lighting designer tells you where to look … and the sound designer controls what your ears hear' (quoted in Cohen 2011, 101). As the designer of the world, the set designer assumes the position of greatest authority below the stage director, followed, in descending order, by the costume designer, the lighting designer, and the sound designer (see Figure 5.1). Each position within the structure informs the extent of the practitioner's artistic independence, as well as their reporting structure and involvement in early conceptual discussions.

Cohen's hierarchy for the 'Big Four' notably excludes the projection designer. Instead, he ranks projection designers in a third creative tier, alongside wig and hair designers, property designers, and Foley artists. Within this lower tier, Cohen suggests that the projection designer should report to the set or lighting designer, rather than to the stage director directly. Lighting designer Graham Walne (1995) makes a similar assessment, noting that the set and lighting designers assume shared ownership over any projections used in a production. Typically, 'the responsibility for acquiring, rigging, focusing, and operating the projectors will fall within the lighting department' but the 'artwork for the slides will tend to be the responsibility of the set designer' (68). As the primary authority within the 'Big Four,' the set designer is responsible for the artistic duties—creating the actual projected

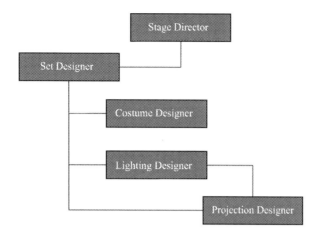

Figure 5.1 Vertical creative hierarchy, as described by Cohen (2011), including projection designer.

content—while the lighting designer coordinates the technical logistics. Walne's explanation was written more than 25 years ago but still tellingly aligns with both Cohen's description and the United Scenic Artists' 2019–2022 bargaining agreement (USA 829 2019).[2]

Cohen's version of the vertical creative hierarchy does not precisely align to opera production. While incorporating a sound designer, his structure omits the musical conductor, a role which, as lighting designer Donald Holder notes, 'often holds an equal or greater leadership role in comparison to the director' due to opera's focus on music (personal communication, June 27, 2020).[3] A more accurate framing for opera might therefore place the stage director and conductor in a position of shared leadership over the overall production, or perhaps even place the musical conductor slightly higher than the director. However, the scenographic elements of an opera remain the purview of the stage director alone, and as such, we can still rely on Cohen's description of their relationship with the designers as a benchmark of historical practice.

Within the traditional vertical hierarchy, the subordinate status of the projection designer is clearly at odds with the creative possibilities for digital scenography. Indeed, projection design is framed, by Cohen at least, as the scenographic equivalent of wigs or props, rather than an independent design field that contributes at an equal level as the other designers. The projection designer's limited communication with the director and absence from creative discussions with the 'Big Four' poses a particular challenge in terms of partial-synthesis or full-synthesis productions. The use of causal interplay generally requires active engagement from the projection designer at an early point in the creative process, which is difficult to achieve within Cohen's third creative tier.

Sven Ortel suggests that the tradition of complete directorial authority limits experimentation with digital scenography, as 'a director basically decides what gets done and how a story gets told' rather than framing all of the practitioners as equal 'storytellers' (personal communication, May 21, 2020). Accordingly, we can see how traditional vertical hierarchies seem to align most naturally to non-synthesis productions that use projections for background scenery or atmospheric effects. In these types of productions, while digital elements play an important visual role as part of the scenographic design, the projection designer is not necessarily needed in the upper tiers of the creative hierarchy.

S. Katy Tucker and projection designer Wendall K. Harrington both suggest that the traditional vertical hierarchy is no longer tenable in practice. Harrington considers the entire concept of directorial authority to be 'outdated' and 'counterproductive,' noting 'I don't see the value of "staying in your lane" if you have valuable ideas to offer' (personal communication, June 27, 2017). Tucker diplomatically observes that only directors 'whose careers began earlier' still seem to operate within this traditional framework (personal communication, September 21, 2017).

Mark Grimmer of 59 Productions suggests that the younger generation of designers is increasingly drawn to 'more collaborative ways of working,' in which projection design is recognised as a discipline in its own right (personal communication, August 15, 2020). He also suggests that expert practitioners are now able to be more selective about the kinds of hierarchies in which they choose to participate (personal communication, June 27, 2017). When 59 Productions was founded in 2006, Grimmer recalls that he and his colleagues had no choice but to work within traditional vertical hierarchies while they were establishing themselves in the field. Once they gained acceptance, however, they were able to avoid dictatorial directors who had 'no patience for, interest in, or understanding of what we do' and instead could 'pick projects based on a degree of certainty that the creative experience [was] going to be one that we [could] contribute value to' (personal communication, May 31, 2017).

The lateral hierarchy: collective directorate

In the twenty-first century, many creative teams have deviated from the traditional vertical hierarchy in favour of a more lateral structure (Howard 2002).[4] Cohen (2011) refers to this kind of lateral hierarchy as a 'collective directorate,' in which the stage director shares creative responsibility with the other members of the artistic team. Cohen explains, 'The director may technically stand atop this hierarchical heap, but the heap is no longer a conical volcano; it's more like a low and windswept dune' (61).

The stage director is still technically the pinnacle of authority in this lateral structure, but the other members of the creative team enjoy increased

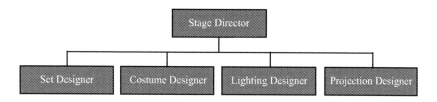

Figure 5.2 Lateral creative hierarchy, as described by Cohen (2011), including projection designer.

creative autonomy, both in their individual fields and in their contribution to the overall scenographic vision (see Figure 5.2). Projection designer Zachary Borovay (2006) suggests that, in this model, the traditional vertical hierarchy is essentially replaced with a 'collaborative dictatorship with many micro-dictatorships within it' (26). Bogart and Gray (2015) concur, proposing a metaphor of multiple windows, in which each member of the creative team views the production from a different, but equally important, perspective (213).

A key element of the lateral creative hierarchy is equality between all members of the design team beneath the director's authority. Stage director Katie Mitchell explains, 'We all work collaboratively together with the tacit understanding that I shape the cohering vision that everyone is working inside' (personal communication, March 10, 2018). The 'director leads,' agrees stage director Roger Hodgman, but 'in a good relationship … it's very much a two-way thing' (personal communication, June 11, 2017).

The set designer is still a key collaborator for the stage director but does not assume a default position of authority over the other designers as in the traditional model (Cohen 2011). Instead, the hierarchy is transformed into a more 'matrixed' structure, in which all of the designers are positioned on a shared plane below the stage director (Grimmer, personal communication, May 31, 2017). The integration of the projection designer into this more democratic structure manifests as an elevation to the second tier of creative authority, or the realm of Cohen's 'Big Four.'

In this capacity, the projection designer no longer reports to the set designer or lighting designer but is positioned equally with the other designers. The projection designer's creative contribution is also perceived as a more integral and potentially autonomous element of the design. Video designer Finn Ross explains, 'you are part of the design team the way any other designer … is part of the team,' instead of 'facilitating the ideas of others' (personal communication, September 12, 2016). S. Katy Tucker agrees, explaining, 'The set designer will contact me while they're coming up with a design: is this a good surface? Does this work for you? And the lighting designer will ask about projector placements. It's more about equality and collaboration' (personal communication, September 21, 2017).

A lateral hierarchy allows for greater creative responsibility and autonomy among the individual designers but can also place the stage director in an awkward position. The director actively collaborates with the other creatives but remains responsible for the overall vision of the production. Regardless of the scope of collaboration within her team, stage director Nancy Black notes that she is 'ultimately responsible' for the final product and 'will take the full blame for everything' (personal communication, May 15, 2017). Cohen (2011) suggests that artistic discussions in lateral hierarchies can be overwhelmed with conflicting opinions. He highlights the issue with a rhetorical question, asking: 'If the designer makes a statement, do the four principal designers make four statements? And does the director make a fifth statement—or a first?' (104).

Animator Paul Barritt argues that the stage director must find a way to balance collaboration and authority within the lateral structure. 'You need leadership but it's senseless for that leadership to be absolute,' he notes. A director 'must always be flexible, must always be prepared to be proven wrong, must always be accepting of new ideas regardless of where or who they come from' (personal communication, June 17, 2017). Projection designer Wendall K. Harrington agrees, declaring that 'the director, of course, is in charge, but good ideas can come from any department.' Harrington notes that she intentionally instructs her projection students at the Yale School of Design to 'think like directors' and 'support the strongest idea wherever it comes from' (personal communication, June 27, 2017).

Nearly all of the practitioners interviewed for this book describe a lateral hierarchy as the ideal creative structure for an opera production that involves projected elements. However, the logistics of integrating the projection designer are not always straightforward. A single practitioner, such as Wendall K. Harrington or Finn Ross, can be easily assimilated into a lateral creative structure, simply joining the other designers on the creative matrix below the stage director. This integration becomes more complicated when projection designs require large teams of animators and programmers, often working for independent companies that have been sub-contracted to provide digital elements. While the primary hierarchical structure for an opera production may be lateral in terms of the lead projection designer or project manager, this creative equality does not necessarily extend beyond the top artistic tier.

When working on large productions, S. Katy Tucker often hires a standard 'team,' which includes a programmer, an animator, a production coordinator, and a systems engineer. These practitioners work directly with Tucker as part of an independent creative hierarchy that stands apart from the rest of the production team (see Figure 5.3). They have no interaction with the stage director or other designers, explains Tucker: 'I am the point of contact … they should never take notes from anyone else other than me' (personal communication, September 21, 2017).[5] In this capacity, Tucker functions as the primary authority within her personal team—'I get to be a

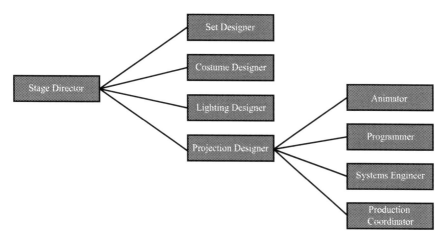

Figure 5.3 Video and projection designer S. Katy Tucker's internal creative hierarchy.

lot like a director'—while the four supporting team members enjoy relative equality with one another (personal communication, September 21, 2017).

Projection designers Sven Ortel and Elaine J. McCarthy also frequently work with their own teams, depending on the scale of the digital design. Ortel notes that he typically engages a compositor, a photoshop artist, and a 3D animator to build assets, while McCarthy uses a combination of assistants, programmers, and artists to support her designs (personal communication, May 21, 2020; personal communication, May 23, 2020). Both note that, like Tucker, they assume the role of the director within their internal teams. 'I wear two hats,' explains McCarthy. 'I'm the designer who has the ideas and then asks for this content, but I'm also the head of the studio creating the content' (personal communication, May 23, 2020).

Mark Grimmer describes a similar scenario for large-scale projects at 59 Productions. Regardless of the number of practitioners involved, each project is overseen by a single creative authority, or project director, who serves as the 'primary liaison for all matters creative' with the stage director, set designer, lighting designer, and costume designer (personal communication, May 31, 2017). 'We've learned that there is a balance to strike between efficient communication and making sure that the key creatives on our team get as much direct exposure to the wider creative process as possible,' Grimmer notes (personal communication, August 15, 2020). Meanwhile, the supporting team members—including programmers, animators, line producers, and technical directors—have little to no communication with the stage director or other designers. 'This whole team structure sits pretty independently within the wider creative team as part of the video designer plane, in much the same way that lighting, set, or costume would also have teams of people,' Grimmer explains (personal communication, May 31, 2017).

As an independent design company that is frequently sub-contracted to provide digital scenography for opera and theatre companies, 59 Productions maintains a significantly larger staff than Tucker, Ortel, or McCarthy. As of August 2020, the company employed 42 staff members, including designers, architects, technicians, producers, directors, administrators, and managers (59 Productions n.d. 'Team'). Given the number of in-house employees, the company's internal hierarchy skews more towards a traditional vertical hierarchy in terms of its reporting structure. The hierarchy is also informed by the size of the commission and can be scaled up or down depending on the needs of a given production.

For example, 59 Productions' digital designs for The Metropolitan Opera's 50th Anniversary Gala in 2017 involved 13 team members, including five animators, two project directors, one technical director, one associate project director, one producer, one programmer, one assistant, and one intern (59 Productions n.d. 'The Metropolitan Opera'). Grimmer outlines a clear hierarchical delineation between the technical and creative personnel for this production, as well as a particular chain of command between varying levels (see Figure 5.4). He clarifies that the hierarchy is not always 'top-down' in practice. However, the number of staff members necessitates a more fixed reporting structure than the creative equality enjoyed by smaller teams like those of Tucker, Ortel, and McCarthy (personal communication, May 31, 2017).

Lateral hierarchies offer significantly more creative autonomy for projection designers than vertical hierarchies. Projection designers are no longer relegated to the lowest creative tier and can communicate directly with the stage director, as well as engage with the other designers as equal artistic contributors. The scope of collaboration still varies, depending

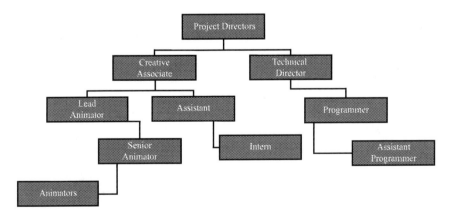

Figure 5.4 59 Productions' internal creative hierarchy.

on the practitioners involved, the components of the scenographic design, and the overall timeline. Production designer Victoria 'Vita' Tzykun notes that the set and costume designers typically still discuss the production design with the stage director first, while the lighting and projection designers will join the discussion after the 'general visual tone of the stage production has already started to take shape' (personal communication, September 8, 2020). Nevertheless, the lateral creative hierarchy reframes the role of the projection designer in a way that better reflects the increased prominence and artistic capabilities of digital scenography. As such, lateral hierarchies naturally align to the use of partial-synthesis, as the close collaboration of the creative practitioners creates the ideal conditions to explore causal interplay.

Hierarchical variation: projection designers as the directorial authority

Vertical and lateral creative hierarchies are most common in opera production, but some projection design practitioners are experimenting with collaborative variations that elevate their roles to positions of greater authority. These experiments can be seen as a reaction to the traditional role of the stage director in that they adapt, adjust, or supplant the director's authority over the rest of the creative team. Such variations explore larger questions about the creative contributions of projection designers and the scope of their artistic ownership over scenographic designs. Many of these variations can also be linked to an extreme use of digital scenography through either partial-synthesis or full-synthesis. This suggests that hierarchical variations may be emerging as a direct result of the technological demands and artistic opportunities inherent to digital scenography.

In each of the three digitally enhanced productions of *The Magic Flute* discussed in Chapter 1, the projection designer assumes a position of directorial authority. Both William Kentridge and Jun Kaneko either replace or supplant the traditional directorial role in their productions for the Théâtre Royal de la Monnaie and San Francisco Opera, respectively. In Barrie Kosky and 1927's *The Magic Flute* for Komische Oper Berlin, Suzanne Andrade of animation company 1927 is elevated to a position of shared directorial authority with Kosky himself. As noted in the earlier chapter, each production also demonstrates a different mode of synthesis in practice: Kaneko's production is non-synthesis, Kentridge's is partial-synthesis, and Kosky and 1927's is full-synthesis. In each case, we can link the mode of synthesis to the subsequent alterations in the hierarchical structure

In his production for La Monnaie (2005), William Kentridge assumed the title and duties of both the stage director and the projection designer. He also credited himself as a 'co-designer' of the set, alongside set designer Sabine Theunissen (Law-Viljoen 2007).[6] As a result, Kentridge had triple authority within the creative hierarchy in which the positions of stage director, projection designer, and set designer were intrinsically combined. Given his status in multiple creative roles, Kentridge was able to ensure that every aspect of the projected imagery was integrated with the set, lighting, and live performers as he intended. By framing himself as co-set designer with Theunissen, Kentridge was also able to avoid some of the traditional tensions between projection and set that can lead to an unintegrated visual design. Most importantly, Kentridge conceived his animations in the context of his staging decisions as director, which supported frequent causal interplay between the live performers and digital elements throughout the production.

Even with these blended roles, Kentridge's production still aligns to a lateral creative hierarchy (see Figure 5.5). Sabine Theunissen describes the creative team as a 'work family' and notes that the first draft of the design concept was determined collaboratively by Kentridge, Theunissen, and video controller and editor Catherine Meyburgh (personal communication, June 10, 2017). She explains: 'the video designer is sitting with the director and the set designer, from day one, in front of the stage model. Ideally also with light[ing] designer and costume designer. It is a team process' (personal communication, June 10, 2017).

Jun Kaneko's production of *The Magic Flute* (2012) for San Francisco Opera also prioritised the projection designer within the creative hierarchy. However, in this case, Kaneko did not assume the mantle of stage director or any other traditional role. Instead he assumed a position of authority *above* the stage director in terms of creative control over the production (see Figure 5.6). Contrary to common practice in which the stage director is first hired by a company's artistic director (Cohen 2011), Kaneko himself was first approached by then general director of San Francisco Opera, David Gockley, to consider the commission (Kaneko 2012). Once Kaneko agreed, Gockley suggested that Kaneko work with stage director Harry Silverstein (Martinfield 2012). In a 2012 interview, Gockley notes that Silverstein's role was to 'adapt the artist's work to the theater,' as Kaneko had little experience with theatrical production (Kaneko 2012, 20). While Silverstein was responsible for staging decisions, Kaneko directly oversaw all other scenographic aspects of the production, including the set, costumes, projections, and props.

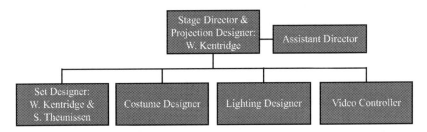

Figure 5.5 Hierarchical variation: William Kentridge and the Théâtre Royal de la Monnaie's *The Magic Flute*.

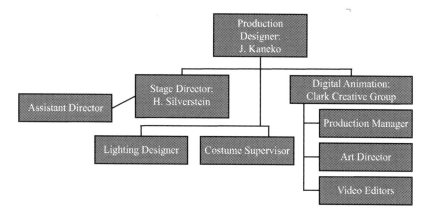

Figure 5.6 Hierarchical variation: Jun Kaneko and San Francisco Opera's *The Magic Flute*.

Rather than assuming a position of creative authority or even equality with the artist driving the projected imagery, Silverstein was established as an adaptor and interpreter of Kaneko's vision. Christopher Maravich, then lighting director of San Francisco Opera, confirmed this unusual creative structure, noting their job was to figure out 'how we're going to produce Jun's vision on stage,' rather than making an independent artistic contribution (Martinfield 2012). As director, Silverstein still took responsibility for the performers on stage, but his creative control in this area was predicated on Kaneko's authority over the other aspects of the production. Although digital animation company Clark Creative Group was hired to work on the production, this team's creative responsibilities were similarly limited. The team members did not conceive any creative content themselves and instead only animated the existing visual designs specified in Kaneko's storyboard (Kaneko 2012).

In both of these productions, the artists driving the digital scenography assumed primacy within the creative hierarchy: in a blended role as stage director, projection designer, and set designer in Kentridge's case, or by circumventing the traditional authority of the stage director as with Kaneko. While Kentridge employed a lateral creative structure, albeit with his own adjustments, Kaneko's hierarchy adheres more closely to a traditional vertical structure, with clear expectations of his authority and an appropriate reporting structure for the members of his team. Kaneko oversaw all visual aspects of the production, much in the same way as Kentridge, but the key difference is that Kaneko was not involved in staging decisions. Instead, Kaneko conceived his designs in isolation from the performers and did not choose to incorporate any causal interplay between the digital elements and live performers. Kaneko's artistic choices in this regard show the importance of the directorial role and active involvement in staging decisions as a means for establishing a production's potential mode of synthesis.

In Komische Oper Berlin's *The Magic Flute* (2012), the projection designer neither supplants nor replaces the role of the stage director but is positioned as an equal collaborator with shared directorial authority (see Figure 5.7). Suzanne Andrade of animation company 1927 and Barrie Kosky are listed as co-directors for the production. All credit listings for the production further state that the production was collectively conceived by 'Suzanne Andrade & Paul Barritt (1927) & Barrie Kosky (Komische Oper Berlin)' (1927 n.d.). Animator Paul Barritt confirms that these credits reflect the reality of the roles and responsibilities undertaken by each member of the creative team. Although the conceptual discussions were collaborative, Andrade and Barritt took the lead on developing the scenographic design, as well as conceiving the relationship between the live performers and digital elements. '[Andrade] and I were allowed to do whatever we wanted. Barrie wanted us to do our thing,' Barritt notes. 'This meant that we very much drove the whole concept and design and certainly always had the final veto power' (personal communication, June 17, 2017).

Like Kentridge, Andrade also took on multiple roles, assuming the traditional directorial duties of staging in addition to driving the digital scenography with Barritt. Barritt notes that the scope of causal interplay in the production required the staging decisions and digital designs to be conceived simultaneously. 'The interaction between animation and live action is an entirely 1927 idea ... It is Suzanne's directing style that makes the show work,' explains Barritt (personal communication, June 17, 2017).

The scope of collaboration between Kosky, Barritt, and Andrade is not surprising given the production's use of full-synthesis. Because the

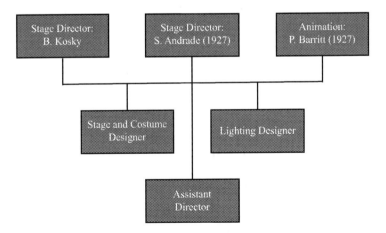

Figure 5.7 Hierarchical variation: Barrie Kosky, 1927, and Komische Oper Berlin's *The Magic Flute*.

production relies so heavily on causal interplay, the structure of its creative hierarchy demands a certain equality between the stage director and the projection designer, or, in this case, the animation team. This kind of full-synthesis production would be untenable in a traditional vertical hierarchy, with the projection designer largely removed from creative discussions and functioning as a subordinate to the set designer. Not only were Barritt and Andrade 'in creative discussions from the very beginning,' but the full-synthesis technique used in the production is one of 1927's own devising (personal communication, June 17, 2017).

While Kosky, Andrade, and Barritt are billed as shared conceptual authors in the production's playbill, however, numerous critical reviews still attribute the production design solely to Kosky. Reviewing the production's premiere at the Edinburgh Festival in 2015, Fiona Maddocks of *The Observer* presented Kosky as the work's driving force, writing 'Kosky has delivered a quixotic enterprise' (Maddocks 2015). Tom Service of *The Guardian* similarly attributed the opera almost entirely to Kosky—'his *Magic Flute*,' 'his globe-conquering production,' 'a Kosky show'—and never mentions Andrade and Barritt except to refer to Kosky's 'collaborators' (Service 2015). In her review of the production's 2019 Australian tour, Diana Carroll (2019) refers to 'Barrie Kosky's fantasy *Flute*' and 'Barrie Kosky's audacious staging' before later acknowledging that the production was produced 'in association' with Suzanne Andrade and Paul Barritt of 1927.

The assumption that Kosky was primarily responsible for the scenographic design reflects a bias towards the historical authority of the stage director within the traditional vertical hierarchy. The pattern also recalls Sven Ortel's acknowledgement that reviewers are most likely to attribute what they see on stage to 'people whose profession they understand' (personal communication, May 21, 2020). This suggests that even digitally enhanced productions that circumvent traditional hierarchies must still contend with deep-rooted expectations about the roles and responsibilities of creative practitioners. The default assumption is still that the stage director is the primary authority in a production, regardless of the dominance of the digital designs.

The evolving role of the projection designer

The hierarchical variations described above remain the exception rather than the rule in digitally enhanced opera production. Sutcliffe (1998) suggests that such variations are usually only possible for prominent artists like Jun Kaneko and William Kentridge who can demand complete creative control from presenting opera companies.[7] He explains: 'Artists who take to designing are usually far more widely famous than professional designers and therefore can do what they artistically want without argument. You do not ask a Picasso for a back-cloth and complain about the result' (87).

While not as internationally renowned as Kentridge and Kaneko, 1927 is an independent theatrical organisation with a history of presenting highly acclaimed artistic work. In addition, Andrade and Barritt relied on their own method for integrating digital animation and live performers, which naturally framed their collaboration with Kosky in terms of their own creative authority.

Other independent companies like 1927 are also experimenting with hierarchical models that replace the traditional role of the director. In 2016, 59 Productions announced its first self-driven digitally enhanced theatrical production, an adaptation of Paul Auster's *City of Glass*, presented in collaboration with HOME in Manchester and the Lyric Hammersmith (Snow 2016). Billed as 'directed, designed and produced by 59 Productions,' the production featured an extensive creative team, in which team members from 59 Productions assumed both traditional roles—such as company director Leo Warner as stage director—as well as more technology-driven positions, such as animators, video designers, and facial tracking developers (59 Productions n.d. 'City of Glass'). Warner explains the rationale for the company's shift to self-production, noting,

> We're now involved with leading the production on a number of projects … and that's very much more where we see ourselves going as a company … being more and more involved in the genesis of things, not just coming in to service somebody else's creative ideas.
>
> (Dong n.d.)

GLMMR,[8] founded by production designer Victoria 'Vita' Tzykun in collaboration with director, designer, and performer David Adam Moore, takes a similar approach to reframing creative collaboration (GLMMR n.d.). Tzykun and Moore work from an integrated model in which 'the video designer and the set designer start at the exact same time, and they have the exact same amount of creative weight' (Victoria 'Vita' Tzykun, personal communication, August 28, 2018). In addition to sharing creative responsibility in a design capacity, Tzykun and Moore also serve as co-directors for most of GLMMR's productions. As a result of these shared roles, 'everything feeds off each other,' notes Tzykun.

> The location of the performer, the shape of the set, the mapping, timing, and intensity of the video … we develop all of these things using an intimately interconnected process, rather than one element being an afterthought to another element.
>
> (personal communication, August 28, 2018)

GLMMR, 59 Productions, and 1927 are all independent organisations with sufficient financial stability and in-house personnel to experiment with new hierarchical forms. Meanwhile, artists like William Kentridge and Jun

Kaneko have the international clout to set their own terms for production design. This is not the case with individual projection designers, who have limited options to deviate from industry expectations, particularly in the early stages of their careers. As a result, the more traditional creative structures, whether vertical or lateral, remain standard among opera companies, practitioners, and unions.

Creative hierarchies and the modes of synthesis

Of the two most common hierarchies in opera, the lateral creative structure unquestionably gives projection designers the most autonomy. In this structure, projection designers function as equal members of the creative team and can play a significant role in driving the overall scenographic design. Nonetheless, the extent of the projection designer's creative involvement is still dependent on hiring practices, timelines, and the scope of the digital designs. According to Victoria 'Vita' Tzykun, the projection designer cannot be a truly equal collaborator unless they are hired as early as possible in the production process and take part in originating the scenographic concept (personal communication, August 28, 2018). This suggests that even in a lateral creative hierarchy, the projection designer may still not have the opportunity to participate on a truly equal artistic level.

Finn Ross believes that the theatrical industry is gradually gaining a better understanding of projection designers and their possible contributions to a scenographic design. 'It is slowly changing, very slowly,' he notes (personal communication, September 25, 2018). S. Katy Tucker believes that the roles of the projection designer and lighting designer may eventually merge into a single position. 'I know a lot of lighting designers who like to use projectors as lights. And I know that I like to use lights a lot. So, I think those two fields are fusing together, and I don't think that's a bad thing,' she explains (personal communication, September 21, 2017).

A continued obstacle to any formalised shift in the way that projection designers are perceived and integrated into creative hierarchies remains the variability that exists from production to production. Creative hierarchies are fundamentally driven by the individual personalities and preferences of the creative practitioners involved, beginning with those who are 'in the room' first. These practitioners are still most often the stage director and the set designer, and their creative choices ultimately shape the responsibilities of the other practitioners. The role of the projection designer is further constrained by the lack of consistent industry standards, in which conditions of employment must be negotiated on a case-by-case basis.

This scope of variation makes it difficult to draw industry-wide conclusions about the potential disruption of digital scenography on creative hierarchies. Here, the modes of synthesis provide an avenue for suggesting a more consistent standard. While no single hierarchy lends itself, without exception, to a particular mode of synthesis, the analysis presented in this chapter suggests a correlation between the mode of synthesis and the creative authority of the projection designer.

In a non-synthesis production, the projection designer does not necessarily need to assume a position of equal creative authority as their designs do not interact with the live performers beyond visual correlation. The performers can be staged as if they are in front of painted backgrounds, and the projection designer can construct their designs in relative isolation from staging considerations and even the other designers. This suggests that non-synthesis productions align most naturally to traditional vertical hierarchies, in which the projection designer has historically held a more subordinate role.

The use of causal interplay, however, does not function as successfully within a traditional vertical hierarchy. Because causal interplay involves interaction between the live performers and digital elements, the projection designer needs to work in close collaboration with the stage director from the early stages of design conception and may even need to participate in staging rehearsals. Partial-synthesis productions are thus best supported by either lateral creative hierarchies, in which projection designers hold equal standing to the other designers, or hierarchical variations in which projection designers assume directorial authority. For full-synthesis productions, the early and extensive involvement of the projection designers—or a totally integrated team—is even more important. The greater the role played by causal interplay in a partial- or full-synthesis production, the more likely the projection designer or projection design team will assume a higher position within the creative hierarchy.[9]

The next chapter will consider another backstage aspect of digital scenography: the production design process. Design processes are closely linked to creative hierarchies in that they are similarly informed by the preferences of the practitioners involved. However, these processes are also critically shaped by the elements of the scenographic design, as well as the external considerations of the presenting companies.

Notes

1 The Broadway League is the 'national trade association for the Broadway industry,' and encompasses more than 700 members including theatre owners, producers, and general managers (Broadway League n.d.).

2 Not surprisingly, the idea that projection design belongs to the realm of either set or lighting design has been contested by projection designers. Borovay (2006) insists,

> I am not a lighting designer, although I use a specialized lighting instrument to convey my design. I am not a scenic designer, although my imagery can be graphic or scenic in nature … I do not see my job as a stepping-stone to any other discipline.
>
> (26)

3 In opera production, the authority of the stage director has been closely linked to that of the musical conductor since the early twentieth century, when both

positions were framed as the artistic guardians of the intentions of the original composer and librettist (Littlejohn 1994). While the conductor is tasked with interpreting a fixed material score, however, the stage director is responsible for realising an ephemeral performative work on stage (Littlejohn 1994). This can lead to conflicts between the fixed artefact of the musical score and its subsequent stage interpretations (Abbate 2003).

4 This shift aligns with a similar flattering of hierarchies in the film industry, which is moving away from the tradition of the sole film director as primary authority. Maule (2008) cites a number of 'new directions in authorial film practice' that 'signal either a rejection or a radical reconceptualization of this model of authorship' (15).

5 Tucker notes that this chain-of-command is not always successful in practice. She recalls a number of occasions when either the stage director or set designer circumvented her authority and attempted to give notes directly to members of her team (personal communication, September 21, 2017).

6 Kentridge used the same hierarchical variation for his productions of *The Nose* (2010), *Lulu* (2015), and *Wozzeck* (2019) for The Metropolitan Opera (Law-Viljoen 2007). With the exception of the lighting designer, the same creative practitioners were also involved in all three productions: set designer Sabine Theunissen, costume designer Greta Goiris, video controller and editor Catherine Meyburgh, and assistant director Luc de Wit (Metropolitan Opera Archives n.d.).

7 Heymont (2012) cites Marc Chagall's *The Magic Flute* (1967), Maurice Sendak's *The Magic Flute* (1981), and David Hockney's *Turandot* (1992) as additional examples of artist-driven opera productions.

8 GLMMR is an acronym for 'Giving Light Motion + Memory + Relevance.'

9 The use of causal interplay does not preclude the possibility of a vertical creative hierarchy. Victorian Opera's *The Flying Dutchman* (2015) is one example of a partial-synthesis production that was designed within a largely traditional vertical structure (see Chapter 2). The scenographic concept was led by the stage director and set designer, who then engaged the Deakin Motion.Lab to build the digital designs to specification. According to stage director Roger Hodgman, 'the projection designers [were] responding to a brief rather than necessarily coming up with ideas' (personal communication, June 11, 2017). However, while acknowledging such exceptions, the analysis still suggests a correlation between the mode of synthesis and the creative hierarchy being employed.

References

1927. n.d. "The Magic Flute." Accessed August 13, 2020. https://www.19-27.co.uk/the-magic-flute.

59 Productions. n.d. "City of Glass." Accessed August 13, 2020. https://59productions.co.uk/project/city-of-glass/.

59 Productions. n.d. "The Metropolitan Opera." Accessed August 15, 2020. https://59productions.co.uk/project/metropolitan-opera-50th-anniversary-gala/.

59 Productions. n.d. "Team." Accessed August 15, 2020. https://59productions.co.uk/team/.

Abbate, Carolyn. 2003. *In Search of Opera*. Princeton: Princeton University Press.

Barbour, David. 2011. "The Prevalence Of Projections: Projection in the Theatre Is Nearly as Old as Theatre Itself, but Recent Technological Advances Have Made It Easier to Use—And Misuse." *American Theatre Magazine* 28, no. 10 (December): 28–33.

Bogart, Anne, and Jackson Gray. 2015. "The Art of Collaboration: On Dramaturgy and Directing." In *The Routledge Companion to Dramaturgy*, edited by Magda Romanska, 213–216. London: Routledge.

Borovay, Zachary. 2006. "I Am Not a Lighting Designer." *Live Design Online*, October 2006: 26–27. https://www.livedesignonline.com/i-am-not-a-lighting-designer.

Broadway League. n.d. "About the League." Accessed August 1, 2020. https://www.broadwayleague.com/about/.

Buntrock, Sam. 2013. "Never Do Projections in Theatre." *PROJCTN*, March 26, 2013. http://projctn.com/never-do-projection-theatre.

Carroll, Diana. 2019. "Review: The Magic Flute, Adelaide Festival." *ArtsHub.com*, March 4, 2019. https://performing.artshub.com.au/news-article/reviews/performing-arts/diana-carroll/review-the-magic-flute-adelaide-festival-257449.

Cohen, Robert. 2011. *Working Together in Theatre: Collaboration & Leadership*. Basingstoke: Palgrave Macmillan.

Dong, Joanna. n.d. "Interview with Leo Warner, Creative Director of 59 Productions." Text by Struan Robinson. Translated by Peng Zuqiang. *Art Zip*, Issue 12. http://www.artzip.org/interview-leo-warner-creative-director-59-production.

Gates, Anita. 2010. "The Screen's Now Setting Many a Stage." *New York Times*, March 7, 2010. http://www.nytimes.com/2010/03/07/theater/07projection.html.

Gendrich, Cynthia M., and Stephen Archer. 2017. *Theatre: Its Art & Craft*. Lanham: Rowman & Littlefield.

Giesekam, Greg. 2007. *Staging the Screen: The Use of Film and Video in Theatre*. Basingstoke: Palgrave Macmillan.

GLMMR. n.d. "About." Accessed August 28, 2018. https://www.glmmr.org/about.

Harrington, Wendall K. n.d. "Biography." http://www.wendallharrington.com/biography/.

Henderson, Mary C. 2001. *Mielziner: Master of Modern Stage Design*. New York: Back Stage Books.

Heymont, George. 2012. "A Most Magic New Flute." *Huffington Post*, August 15, 2012. http://www.huffingtonpost.com/george-heymont/a-most-magical-new-flute_b_1783067.html.

Howard, Pamela. 2002. *What Is Scenography?* New York: Routledge.

Howard, Pamela. 2006. "Directors and Designers: Is There a Different Direction?" In *The Potentials of Space: The Theory and Practice of Scenography and Performance*, edited by Alison Oddey and Christine White, 25–32. Bristol: Intellect.

Johnson, David. 2003. "The Next Generation of Projection Design." *Live Design Online*, May 1, 2003. https://www.livedesignonline.com/next-generation-projection-design.

Kaneko, Jun. 2012. *The Magic Flute*. London: Laurence King.

Law-Viljoen, Bronwyn. 2007. *William Kentridge: Flute*. Johannesburg: David Krut Publishing.

Littlejohn, David. 1994. *The Ultimate Art: Essays Around and About Opera*. Berkeley: University of California Press.

Luke Halls Studio. n.d. "About." Accessed November 22, 2018. http://lukehalls.com/about/.

Maddocks, Fiona. 2015. "The Magic Flute at Edinburgh Festival Review—Unforgettable and Exhausting." *The Observer*, September 30, 2015. https://www.theguardian.com/music/2012/sep/16/magic-flute-eno-bartered-bride-byo.

Martinfield, Sean. 2012. "Jun Kaneko's 'Magic Flute' Is Stunningly Visual." *Huffington Post*, June 28, 2012. https://www.huffpost.com/entry/magic-flute-jun-kaneko_b_1633445.

Maule, Rosanna. 2008. *Beyond Auteurism: New Directions in Authorial Film Practices in France, Italy and Spain Since the 1980s.* Bristol: Intellect.

McElroy, Steven. 2008. "From Afterthought to Essential." *New York Times*, May 18, 2008. https://mobile.nytimes.com/2008/05/18/theater/18mcelroy.html.

Metropolitan Opera Archives. n.d. Accessed April 2017. http://archives.metoperafamily.org.

Napoleon, Davi. 2017a. Projection Design: A Primer For Tony Voters and Critics, Part Two." *Live Design Online*, November 29, 2017. https://www.livedesignonline.com/theatre/projection-design-a-primer-for-tony-voters-and-critics-part-two.

Napoleon, Davi. 2017b. "Projection Design: A Primer for Tony Voters and Critics, Part One." *Live Design Online*, November 27, 2017. https://www.livedesignonline.com/theatre/projection-design-primer-tony-voters-and-critics-part-one.

Newman, Mark A. 2004. "The Stage as Screen." *EntertainmentDesignMag.com*, September 3, 2004.

Official London Theatre. n.d. "Olivier Awards 2019 Winners & Nominees." https://officiallondontheatre.com/olivier-awards/year/2019/.

Oliszewski, Alex, and Daniel Fine. 2018. *Digital Media, Projection Design, & Technology for the Future.* New York: Routledge.

Ortel, Sven. n.d. "Projection Design." Accessed November 22, 2018. https://www.svenortel.com/projection-design-as-design-discipline/.

Pesner, Ben. 2009. "The Tony Awards—Category by Category." https://www.tonyawards.com/news/the-tony-awards-category-by-category/.

Pilbrow, Richard. 2011. *A Theatre Project: A Backstage Adventure—Triumph, Disaster, and Renewal that Changed Stage Lighting and the Shape of Theatre.* New York: Plasa Media.

Ross, Finn. n.d. "Finn Ross." Accessed November 22, 2018. https://www.behance.net/finnross.

Service, Tom. 2015. "Barrie Kosky: 'When I First Saw The Magic Flute, I Didn't Get It and I Didn't Like It.'" *The Guardian*, July 13, 2015. https://www.theguardian.com/music/2015/jul/13/barrie-kosky-the-magic-flute-i-was-like-euggh.

Snow, Georgia. 2016. "Projection Designers 59 Productions to Create Its First Theatre Show." *The Stage*, September 8, 2016. https://www.thestage.co.uk/news/projection-designers-59-productions-to-create-its-first-theatre-show.

Sutcliffe, Thomas. 1998. *Believing in Opera.* London: Faber and Faber.

Swain, Rob. 2011. *Directing: A Handbook for Emerging Theatre Directors.* London: Methuen Drama.

Tucker, S. Katy. n.d. "Biography." Accessed November 22, 2018. http://www.skatytucker.com/biography/.

USA 829 (United Scenic Artists). 2019. *Agreement Between United Scenic Artists and the Broadway League, Inc, 2019–2022.* https://www.usa829.org/Portals/0/Theatre%20Opera%20Dance/Temp%20-%20Broadway%20Agreement%202019-2022%20Fully%20Executed.pdf?ver=2019-07-02-135715-170.

Walne, Graham. 1995. *Projection for the Performing Arts.* Waltham: Focal Press.

Williams, Simon. 2012. "Opera and Modes of Theatrical Production." In *The Cambridge Companion to Opera Studies*, edited by Nicholas Till, 139–158. Cambridge: Cambridge University Press.

6   Digital scenography and evolving production design processes

As outlined in the previous chapter, creative hierarchies for digitally enhanced productions vary, depending on preferences and personalities. The hierarchy that ultimately emerges directly influences the production design process, or the logistics of realising a theatrical work on stage. These logistics include developing the design concept, drafting preliminary artwork, building scale set models and storyboards, finalising physical and digital set components, and transferring all elements into the theatrical venue for technical rehearsals. Design processes are shaped by technological considerations—such as the equipment and the form of digital elements being used—as well as the dramaturgical requirements of the work and the ways that projections will be used to support the narrative. Most of all, processes are driven by the practitioners involved and their preferred method of working.

These variables lead to unlimited possibilities for how a digitally enhanced production might progress from concept to stage. As Mark Grimmer of 59 Productions explains, 'the truth is, it's different every time' (personal communication, May 31, 2017). This lack of consistency poses yet another challenge for establishing an industry benchmark for these productions, as each creative process is arguably unique. Defining a baseline of practice for individual designers is similarly difficult, since their work is framed to a different set of conditions for every production.

Production design processes are further complicated by the requirements and expectations of presenting opera companies. Depending on its infrastructure, production schedule, and funding model, a presenting company will establish key milestones in a given design process, including the timeline for hiring designers, the scheduling of technical and staging rehearsals, and the coordination of on-site workshops. The company is also responsible for setting design deadlines, arranging rehearsals with live performers, and overseeing the budget, among other administrative obligations. These factors, driven by company management rather than creative practitioners, fundamentally shape the scope and scale of a production design process.

What emerges is an interesting dichotomy of influence: the first driven by creative practitioners and their vision for a scenographic design, and the second determined by the administrative authority of the presenting

DOI: 10.4324/9781003093305-6

company. Trevisan (2017) suggests that administrative power always limits 'the autonomy of the artists and their creative impulse,' as directors and designers must adhere to managerial considerations when realising their artistic visions (2). The potential tension between artist and administration is also exacerbated by the economic instability of many opera companies. Because companies must prioritise budgetary concerns, the result is an 'increasing disregard for the artistic interests and ambitions of creative arts professionals' involved in their productions (Trevisan 2017, 2–3).

Administrative authority is a complicating factor for any production design process. However, it raises particular issues for digital scenography. The previous chapter highlighted how creative hierarchies are evolving with advancing technologies. But there is little evidence that opera companies are similarly adapting their administrative procedures with the increasing use of digital scenography. Instead, digitally enhanced opera productions are generally held to the same standards as productions that use traditional physical sets.

This chapter examines this conundrum by considering both the creative and administrative impacts on production design processes and the ways these influences can manifest in practice. The chapter begins with an overview of common organisational and funding models for opera companies and their effects on production design. The twentieth-century standard for production design described by scenographer Günther Schneider-Siemssen in 1977 is fundamental to this analysis. As his production design process notably omits any significant consideration of projection design, his description establishes a benchmark for a design process that predates the use of digital scenography.

I then analyse the design processes used in five opera productions that incorporate digital elements: Washington National Opera's *Das Rheingold* (2016), the Théâtre Royal de la Monnaie's *The Magic Flute* (2005), Dutch National Opera's *The Magic Flute* (2012), Santa Fe Opera's *The (R)evolution of Steve Jobs* (2017), and Komische Oper Berlin's *The Magic Flute* (2012). Drawing on interviews with S. Katy Tucker, Sabine Theunissen, Finn Ross, Victoria 'Vita' Tzykun, and Paul Barritt, among others, I identify common trends across digitally enhanced production design and discuss whether existing administrative structures are adequately responding to the demands of digital scenography.

A benchmark of organisational and funding models

In her overview of arts management in opera, Trevisan (2017) suggests that the biggest differences between opera companies are related to structure, governance, and finance. She explains: 'The organization's size, production values, and of course its local context influence each opera house's organizational structure and budget levels, while different national contexts influence its legal status, governance, production strategy, and financial structure' (15). Despite the variations that can exist from company to company, Trevisan notes that all opera companies must provide the same basic resources to any production presented under their auspices: 'manpower (employed staff and guest artists), time and space (a rehearsal schedule), and financial resources (a dedicated budget)' (17).

These three resources provide an avenue for considering differences across production design processes from an administrative perspective. The number of creative personnel, or 'manpower,' hired by a company, for example, will have an impact on design logistics, determining the nature of the creative hierarchy and the scope of collaboration between practitioners. Time and space are equally important, as they determine design deadlines as well as any opportunity for on-site experimentation or workshops. Most of all, design processes are driven by financial considerations, as a company's budget will directly affect personnel and timeline. The budget also informs the artistic components of the design itself, with cost often determining the choice between a functionally interactive digital set and a non-synthesis scenic background.

As a way of codifying how financial and staffing resources can be distributed by different companies, I draw on Cohen's (2011) description of three common models for theatrical organisations: the institutional model, the single-production model, and the regional theatre model. The *institutional model,* according to Cohen, describes a company with the financial stability to support full-time administrators as well as 'the majority of the artistic staff (directors, designers, actors) and virtually all of the production staff (technicians, dramaturges, business and publicity offices)' (93). As the majority of the creative team are on full-time salaries, they are available for the entirety of the production design process, beginning from the earliest design discussions, and can collaborate with the other creative practitioners both in person and on site. The model's financial stability also lends itself to an extended timeline, as the company can support additional staging rehearsals and design workshops and modify scheduling as needed.

The *single-production model* involves assembling an entire creative and administrative team at the start of each production. This includes producers, administrators, stage director, designers, and all performers. The single-production model is most commonly seen on Broadway, where productions are usually presented under the auspices of external producers rather than independent theatre companies (Cohen 2011). A creative benefit of the model is that specific designers are hired based on their appropriateness for a given project. Nonetheless, the design process is limited by a lack of infrastructure and financial support. Many of the designers will be based in different locations or working on other projects simultaneously when conceiving the production design. Cohen (2011) notes that the practitioners involved in a single-production model work in relative isolation and may only meet in person at the first technical rehearsal.

The third theatrical model, which Cohen suggests is most common among professional opera and theatre companies, is the *regional theatre model*. The model functions similarly to the institutional model but without the same funding support. Regional models maintain a small number of permanent staff members, including an artistic director, managing director, and critical administrative staff, but the rest are hired on a short-term basis, including a production's 'director, many of its designers, and most, if not all, of its cast' (Cohen 2011, 94). Depending on the resources of the company and the location of the designers, some stages of the design process may take place on site, including workshops and initial creative meetings. As in the single-production model, though, the majority of the design process will occur through remote communication until the first rehearsals in the venue (Cohen 2011). Given these limitations, both the single-production and regional theatre models generally have shorter production timelines and involve fewer team members than the institutional model.

The role of funding in each of these organisational models leads to certain location-specific trends. Given the scale of financial resources required to support full-time designers, technicians, and craftsmen,[1] the institutional model is most commonly found in Europe, where opera companies are subsidised by the government under what Ertman (2012) terms the 'statist model' (26).[2] The extent of government funding varies by country, but, using the most recent comparative data from 2005, Mariani (2009) finds that government support for opera companies ranges from 56 per cent of funding in the United Kingdom to as high as 80 per cent in Sweden. Mariani's data does not reflect recent austerity movements, and Trevisan (2017) confirms that subsidies for the arts in Europe have been steadily decreasing since the 1990s. However, European opera companies continue to benefit from significant government support. In 2015, nearly 75 per cent of the Théâtre Royal de la Monnaie's total operating budget was provided by the Belgian federal government (Loomis 2014). In the same year, English National Opera received a multimillion-dollar government subsidy, which amounted to more than a third of its annual operating budget (English National Opera 2016).

In the United States, opera companies operate on a non-profit basis, with private donors and grants providing the majority of financial support. Ertman (2012) refers to this as an 'impresarial model' of funding, in which companies are not subsidised by the government and instead rely on 'a tradition of cultivating wealthy donors' (35). As a result, American opera companies are more vulnerable to economic instability than their European counterparts. Agid and Tarondeau (2010) note, 'when an American opera house feels that it cannot sustain its box office expectations and notices some drop in contributions, it has to rapidly adjust its overall cost situation just to survive' (180).

Without the guarantee of government support, companies in the United States adhere most closely to the regional theatre model, in which the majority of creative practitioners are hired per production, rather than serving as full-time employees. In the 2006/7 season, for example, Houston Grand Opera in Texas maintained 120 permanent staff members and hired approximately 550 temporary staff members for 46 opera performances. In comparison, during the same season, the Semperoper Dresden in Germany maintained 787 permanent staff members for 176 opera performances (Agid and Tarondeau 2010).

Total production timelines are also typically shorter in the United States, as companies enact cost-cutting measures where possible. In the United States, 'funding is usually in short supply, production budgets are very tight, [and] available stage time to create the work [is] precious,' explains lighting designer Donald Holder (personal communication, June 27, 2020). 'Any minute you're in a place like [Washington National Opera] or the Met, it costs tens of thousands of dollars just to be in that space,' agrees video and projection designer S. Katy Tucker (personal communication, September 21, 2017). Given these financial constraints, opera companies can only offer limited time for technical and staging rehearsals, and every production design process must fit within a fixed scheduling framework. 'Time is money,' notes projection designer Elaine J. McCarthy. 'It definitely feels like a luxury when I work in situations where it's more government-funded, typically outside the United States' (personal communication, May 23, 2020).

These theatrical models and associated funding implications allow us to consider the larger administrative impacts on production design processes. Regardless of the preferences of the creative practitioners involved, designs are unavoidably affected by the infrastructure of the presenting company. Before examining the potential disruption posed by digital scenography, however, a benchmark for the production design process itself—that is to say, 'traditional' twentieth-century standards for production design—must first be established.

The twentieth-century standard for production design

In his 1977 essay 'From Drawing-Board to Workshop,' scenographer Günther Schneider-Siemssen outlines a detailed design process, which he claims is standard for any opera production (Schneider-Siemssen 1977a). This design process is outlined in brief below.

Schneider-Siemssen notes that a design process will always begin with a creative discussion between the stage director and the set designer. He proposes three potential scenarios for this initial discussion. First, the director may provide the set designer with a specific vision to implement. Second, the set designer may present their own proposal and, with the stage director's approval, drive the creative vision. Third, the two practitioners may work collaboratively until it is 'impossible to tell what ideas were contributed by whom' (29).

Once the design concept is confirmed, Schneider-Siemssen notes that the set designer and director will agree on a 'ground plan' for next steps

(30). The set designer will then build a small scale model of the proposed design to be reviewed by the director. Once the scale model has been approved, the set designer and their assistants will draw architectural plans for the physical set pieces that will require construction. The assistants will create a second, larger scale model of the set, while the set designer selects the materials and colours for the actual construction. Throughout this process, the stage director will be repeatedly consulted to ensure their 'wishes can be taken into consideration … and the model changed accordingly' (30).

After the second scale model has been approved, the other designers will formally join the production discussions. Schneider-Siemssen notes that the lighting designer and technical director are the first to be involved, as they need to review the technical requirements for the finalised design. These meetings are followed by additional discussions between the set designer and 'the stage manager, the technical director and the heads of the painting, carpentry, metalwork, sculpture, upholstery and other workshops' to confirm 'all outstanding architectural, artistic and technical details,' as well as budget and timeline (30). With the design now finalised, the process of construction can begin, and the physical set will be assembled in the theatrical venue prior to the start of technical rehearsals.

Writing more than 50 years ago, Schneider-Siemssen's process is a reflection of what Lester (2015) terms the 'twentieth-century historical model' for production design (228). With a fixed timeline, structured duties for each member of the creative team, and clearly defined expectations for every stage of design development, the process is grounded in a predictability that can be replicated from production to production. Baugh (2013) stresses the importance of the fixed and replicable timeline of this traditional model, meant to align with a company's set production schedule for musical, staging, and technical rehearsals.

Schneider-Siemssen's process clearly aligns to a vertical creative hierarchy. Not only do the stage director and set designer conceive the design on their own, but the other designers do not participate in any creative discussions until the set design has already been finalised. Schneider-Siemssen's set designer is framed as the highest authority among the 'Big Four' designers and explicitly instructs the other practitioners on how to proceed with their work.

Schneider-Siemssen's process also occurs in isolation from the performers, and the set is finalised before staging rehearsals begin. Only at the start of technical rehearsals is Schneider-Siemssen's physical set combined with the rest of the design—lights, costumes, and props—as well as the actual performers. This reflects a longstanding tradition of set designers working independently from staging rehearsals. Scenographer Pamela Howard (2002) explains that, historically, 'designers were kept at a distance and expected not to interfere or be present at rehearsals.' Instead, the 'domain of the designer was The Workshop' (75).[3] Accordingly, Schneider-Siemssen's finished set design is not seen by the performers, let alone the other design-ers, until the load in[4] into the theatre (Cohen 2011).

Schneider-Siemssen does not specify a particular opera company in his text, but we can infer that his description is drawn from his experiences as Head of Stage Design for the three federal theatres of Austria, a position which he held from 1962 to 1986 (Osterfestspiele Salzburg n.d.). The logis-tics of his design process are clearly shaped to an institutional theatrical model that benefits from significant government support. Each of the vari-ous assistants and artisans that he references can be identified as full-time and permanent employees of the presenting opera company, rather than hired on short-term contracts. With all of the practitioners available from the start of the production process, Schneider-Siemssen can organise fre-quent creative meetings and outsource tasks to his large team of assistants. Schneider-Siemssen does not provide any indication of timeline in his de-scription, but his references to multiple scale models and numerous meet-ings prior to physical set construction further suggests an extended schedule consistent with the institutional model.

As noted earlier, Schneider-Siemssen omits any reference to projection design in his description of this standard process. Instead, he provides an addendum in another practical essay from 1977 for set designers who may want to use projected elements (Schneider-Siemssen 1977b). Any use of pro-jected scenery, he notes, necessitates additional tests before the start of tech-nical rehearsals, as well as discussions with the lighting designer to confirm projector locations and other technical logistics. Once these logistics have been finalised, the set designer can begin to create the glass slides for the projectors.

Schneider-Siemssen's instructions reinforce the historical expectations cited in the previous chapter, in which the lighting designer is responsible for the technical aspects of projection design while the set designer is re-sponsible for the creative content. There is no mention made of a projec-tion *designer*, only the technology as a potential tool to be implemented by the set designer. Schneider-Siemssen's instructions also frame projected imagery as a scenographic element that can be easily integrated into the standard production design process. In his view, projections require some advance preparation, plus additional discussions with key practitioners, but still largely fit within the process that he outlines for physical sets.

Schneider-Siemssen's process is shaped by both the production's creative practitioners and its overseeing company. In his case, the combination of a traditional vertical hierarchy and an institutional model function in com-plementary ways, supporting an extended design process led by the stage director and set designer. In the present day, production design processes are similarly impacted by the combination of these two influences: creative and administrative. Yet, while creative practitioners and creative hierar-chies have adapted and evolved with the increasing prominence of digital designs, administrative procedures have not necessarily shifted accordingly.

This creates a potential conflict between the creative possibilities of digital scenography and the expectations of the presenting company.

The following section will consider five recent digitally enhanced opera productions and their production design processes. Drawing on interviews with practitioners involved in each production, I consider the impacts of both creative and administrative factors in driving design processes and the degree to which practitioners are forced to adapt to organisational constraints.

Washington National Opera's *Das Rheingold* (2016)—non-synthesis

In 2016, Washington National Opera presented director Francesca Zambello's production of Wagner's *Ring* cycle, featuring digital projections and video by S. Katy Tucker (Smith 2016). Tucker had collaborated with projection designer Jan Hartley for the original premiere of Zambello's production at San Francisco Opera in 2011 (San Francisco Opera Archives n.d.). When the production was revived at Washington National Opera, Tucker was hired to redesign *Das Rheingold* and update the projection designs for *Die Walküre*, *Siegfried*, and *Götterdämmerung*. Because *Das Rheingold* constituted the only wholly new design among the four, the production served as the primary topic of discussion during our interviews.

From Tucker's perspective, the production design process for *Das Rheingold* began with a meeting with Zambello approximately one year before the production's premiere. Tucker explains her process for this kind of initial discussion, noting:

> Before my meeting, I'll write a breakdown of when I think stuff should be, what I think it should look like. Then we'll meet, and I'll either be right on track, or we'll scratch everything and start over. Ideas first.
> (personal communication, September 21, 2017)

Based on this initial meeting and a subsequent group meeting involving set designer Michael Yeargan and lighting designer Mark McCullough, Tucker constructed a digital storyboard with her proposed projections overlaid onto the physical set. This storyboard was then presented to the rest of the creative team for feedback and discussion. Once approved by Zambello and the other designers, Tucker's design was considered finalised, and she began the process of constructing the projected imagery.

Tucker recalls that she began to build the actual projections approximately two months before technical rehearsals began.[5] As part of the process, Tucker collaborated with her animator, Robert Figueira, for nearly six weeks before travelling to Washington, DC for the start of technical rehearsals. 'I don't show up until they load in scenery,' she confirms (personal communication, September 21, 2017). Once on location in the theatre at the

Figure 6.1 Alberich kneels to Wotan in Washington National Opera's *Das Rhein-gold.* Photograph © Scott Suchman for Washington National Opera.

Kennedy Center, the next step was to upload Tucker's content onto the media servers, focus the projectors, and analyse the result (see Figure 6.1).

Since Tucker's projections were not incorporated with the actual physical set until this point in the process, the technical rehearsal presented the first opportunity for the designers to consider the collective scenographic design in person, 'looking at what we made and saying, this failed, or this worked out well' (personal communication, September 21, 2017). Tucker recalls that some of her designs did not work as expected when incorporated into the physical stage space. 'My original concept was horrible. Scene one was atrocious,' she recalls. 'And we were all sitting there before Zambello came, and we were like, "why doesn't this work?" And then we figured it out together' (personal communication, September 21, 2017).

Das Rheingold employed a lateral creative structure, in which Tucker served as an equal and autonomous member of the creative team. While Tucker initially met only with Zambello, the design process quickly became more collaborative, with Tucker discussing her concept with the other creative practitioners before finalising the design. The collaborative nature of the process was also evident in the way Tucker and her colleagues worked to revise the projections at the start of technical rehearsals: they 'figured it out together.'

The design process that Tucker describes was also shaped by Washington National Opera's theatrical model and financial resources.

The company aligns most closely to a regional theatre model, rather than Schneider-Siemssen's institutional model. While Washington National Opera maintains a large administrative staff, the company hired Tucker and the other designers on short-term contracts specifically for the *Ring* cycle, rather than appointing them to permanent roles. As such, Tucker's process was limited to a fairly short timeframe, as noted above. The majority of her design development also occurred in isolation from the other practitioners. Other than a few meetings with the other designers, Tucker primarily worked from her residence in New York and relied on remote communication until arriving on site for technical rehearsals in Washington, DC.

Tucker was also not involved in any staging rehearsals with the performers for *Das Rheingold* and only arrived after staging had already been finalised by Zambello. Because *Das Rheingold* is a non-synthesis production without causal interplay, Tucker's absence from staging rehearsals did not have a major impact on the final design. Tucker acknowledges that instances of causal interplay would ideally require her involvement at an earlier stage of the process. 'You can get some of those ideas in there if you're coming in at tech or seeing a few room runs ... but I would say it happens less when you're coming up with your ideas in advance' (personal communication, September 21, 2017).

An example of the 'impresarial model' for funding, Washington National Opera relies on private donors rather than government subsidies for the majority of its operational activities (Pierce 2000). Nevertheless, the company is very highly funded by American standards. National organisation Opera America ranks the company as one of 11 within its 'Budget Level 1' category, with an annual operating budget of more than USD 15 million (Opera America n.d.). Tucker confirms that Washington National Opera was able to provide sufficient funding for her to hire her standard internal team, including systems designer and engineer Russell Adamson, associate projection designer and animator Robert Figueira, and projection coordinator Maria T. Mendoza (personal communication, September 21, 2017).

Despite this funding support, the design process was still limited by Washington National Opera's infrastructure, particularly in terms of the amount of time available for Tucker to workshop her designs in the venue. Like many companies, Washington National Opera conducts the majority of its staging and musical rehearsals at an off-site location and only moves to the theatrical venue after load in, typically one week before a production premieres (Agid and Tarondeau 2010; Trevisan 2017). Only once she saw her designs overlaid with the physical set on stage did Tucker realise that she needed to make substantial changes. Accordingly, Tucker refers to the 'luxury' of European production processes, which enable projection designers to work on site long before the first technical rehearsal (personal communication, September 21, 2017).

Théâtre Royal de la Monnaie's *The Magic Flute* (2005)—partial-synthesis

William Kentridge's production of *The Magic Flute* for the Théâtre Royal de la Monnaie benefited from a more flexible timeline than Washington National Opera's *Das Rheingold*, as well as a government-subsidised budget. As noted earlier, nearly 75 per cent of La Monnaie's annual operating budget was subsidised by the federal government in 2015, and the company is thus able to provide extensive organisational support for its productions (Loomis 2014). Drawing on these company resources, *The Magic Flute* employed a variation of the lateral creative hierarchy, as discussed in Chapter 5, in which Kentridge served in multiple roles as stage director, projection designer, and co-set designer with Sabine Theunissen, who was interviewed about the production design process (Law-Viljeon 2007).

Asked to describe the ideal timeframe for a digitally enhanced opera production, Theunissen proposes a period of two-and-a-half years—more than twice the amount of time available for Tucker—which she confirms is the typical timeline for Kentridge's productions. For *The Magic Flute*, Theunissen breaks down this period into seven stages, spanning from initial design discussions to the production's premiere (personal communication, June 10, 2017).

The first stage of the process described by Theunissen was a brainstorming session with all members of the creative team, participating either in person or remotely. Theunissen emphasises the importance of this first session to clarify initial ideas about the production and introduce potential reference materials. The second stage of the process involved only Kentridge, Theunissen, and the video editor and controller, Catherine Meyburgh, who collectively constructed a scale model of the proposed physical set and began to test video imagery. This was followed by a week-long workshop, in which the full creative team participated in what Theunissen terms a 'Doing/Watching/Talking' session with the set model (personal communication, June 10, 2017).

The next stage of the design process was to construct a storyboard for the projected imagery and build a more precise scale model of the set. Once complete, these developments were considered and discussed in a second full-scale workshop with all members of the creative team. This session included a technical run-through of the set design with live actors and discussion about possible causal interplay between live performers and digital elements. All members of the creative team were then 'in the room' from the second week of staging rehearsals with the performers. Following the move into the venue for technical rehearsals, the full creative team again worked collaboratively to refine the overall scenographic design. This included adjusting the technical specifications of the physical set and projected imagery, coordinating musical timings, balancing the lighting design with the projections, and 'simplify[ing]' the designs as needed (personal communication, June 10, 2017).

Theunissen's description of this extended production design process is in stark contrast to the process that S. Katy Tucker describes for *Das Rheingold*. While both productions reflect a lateral creative hierarchy, *The Magic Flute* involved significantly more personnel and creative collaboration at a much earlier stage in the process. In addition to beginning their creative discussions two-and-a-half years in advance of the premiere (compared to Tucker's single year), the members of Kentridge's creative team met multiple times before the rehearsals with the performers even began. The development stage also involved lengthy trial periods to test digital content and experiment with the relationship between the live performers and digital elements.

In contrast to *Das Rheingold* and departing from Schneider-Siemssen's traditional process, the creative practitioners for La Monnaie's production were also involved in staging rehearsals and attended what Theunissen describes as 'creation' from the second week with the live performers (personal communication, June 10, 2017). This provided the opportunity to build on the developments of their earlier workshops in terms of the performers' interactions with the digital elements. Theunissen confirms that the creative practitioners still worked remotely at times, as these scheduling 'gaps' allowed the designers to 'consolidate the discoveries made together' in their own areas of the production (personal communication, June 10, 2017). Yet, the creative team still assembled on location for multiple extended periods before technical rehearsals began.

The extended timeline and number of personnel involved in Kentridge's production suggest significant support from an institutional theatre model and a corresponding scale of funding. This support provided time and opportunity for extensive collaboration and experimentation, which, in turn, helped to support Kentridge's partial-synthesis vision and the degree of causal interplay used in the production. Rather than being driven by institutional necessity, the timeline for the scenographic design was framed to the needs of the creative practitioners.

The institutional model also provided additional support for Theunissen in her capacity as a creative practitioner. Theunissen was a full-time salaried employee at La Monnaie when *The Magic Flute* was staged in 2005 and received a separate contract for her work as Kentridge's co-designer (personal communication, May 1, 2018). While Theunissen likely had other duties related to her position at La Monnaie, the financial security of this salaried position undoubtedly contributed to her ability to participate in a lengthy development process with Kentridge. In contrast, consider Tucker, whose work as a freelance designer within a regional theatre model necessitated her working remotely from home until the start of technical rehearsals for *Das Rheingold*.

Despite the benefits provided by La Monnaie's infrastructure, Theunissen notes certain limitations due to the company's production timeline. After the start of technical rehearsals, *The Magic Flute* was restricted to essentially the same timeline as other company productions: approximately one week in the venue prior to the premiere. Theunissen expressed a desire to have had additional time once all of the scenic elements were combined on stage. 'There is a very small window to work light, video, and set transitions together ... we have too often the feeling [of needing] to fight for a dedicated time,' she explains. 'To me, when we try to achieve an opera production where all is interdependent and coordinated ... the limit is less technology than people, organisation, and time' (personal communication, June 10, 2017). Even though Theunissen's design process was more than twice the length of Tucker's process for *Das Rheingold*, both productions were constrained by limited time in the venue during the final stages of the process.

Dutch National Opera's *The Magic Flute* (2012)—partial-synthesis

Co-commissioned by Dutch National Opera, English National Opera, and Festival d'Aix-en-Provence, *The Magic Flute* (2012) was director Simon McBurney's first foray into operatic repertoire (Jeffries 2013). McBurney is better known for his work with experimental theatre company Complicité, which he founded in 1983 under the premise of what is termed 'devised theatre.' Within this framework, all members of the creative team, including designers, writers, and performers, work collaboratively over an extended period of time to develop a new work (Complicité n.d.). In our interviews, video designer Finn Ross notes that McBurney applied this practice of devised theatre to the production design process for *The Magic Flute*. He explains,

> you turn up on day one of rehearsals with nothing really designed, just a subject matter and notion of where you are going with it. Then over a number of weeks you try various ideas out until you have a show. From this process very organic, intuitive, and raw works usually emerge.
> (personal communication, June 20, 2017)

Ross recalls that he was first involved in production discussions approximately one year before *The Magic Flute* premiered, similar to Tucker's timeline for *Das Rheingold*. However, Ross clarifies that no design work occurred during any of these initial meetings. Instead, McBurney and Ross, along with set designer Michael Levine and lighting designer Jean Kalman, simply discussed the technical logistics for the production. 'We knew it was *Magic Flute*, and we knew what the set looked like. That was about it' (personal communication, September 12, 2016). Ross' actual design work did not begin until the second week of staging rehearsals with the performers, approximately four weeks before the production premiered.

Describing the short timeline as 'terrifying,' Ross recalls that these four weeks involved extensive 'watching, listening, responding ... until there was an idea of a design in our heads.' Ross then experimented with different kinds of video content and would 'throw it into rehearsals' to see how McBurney and the other designers responded (personal communication, September 12, 2016). 'The process of working with Simon is not a formal process. It is very erratic and unplanned,' Ross explains. 'It is much more about being there, watching what the performers are doing and designing something around that' (personal communication, September 12, 2016).

Ross' explanation is consistent with the production's use of causal interplay, which necessitated his active engagement during staging rehearsals. While William Kentridge's creative team tested instances of causal interplay in a series of workshops before staging rehearsals, McBurney's production relied on a more improvisatory approach. Rather than being conceived in advance, the relationship between the live and the digital was established through experimentation in real time. However, both productions relied on faux-interactivity, rather than functional interactivity. As such, both design processes required the projection designer to work closely with the performers and digital elements to maintain the intended visual illusion.

Ross acknowledges that the production design process for *The Magic Flute* deviated from the 'normal video experience of the opera house' (personal communication, September 12, 2016). He frames the process as running particularly counter to the structured timeline described by both S. Katy Tucker and Sabine Theunissen, in which the projection designs were conceived months and even years in advance. Ross did not participate in any standard conceptual or preparation stages, including constructing visual storyboards or discussing concept imagery with the other designers. Instead, the entire production design process—from conception to construction— was consolidated into the few weeks before technical rehearsals and overlapped with staging rehearsals.

As with the other two productions, Dutch National Opera's *The Magic Flute* reflects a lateral creative hierarchy. All members of the creative team worked collectively to conceive the overall scenographic design. 'Working with Simon ... the lines of your roles and responsibilities are blurred sometimes. Broadly, you sit in the rehearsals, listen, offer up ideas, take in others' ideas, mix them all together and develop a show,' Ross notes (personal communication, June 20, 2016).

The production was also presented under the auspices of an institutional theatre model with its three co-commissioning companies based in Europe. As noted earlier, despite a recent push for austerity in government arts funding in England, more than 30 per cent of English National Opera's operating budget was subsidised by the government as of 2016 (English National Opera 2016). Dutch National Opera is similarly the recipient of long-term government subsidies (BeroepKunstenaar n.d.). Given this funding support, the commissioning companies could potentially have provided a more extended design timeline for planning and preparation, such as that described by Theunissen.

Yet, this opportunity for advance planning may not have been appealing to McBurney, given his preference for a devised theatrical model that involves close collaboration with performers. In McBurney's work with Complicité, performers are involved at a much earlier point in the design process, extending months if not years in advance of a production's premiere. As neither English National Opera, Dutch National Opera, nor Festival d'Aix-en-Provence would typically contract performers so early in the process, McBurney had limited time to work with his performers and designers simultaneously. From this perspective, despite his creative preference, McBurney still had to adhere to the logistical expectations of the presenting companies for his production design process.

Santa Fe Opera's *The (R)evolution of Steve Jobs* (2017)—non-synthesis

Co-commissioned by Santa Fe Opera, Seattle Opera, and San Francisco Opera, *The (R)evolution of Steve Jobs* (2017) is something of an outlier from the other productions discussed in this chapter because the work was a world premiere opera written by composer Mason Bates and librettist Mark Campbell (Serinus 2017). This provides an interesting analytical perspective, as the production design process was initiated before the opera itself had been fully written. *The (R)evolution of Steve Jobs* was also first premiered by a summer festival, Santa Fe Opera, rather than a company that operates over an entire season (Smith 2015). Both factors had implications for the production design process.

In our interviews, production designer Victoria 'Vita' Tzykun notes that the design process began with a series of discussions with stage director Kevin Newbury approximately 18 months before the production premiered. After discussing the 'kind of role the video would play' and reviewing a number of digital set models, Tzykun and Newbury 'eventually landed on an idea that we liked' (personal communication, August 28, 2018). Lighting designer Japhy Weideman joined the creative discussions before the design was finalised, as Tzykun realised the proposed video content would need to be closely integrated with the lighting effects (personal communication, August 28, 2018). The projection designer, Benjamin Pearcy of 59 Productions, was then involved approximately one year before the production premiered.

By this point, the general scenic concept was finalised, and Tzykun and Newbury were considering the kinds of projections that would most benefit the vision for the production. Tzykun's design involved large set pieces, or 'monoliths,' that moved independently around the stage, and Pearcy's role was to conceive and create video sequences to align with the constantly shifting set (see Figure 6.2). Tzykun outlined the specific set configurations

Figure 6.2 Steve Jobs meets his younger self in Santa Fe Opera's *The (R)evolution of Steve Jobs*. Photograph © Ken Howard for Santa Fe Opera.

for each scene, and the two designers 'went on to storyboard the show together' (personal communication, August 28, 2018).

The next stage of the process was a series of digital workshops held at Pearcy's studio in New York. These sessions were attended by most of the creative designers, along with the production's choreographer Chloe Treat, and were fairly casual. 'Ben [Pearcy] would just play sequences on his computer, and we would look at the animation and comment on it and decide what works and what doesn't work,' recalls Tzykun (personal communication, August 28, 2018). The workshops enabled the creative team to finalise the digital elements of the overall design well in advance of the first technical rehearsal. 'We essentially teched the show in virtual reality before we ever got to stage,' notes Tzykun (personal communication, August 28, 2018). The full creative team then arrived at Santa Fe Opera approximately one month before the production's premiere.

Tzykun confirms that the logistics of the scenographic design demanded close collaboration within the creative team 'because everything was so tightly interwoven' (personal communication, August 28, 2018). The moving set pieces required their own designated staging as well as specific technical considerations: in addition to serving as a projection surface for Pearcy's video designs, each set piece contained thousands of remote-controlled LED lights. As such, once the scenic design was finalised, it was critical to include Weideman, Pearcy, and Treat in the ongoing creative discussions and 'virtual' workshops (personal communication, August 28, 2018).

Tzykun notes that she was involved in a number of staging rehearsals and occasionally needed to adapt the positioning of the physical set pieces due to staging considerations. However, she confirms that the digital designs, while extensive, were non-synthesis. 'It didn't work in a sense that they would touch a screen and then something would respond,' she explains. Instead, Tzykun refers to the use of visual correlation, in which 'the video responded to the internal mood of the characters' (personal communication, August 28, 2018).

Like Washington National Opera's production, the production design process for *The (R)evolution of Steve Jobs* was shaped by both the regional theatre model and the impresarial funding system, with a reliance on private donors over government support. Tzykun recalls active fundraising efforts from Santa Fe Opera's executive leadership in order to provide the necessary financial support for the production. Because of the subject matter of the opera—Steve Jobs, the founder of tech giant Apple—the company's leadership recognised that the production needed to be technologically advanced and were prepared for the accompanying cost. 'I have to say we needed a lot. It was very expensive, and they came on board and they raised the money,' Tzykun recalls (personal communication, August 28, 2018).

This funding provided sufficient support for the creative team to engage in off-site workshops as part of the production design process. Even though the designers still primarily worked remotely, these workshops allowed them to see how the physical and projected elements would be integrated in the venue and to make revisions at an early stage in the process. This runs contrary to S. Katy Tucker's design experience for *Das Rheingold*, in which the technical rehearsal was the first opportunity for the designers to see their individual contributions combined in the theatrical space. While less formalised than Theunissen's week-long workshops for *The Magic Flute*, Tzykun's production design process benefited from the same advanced planning and opportunity for discussion within the creative team.

Like the other practitioners, Tzykun describes the timeline as a particular challenge for the production design process. World-premiere productions generally have one or two years for development, she notes, but Santa Fe Opera's timeline was unusually short. She recalls, 'I probably had about 7–8 months before the final design presentation. It's actually a short turnaround in opera terms, especially when you're trying to do something that's a world premiere' (personal communication, August 28, 2018).

The schedule was also constrained by Santa Fe Opera's festival model, in which the company rehearses and techs four opera productions simultaneously. As a result, there were long gaps between subsequent technical sessions for *The (R)evolution of Steve Jobs*. Although the creative team arrived one month before the premiere, they still had limited opportunities to test in the theatrical space. Tzykun explains,

> you would have tech and then you wouldn't be on stage for maybe a week and a half or two weeks or something. Then you would get back on stage and then you wouldn't be back on stage for ten days.
>
> (personal communication, August 28, 2018)

The impact of this limitation, however, was largely offset by the 'virtual' workshops in Pearcy's studio, which had enabled the team to work through the set design in advance.

Komische Oper Berlin's *The Magic Flute* (2012)—full-synthesis

As outlined in Chapter 5, Barrie Kosky and 1927's production of *The Magic Flute* for Komische Oper Berlin employed a variation of the lateral creative hierarchy, in which Suzanne Andrade of 1927 shared directorial authority with Kosky. The production was also presented under the auspices of an institutional theatrical model and benefited from significant financial support. Komische Oper Berlin is Berlin's smallest opera company but maintains a large permanent staff and, as of 2014, received nearly 90 per cent of its annual operating budget from government subsidies (Taylor and Croggon 2014). Animator Paul Barritt was interviewed about the production design process, as well as Tobias Ribitzki, who served as assistant director for the premiere production, and tenor Aaron Blake, who has performed the role of Tamino in five different revivals of the production since 2014.

Barritt describes a lengthy production design process that extended nearly three years. This timeframe aligns roughly to Theunissen's account of La Monnaie's production of *The Magic Flute*. However, given the shared authority over the scenographic design between Kosky, Andrade, and Barritt, the production involved even closer collaboration than Kentridge's production (Albert 2019). Concept discussions were primarily driven by the 1927 team, with Andrade and Barritt proposing ideas for scenes and Kosky serving as 'an overseer' in consultation with the production's dramaturge, Ulrich Lenz (Barritt, personal communication, June 17, 2017). As an example of this in practice, Barritt describes the development of the opening scene with Tamino:

> I came up with the idea of Tamino getting swallowed by the dragon and we all liked that. I then made a dragon and we watched it but Suze [Andrade] thought it looked like a turtle. Barrie quite liked it. Suze then wanted to turn it black but Barrie insisted it be red. I, too, wanted it to be red so we decided on that and I changed its look to make it more like a Spice Worm out of Dune. That was kind of how the process worked ... We always resolved it with something we all liked.
>
> (personal communication, June 17, 2017)

After finalising the concept designs, Barritt and Andrade constructed a detailed storyboard and Barritt began constructing the actual animations in 1927's London studio. This process took approximately one year, Barritt recalls.

The production's use of full-synthesis required careful consideration of the live performers from the earliest stage of the process. 'The actor is always taken into account,' confirms Barritt (personal communication, June 17, 2017). However, no performers were physically involved in this stage of the design process. Instead, the digital animations were conceived with clear spatial vacancies for the performers. Then, as Andrade notes in a 2019 interview, 'it was a case of, when we got to rehearsal, teaching the singers where they stood and what they were doing' (Jirik 2019).

Tobias Ribitzki emphasises the difficulty of the staging process and the challenge of coordinating the performers' movements with the production's approximately 900 cues of animation (personal communication, February 19, 2019; Albert 2019). Tenor Aaron Blake notes that the staging requirements were completely different from any other opera he had performed (personal communication, February 28, 2019). Part of the challenge, he notes, stemmed from the production's stylistic homage to silent film, which required the performers to limit their movement to carefully coordinated gestures. Blake asserts that this mode of acting is in contrast to standard operatic staging, in which performers are often given a rough 'shape' for a scene and then allowed to improvise according to their understanding of the character (personal communication, February 28, 2019).

Another significant challenge related to the logistics of performing alongside the digital animations. Blake notes that the performers in the production must remain within 15 centimetres of the projection surface in order to avoid casting shadows and ruining the full-synthesis illusion. In addition, the performers can never look directly at the digital elements with which they are interacting, as this similarly disrupts the effect. When performers are first learning the choreography for the production, Blake explains, their natural instinct is to turn and look at the digital elements, essentially treating them as they would any other performer on stage (personal communication, February 28, 2019). However, the performers must always remain perpendicular to the projection surface and rely on their peripheral vision and musical cues to maintain the visual synthesis. 'It has to be perfect because you can see every mistake,' confirms Ribitzki (personal communication, February 19, 2019).[6]

While the scenographic logistics of the production are at odds with Schneider-Siemssen's historical model for a physical set, the collaborative nature of the design process and its organisational model show certain parallels. As in Schneider-Siemssen's model, *The Magic Flute* benefited from an institutional theatrical model and significant government funding, both of which supported a lengthy design process and extensive collaboration between its creative practitioners. Just as Schneider-Siemssen worked in close collaboration with the stage director, Barritt and Andrade developed their designs with Kosky over the course of several years.

As with the other productions discussed in this chapter, however, Komische Oper Berlin's *The Magic Flute* still adhered to the same standard timeline for technical rehearsals. The only significant difference stems from the production's use of digital scenography. Contrary to the other four productions, Ribitzki notes that *The Magic Flute* does not incorporate lighting design in a traditional way and instead primarily relies on the digital projections to illuminate the performers. As a result, Ribitzki confirms that the production's technical rehearsals required less time to coordinate lighting logistics than in standard productions (personal communication, April 1, 2019).

Commonalities across the five production design processes

Each of these case studies reflects a very different production design process, one that is informed by the individual practitioners, the creative hierarchy, and the organisational structure of the presenting company. La Monnaie's *The Magic Flute* with director William Kentridge was conceived and designed collaboratively over the course of nearly three years (Law-Viljoen 2007). In contrast, the entirety of Simon McBurney's design process for Dutch National Opera's *The Magic Flute* took place over four weeks in the midst of staging rehearsals. Komische Oper Berlin's full-synthesis *The Magic Flute* roughly aligns to Kentridge's production in terms of timeline, but the production design process was significantly different, prioritising design conception between the three primary creatives before the start of staging rehearsals.

All three productions of *The Magic Flute* involved extensive causal interplay between live performers and digital elements. All three productions also benefited from institutional theatre models with government funding. However, the scope of support varied significantly. Komische Oper Berlin and La Monnaie are both subsidised at high levels by government funding. Not surprisingly, both productions benefited from the most extended timelines out of the five case studies discussed. In comparison, English National Opera is subsidised at only 30 per cent, a level which, while still significant, is reflected in the scope of support available for its co-production of *The Magic Flute* with Dutch National Opera.

The other two productions discussed in this chapter, Washington National Opera's *Das Rheingold* and Santa Fe Opera's *The (R)evolution of Steve Jobs*, were both presented by opera companies in the United States that adhere to regional theatre models and rely primarily on donor funding. While both productions employed lateral creative hierarchies, most of the collaboration for *Das Rheingold* occurred remotely prior to the first technical rehearsal, while *The (R)evolution of Steve Jobs* incorporated a combination of in-person collaborations and 'virtual' workshops several months before technical rehearsals began. Both productions relied on significantly shorter production design timelines than the three European productions. Both also employed digital scenography in a non-synthesis way, with dramaturgical objectives based on visual correlation rather than interaction between the performers and digital elements.

These five productions demonstrate the scope of variation for design processes that use digital scenography, as well as the degree to which processes can deviate from Schneider-Siemssen's historical model. As with the varying creative hierarchies considered in Chapter 5, this makes it difficult to establish a consistent industry benchmark. However, a comparison of the five processes highlights some recurring themes.

Three of the five productions actively incorporated a visual storyboard during the design process: Washington National Opera's *Das Rheingold*, Santa Fe Opera's *The (R)evolution of Steve Jobs*, and Komische Oper Berlin's *The Magic Flute*. For both S. Katy Tucker and Victoria 'Vita' Tzykun, these storyboards were computerised, used in concert with virtual set models, and designed to reflect the narrative progression of the projections. In contrast, Barritt's storyboards for Komische Oper Berlin's *The Magic Flute* were illustrated by hand, reflecting his background as an animator (Albert 2019). While Finn Ross notes that he did not use storyboards for Dutch National Opera's *The Magic Flute*, he confirms that he usually creates them for digitally enhanced productions that follow more standardised design processes. Of the five designers, only Sabine Theunissen describes using physical scale set models akin to those used in Schneider-Siemssen's historical process, rather than digital storyboards.

The use of storyboards can be linked to the film and animation industry, in which pre-visualisation imagery is a crucial part of the production process (Finance and Zwerman 2010). This suggests that designs for digitally enhanced opera productions are beginning to align to the practices used in the film industry. The role of storyboards also speaks to the increasing prominence of digital scenography. Rather than functioning as static background scenery, digital elements can serve an independent narrative function, just as Edward Gordon Craig envisioned with his 'thousand scenes in one' (Craig 1915, 139).

The creative possibilities for digital scenography are also now sufficiently complex that digital elements need to be plotted separately from any physical set. Consider Tzykun's use of a designated choreographer for the physical set in concert with a detailed storyboard for Pearcy's video content. While reinforcing the important dramaturgical role that digital scenography plays, this deviates from Schneider-Siemssen's historical process. Projections are no longer visual accessories that can be easily integrated into an existing design progress, as Schneider-Siemssen suggests. Instead, digital scenography requires a customised approach in which projected elements are treated as a separate design tool with unique requirements.

The 'virtual' workshops used for *The (R)evolution of Steve Jobs* suggests that design processes themselves are also becoming more technologically driven. These workshops allowed the creative practitioners to consider the visual integration of Tzykun's and Pearcy's designs in virtual reality and to experiment with different configurations in real time, long before the first technical rehearsal in the physical venue. Although the creative practitioners had to travel to Pearcy's studio in New York, the workshops required limited time, funding, and staffing on behalf of the presenting company: the designers simply reviewed, discussed, and modified the designs in a computerised form. In comparison, the week-long workshops for La Monnaie's *The Magic Flute* required significant resources, including physical set models, live performers, and multiple days on location. Tzykun's digital version thus presents an economical alternative to the resource-heavy version described by Theunissen.

Another recurring theme among the five case studies relates to the technical challenge of combining projections with the physical set and live performers. Regardless of the amount of time spent preparing and testing projected content, the technical rehearsal is still generally the first opportunity for all of the scenic elements to be physically combined in the theatrical space. Tucker and Theunissen both reference the need to make revisions of varying scope to the projection design at this late stage of the process, from Tucker's complete revision of the first scene of *Das Rheingold* to Theunissen's reference to 'simplifying' elements for *The Magic Flute*. Ross and Barritt similarly allude to the need for last-minute adjustments in the days before their productions' respective premieres, with Ross noting that the design for Dutch National Opera's *The Magic Flute* was only 'finalised on opening night' (personal communication, June 20, 2017).

Only Tzykun did not explicitly mention the need to make significant revisions during the technical rehearsal and notes that major changes to the video design had already been made during the virtual workshops. This suggests that incorporating technology into the production design process itself (e.g., workshopping a virtual version of a physical set with overlaid projections) can resolve some of the issues that emerge during the technical rehearsals for digitally enhanced productions. At the very least, Tzykun's experience suggests that some of the problems specific to the integration of projections, set, and lighting could be identified at an earlier stage in the design process.

Tellingly, four of the five designers emphasised a desire for more time, particularly on location in the venue or working with live performers. S. Katy Tucker refers to the extended timeline of European companies with some chagrin, noting 'if it were the European style, I would be in the rehearsals, so we would be building the show all together' (personal communication, September 21, 2017). Ross, tasked with McBurney's condensed production process, acknowledges the difficulty of working with a 'very tight schedule for a very demanding show,' and then wryly asks, 'But when isn't there?' (personal communication, September 12, 2016). Tzykun describes the timeline for *The (R)evolution of Steve Jobs* as 'stressful' and notes she would have preferred more time to 'actually design' (personal communication, August 28, 2018). Even Theunissen, who benefited from one of the longest timelines out of the five productions, refers to the limitations of the schedule in the final stages of the production design process. Only Barritt did not explicitly mention the timeframe as a particular challenge. Because nearly all of the animations for *The Magic Flute* were conceived and finalised in the three years before staging rehearsals, the 1927 team may not have felt as much time-related pressure when combining the scenographic elements on stage.

Production design processes and the modes of synthesis

A comparison of the five design processes shows a correlation between the infrastructural model of the presenting company and the amount of time available for design work. Theunissen, Ross, and Barritt all worked within institutional theatre models for their productions of *The Magic Flute*. This created the possibility for an extended timeline in the early stages of planning and design. All three practitioners were also able to be involved in staging rehearsals, which supported the use of partial- or full-synthesis techniques in their productions. Tzykun's and Tucker's work within the regional theatre model was subject to more constrained schedules, with both practitioners allotted less than a year to complete their designs. Neither production involved causal interplay between the live performers and digital elements and only Tzykun, in her capacity as production designer, attended staging rehearsals.

This suggests a further correlation between the production design process and the mode of synthesis being employed. As the design processes for the three productions of *The Magic Flute* demonstrate, the use of causal interplay benefits from projection designers who can either collaborate closely with the director or serve in positions of directorial authority *and* are able to actively engage with live performers in staging rehearsals. Accordingly, nearly all of the partial-synthesis and full-synthesis productions discussed in this book were either presented by institutional theatre models or benefited from an unusual amount of funding support. Although neither Tzykun nor Tucker employ causal interplay in their productions, the regional theatre model does not necessarily preclude the use of partial-synthesis. Rather, the funding and scheduling limitations of this model simply present more of a challenge for integrating live performers with digital elements.

The analysis also highlights the degree to which digital scenography may clash with the traditional expectations of the production design process. This is most evident in the final stages of the process, including staging rehearsals, load in, technical rehearsals, and dress rehearsals. While the planning and development stage of an opera production can follow a somewhat flexible timeline depending on funding and personnel—extending one, two, or even three years before a production premieres—the final stages of the process are generally fixed across the wider industry. However, these industry standards are still largely based on Schneider-Siemssen's twentieth-century historical model, in which a physical set is constructed before technical rehearsals begin.

Lighting designer Donald Holder acknowledges that opera has a 'much tighter schedule' and 'significantly less time available for technical rehearsals' compared to standard theatre (personal communication, June 27, 2020). At The Metropolitan Opera, he notes as an example, designers can have as little as 20 hours of stage time to work through their designs with the performers before the production premieres. This timeframe is even more problematic in productions that involve digital scenography. Projection designers can only finalise their designs after they have been integrated with the physical set, lights, and live performers in the venue, which most often occurs after load in. This leaves designers with extremely limited time to implement any necessary design changes, let alone experiment with the visual synthesis of the digital scenography.

Projection designer Wendall K. Harrington highlights this disconnect between standard industry practice and the reality of digital scenography.

> More tech time is always valuable, and the most valuable but rarely available is a tech *after* the 'orchestra dress' when everything finally comes together. Now that you see what you have, a lot of new ideas advance, but there is never time to insert them.
>
> (personal communication, June 27, 2017)

S. Katy Tucker agrees with the need for additional time for experimentation: 'with projection, you come up with some new idea, and you can't know if it is successful until you're in the room and you're running it' (personal communication, September 21, 2017). Projection designer Sven Ortel similarly cites the importance of 'iteration' as part of the production design process: 'You have to try and often fail and then try something else, come back to it, and then sometimes a week later you remember something that didn't work so well, but it might be good for something else' (personal communication, May 21, 2020).

These practitioners point to the need for a re-evaluation of the production process from an administrative perspective. While the integration of digital scenography has shifted aspects of Schneider-Siemssen's standard, the final stages of the design process remain firmly entrenched in the historical model. Just as current union standards default to traditional creative hierarchies, production practices default to similarly outdated expectations based on the use of physical sets. This not only limits the opportunities for experimentation with digital scenography but also places administrative procedures at odds with the artistic capacity of the creative team. Accordingly, the use of digital scenography does not necessary pose a disruption to the production design process in itself. Instead, it is the administrative procedures and expectations of presenting companies that function as the 'disruption,' undermining the scope of possibilities for digital scenography in practice.

Notes

1 Trevisan (2017) notes that up to three-quarters of an opera company's budget can be designated to personnel costs.
2 See Ertman (2012) for a detailed overview of the origins of the 'statist model' and its current manifestations and challenges. See also Agid and Tarondeau (2010) for a comparative study of opera management and funding by country.
3 A 'workshop,' also known as a 'scene shop' or 'scenery shop,' is a specialised space where elements of a set are physically constructed, including flats, platforms, and backdrops.
4 Also called 'bump in,' 'load in' is when all of the production materials (e.g., sets, props, costumes) are moved onto the stage from their various workshops in preparation for technical rehearsals.
5 Tucker notes that she usually streamlines this stage of the process by building useable content (i.e., in a 'workable resolution') directly into her digital storyboard (personal communication, September 21, 2017).
6 This perfection can be difficult to achieve in live performance. Blake recalls one performance when his shoe slipped while he was 'dodging' the Queen of the Night's digital spider legs, and he was briefly 'impaled' from the perspective of the audience (personal communication, February 28, 2019).

References

Agid, Philippe, and Jean-Claude Tarondeau. 2010. *The Management of Opera: An International Comparative Study.* Basingstoke: Palgrave Macmillan.
Albert, Jane. 2019. "Barrie Kosky's The Magic Flute Opera Heads for Australia." *Financial Review*, January 29, 2019. https://www.afr.com/lifestyle/arts-and-entertainment/music/barrie-koskys-the-magic-flute-headed-for-australia-20190112-h1a06u.
Baugh, Christopher. 2013. *Theatre, Performance and Technology: The Development of Scenography in the Twentieth Century.* New York: Palgrave Macmillan.
BeroepKunstenaar. n.d. "Theatre and dance in the Netherlands." Accessed June 12, 2018. https://www.beroepkunstenaar.nl/en/disciplines/theatre-and-dance-in-the-netherlands/.
Cohen, Robert. 2011. *Working Together in Theatre: Collaboration & Leadership.* Basingstoke: Palgrave Macmillan.
Complicité. n.d. "About Us: The Company." Accessed October 25, 2017. http://www.complicite.org/about.php.
Craig, Edward Gordon. 1915. "The Thousand Scenes in One Scene." *The Mask* 7, no. 2 (May): 139–158.
English National Opera. 2016. *2015/16 Annual Report.* https://www.eno.org/news/annual-review-201516-update-ceo/.
Ertman, Thomas. 2012. "Opera, the State and Society." In *The Cambridge Companion to Opera Studies*, edited by Nicholas Till, 159–178. Cambridge: Cambridge University Press.
Finance, Charles, and Susan Zwerman. 2010. *The Visual Effects Producer: Understanding the Art and Business of VFX.* Burlington: Focal Press.
Howard, Pamela. 2002. *What is Scenography?* New York: Routledge.

Jeffries, Stuart. 2013. "Simon McBurney: The Age of Enlightenment." *The Guardian*, November 5, 2013. https://www.theguardian.com/music/2013/nov/04/simon-mcburney-mozart-magic-flute-english-national-opera.

Jirik, Kim. 2019. "Acclaimed Director Barrie Kosky Enlisted a Pair of Opera Newbies to Tackle Mozart's 'Impossible' Magic Flute." *ABC News*, February 21, 2019. https://www.abc.net.au/news/2019-02-20/the-magic-flute-barrie-kosky-and-1927-tackle-mozart-opera/10826942.

Law-Viljoen, Bronwyn. 2007. *William Kentridge: Flute.* Johannesburg: David Krut Publishing.

Lester, Gideon. 2015. "Dramaturgs as Artistic Leaders." In *The Routledge Companion to Dramaturgy*, edited by Magda Romanska, 225–229. London: Routledge.

Loomis, George. 2014. "Belgian Opera House Copes With Cuts." *New York Times*, December 22, 2014. https://www.nytimes.com/2014/12/23/arts/international/belgian-opera-house-copes-with-cuts.html.

Mariani, Marcello. 2009. *Live Classical Music Organisations in Europe: An International Comparison of Funding Trends, Governance Mechanisms and Organisational Structures.* Amsterdam: European Cultural Foundation and Bank of Sweden Tercentenary Foundation.

Opera America. n.d. "Membership Directory: Washington National Opera." Accessed October 30, 2018. https://www.operaamerica.org/applications/Membership/index.aspx?id=3092#details.

Osterfestspiele Salzburg. n.d. "Günther Schneider-Siemssen." Accessed October 11, 2018. https://www.osterfestspiele-salzburg.at/programme-festival-performances/kuenstlerdatenbank/guenther-schneider-siemssen.html.

Pierce, J. Lamar. 2000. "Programmatic Risk-Taking by American Opera Companies." *Journal of Cultural Economics* 24: 45–63.

San Francisco Opera Archives. n.d. Accessed April 2017. http://archive.sfopera.com.

Schneider-Siemssen, Günther. 1977a. "From Drawing-Board to Workshop." In *Opera*, edited by Rudolf Hartmann, 29–30. New York: W. Morrow & Co.

Schneider-Siemssen, Günther. 1977b. "Lighting and Projection." In *Opera*, edited by Rudolf Hartmann, 38–42. New York: W. Morrow & Co.

Serinus, Jason Victor. 2017. *"The (R)evolution of Steve Jobs* is (R)evelatory in Santa Fe Premiere." *San Francisco Classical Voice*, July 24, 2017. https://www.sfcv.org/reviews/opera-santa-fe/the-revolution-of-steve-jobs-is-revelatory-in-santa-fe-premiere.

Smith, Craig A. 2015. *A Vision of Voices: John Crosby and the Santa Fe Opera.* Santa Fe: University of New Mexico Press.

Smith, Tim. 2016. *"Das Rheingold* (4/30/16), *Die Walküre* (5/2/16), *Siegfried* (5/4/16), *Götterdämmerung* (5/6/16)." *Opera News*, June 2016. https://www.operanews.com/Opera_News_Magazine/2016/8/In_Review/WASHINGTON_DC__The_Ring.html.

Taylor, Anna Frey, and Alison Croggon. 2014. "Barrie Kosky on Arts Funding in Europe and Australia." *ABC News*, September 1, 2014. https://www.abc.net.au/radionational/programs/booksandarts/barrie-kosky-snakecharmer/5710536.

Trevisan, Paola. 2017. *Reshaping Opera: A Critical Reflection on Arts Management.* Newcastle upon Tyne: Cambridge Scholars Publishing.

Conclusion
The future evolution of digital scenography

As a practical tool, the modes of synthesis not only identify and contextualise the possibilities for digital scenography in opera but can also anticipate the extent to which digital scenography may be disruptive to production conventions. In the course of the discussion, I find that the use of digital scenography has far greater implications for offstage processes than it has from an onstage perspective. In the previous two chapters, I identified certain correlations between the mode of synthesis used in a production and both the associated creative hierarchy and the production design process. Partial-synthesis and full-synthesis productions are more likely to place the projection designer in a position of authority within the creative team. Partial-synthesis and full-synthesis productions also generally benefit from more extended design timelines and funding resources from presenting companies.

Regardless of funding or theatrical model, however, the use of digital scenography remains limited by outdated industry standards. The timeline used for technical rehearsals and other final stage logistics in opera production remains driven by the premise of a physical set. This process has not been adapted to address the additional dramaturgical requirements of digital scenography, such as the need for further experimentation and revision once all scenic elements are combined in the theatre space. Employment practices and union protections for projection designers are inconsistent and subject to negotiation from production to production, and thus are similarly outdated.

The modes of synthesis present an opportunity to identify and modify existing standards that are at odds with the use of digital scenography in practice. Mode classifications, for example, could provide a basis for establishing a consistent benchmark for projection designers by labour unions. Rather than leaving work conditions subject to negotiation, the extent of causal interplay could inform general expectations of work conditions and responsibilities across the industry. Projection designers could then leverage this benchmark to outline the scope of their potential work on a given production.

The modes could also be applied to re-evaluate aspects of the production design process. The use of causal interplay could, for example, prompt

DOI: 10.4324/9781003093305

modification to anticipated production schedules, providing more opportunity for projection designers to integrate their designs with the other scenic elements. Budgetary restrictions would no doubt limit this shift in practice, particularly in the United States. However, pending available resources, one or more additional technical rehearsals could be added to the standard schedule after the orchestra dress rehearsal, as projection designer Wendall K. Harrington suggests (personal communication, June 27, 2017). This would give practitioners more time to explore the synthesis of the performer, stage setting, and spectator in a rapidly evolving field.

Lighting designer Japhy Weideman suggests that the possibilities for digital scenography in opera are in a state of flux. As technology continues to advance, the dramaturgical potential for its use will 'continue to evolve and continue to expand' (personal communication, June 1, 2020). Lighting designer Donald Holder agrees, recalling the speed at which digital scenography has already developed over the course of his career. He cites the increasing use of live-action video feeds in productions as one example, noting, 'It's an exciting new addition to the visual storyteller's toolkit, and I look forward to seeing how it evolves over time' (personal communication, June 27, 2020).

Projection designer Sven Ortel suggests that technological advancements will have a direct impact on how digital scenography is used for opera production in the future. He notes that many of the creative choices involving digital technology are still currently informed by risk management strategies, with concerns about reliability outweighing questions of cost. Outlining his preference for faux-interactivity over functional interactivity as an example, he explains, 'I'd rather risk a cue being off once every 30 performances than entire shows being cancelled because the computer doesn't start up' (personal communication, May 21, 2020). As technology becomes increasingly reliable and efficient, scenographic practices that were once too 'risky' to implement will become more widely accepted by both practitioners and presenting companies.

Given that technological advancements will continue to occur in the future, one suspects that the next stage of evolution for digital scenography in opera will be one of increasing extremes, in which the use of causal interplay will expand beyond its current limitations. There have already been a number of experiments in this space outside the confines of the traditional opera house. In 2018, Los Angeles-based company BASE Hologram premiered *Callas in Concert: The Hologram Tour*, a 90-minute concert that combines a 'hologram' of dead soprano Maria Callas with a live orchestra (Huizenga 2018). Evoking the Pepper's Ghost illusion of the nineteenth century (Schein 2014), the holographic Callas sings, smiles, and pauses between arias, while the conductor and instrumentalists perform as if they are accompanying the singer in real time.

BASE Hologram has created a number of other productions based on dead performers, including *An Evening with Whitney: The Whitney Houston*

Hologram Tour and *In Dreams—Roy Orbison in Concert* (BASE Hologram n.d.). Thus far, the technique has remained limited to concert settings. However, it is not difficult to conceive the effect's potential application to the operatic stage. Holographic performers based on Maria Callas, Luciano Pavarotti, and Joan Sutherland could be integrated with physical stage settings and live performers for productions of standard operatic repertoire in traditional venues. Much like the digital avatars employed in Victorian Opera's *The Flying Dutchman* or Opéra de Lyon's *L'Enfant et les Sortilèges*, the technique would function as an extended variant of causal interplay, in which digital technology augments and replaces the live performing body.

Another technology with the potential to augment live performers in the opera house is VOCALOID, a singing synthesiser application software released by Yamaha in 2004. VOCALOID creates digitalised versions of the human voice which can be adapted to suit certain genres of music (Kenmochi 2010). Vibrato, dynamics, tone, and syllabic pronunciation can be individually adjusted according to the melody and lyrics inputted into the software. Marketed as 'a singer in a box,' the technology has already produced a number of digital performers, or 'virtual idols,' who perform in concert for live audiences (Complex 2016). One such 'virtual idol,' Hatsune Miku, was even included on the performer line-up for California's Coachella Valley Music and Arts Festival in 2020 (Shaffer 2020). Like the holographic Maria Callas, VOCALOID could potentially be applied to a traditional operatic setting and used to replace the live performing voice.

These kinds of technological approaches would expand upon existing techniques for causal interplay that augment the onstage performer. With live performers physically replaced by holographic avatars or digitalised voices, the role of the projection designer—or in this case, the holographic designer or software engineer—would become even more critical within the creative hierarchy. The production design process would be similarly impacted, with particular implications for staging and technical rehearsals, as well as employment practices and the wider operatic labour force.

Scenic settings in opera production are in a particular state of fluidity as a result of advancing technologies. Growing interest in virtual and augmented realities has shifted expectations of scenography and the traditional confines of proscenium-based performing venues (Ille 2018). In 2016, United States-based company Opera on Tap collaborated with Samsung VR to present the 'world's first VR opera' (The Parksville Murders n.d.). Composed by Kamala Sankaram to a libretto by Jerre Dye, *The Parksville Murders* (2016) follows two performers through a surrealist ten-minute VR experience. In 2018, the United Kingdom's The Space similarly commissioned VR studio Relative Motion to produce 15 minutes from the first act of Puccini's opera *Tosca* as a 360 VR experience (Relative Motion n.d.). Composer Michel van der Aa is a particular forerunner in experiments with extended reality in opera: his 15-minute interactive VR opera *Eight* premiered at the Festival d'Aix-en-Provence in July 2019 (Barone 2019).

In these examples, the scenic design is mediated into a digital form through virtual reality. This has direct implications for the three-way interplay between the performer, stage setting, and spectator. Since the performers are no longer 'live' but exist within the same digital realm as their scenic surroundings, the two components are truly 'synthesised' within the VR experience. Meanwhile, the spectator—whether viewing the content through a VR headset or their computer screen—can not only visually engage with the performance but also actively drive their own experience.

Large-scale opera companies have been more conservative in their use of extended realities, particularly as a replacement for traditional staged productions (Dixon 2006). In addition to the expense and logistical challenges associated with such technologies, a shift away from live performance represents a significant artistic and financial risk for any presenting company (Sgourev 2013). VR experiences are unavoidably limited to a small number of viewers, and companies would undermine their own ticket revenue by replacing live performances with VR versions. Companies also risk alienating traditionalist audience members for whom both the 'liveness' of the operatic event and its adherence to the intentions of the original creators remain paramount.

Instead, extended realities have been most frequently used by major opera companies as part of digital marketing strategies. In 2016, The Royal Opera, Covent Garden released a short VR experience on YouTube that invited viewers to 'Join the Royal Opera Chorus' and participate in staging rehearsals leading up to opening night (Royal Opera House 2016). The Opéra National de Paris released a VR experience in 2019 that travels through the various spaces of one of their venues, the Palais Garnier (Opéra National de Paris 2019), while an experience released by the Bayerische Staatsoper takes its viewers on stage at the Nationaltheater in front of an audience of 2,000 (Bayerische Staatsoper 2018).

However, in early 2020, the potential for VR and other mediated forms of scenography in opera underwent a marked shift as a direct result of the COVID-19 pandemic. Opera companies worldwide were forced to close their physical venues and cancel in-person seasons of staged performances. For many companies, digital platforms became the only avenue for engaging with their audiences and augmenting lost revenue (Vincent 2020).

A number of companies began to stream archival recordings from past productions for free-to-access viewing on social media platforms. Others engaged in more experimental uses of digital technology to engage their audiences. The Metropolitan Opera's annual fundraising gala for 2020 was marketed as a 'virtual at-home gala' and featured live streaming performances from the homes of 40 international artists (The Metropolitan Opera 2020). Following the cancellation of its live production of Beethoven's *Fidelio* in October 2020, Washington National Opera partnered with Montreal-based Felix & Paul Studios to develop a VR experience based on one of the opera's arias (Salazar 2020). Fort Worth Opera similarly commissioned

Bernadette's Cozy Book Nook, a comic chamber opera about an online book club by composer Joe Illick and librettist Mark Campbell, designed to be performed via Zoom (Ryan Lathan, Fort Worth Opera, personal communication, November 3, 2020). As in the productions described above, these examples rely on a scenic setting that is mediated through a digital platform. This establishes an unavoidable visual synthesis with the 'live' performers, who are themselves mediated from the viewer's perspective.

Many of these digital strategies can be seen as a stopgap, designed to sustain company operations until the resumption of in-person activities post-pandemic. Yet, we can see how the shift to digital performance platforms and a mediated relationship between the performer, scenic setting, and spectator has the potential to transform opera production at a fundamental level. This book's discussion of digital scenography is focused on operatic venues that uphold the spatial tradition of this three-way relationship. Even within these standard spaces, however, digital scenography can cause significant disruptions to opera's backstage processes. An expansion beyond traditional venues and formats poses far greater consequences for both the scenographic expectations and administrative realisations of digitally enhanced opera.

To that end, this discussion constitutes only a starting point in an exploration of digital scenography in opera production. The modes of synthesis provide a means for identifying and evaluating current scenographic trends, as well as highlighting opportunities to adjust and revise existing industry standards accordingly. Drawing on this initial framework for critical analysis, both scholars and industry practitioners will be in a position to achieve the 'better understanding of technology and its capabilities—and limitations' that Stacey Kors outlined in her 1999 review of *Monsters of Grace* (Kors 1999). This, in turn, will pave the way for future considerations of digital technology and performance both in the opera house and beyond.

References

Barone, Joshua. "'Eight' Is a Breakthrough for Virtual Reality in Classical Music." *New York Times*, July 10, 2019. https://www.nytimes.com/2019/07/05/arts/music/michel-van-der-aa-eight.html.

BASE Hologram. n.d. "Productions." Accessed August 13, 2020. https://basehologram.com/productions.

Bayerische Staatsoper. 2018. "V-Aria—Opera in VR and 360° from Munich." YouTube video, 4:38. https://www.youtube.com/watch?v=b1DOoAwkeN4.

Complex, Valerie. 2016. "Diving into the World of Vocaloid's Hologram Performance Artists." *Nerdist*, May 9, 2016. https://archive.nerdist.com/hatsune-miku-and-the-vocaloid-idol-revolution/.

Dixon, Steve. 2006. "A History of Virtual Reality in Performance." *International Journal of Performance Arts and Digital Media* 2, no. 1: 23–54.

Huizenga, Tom. 2018. "Raising The Dead—And a Few Questions—With Maria Callas' Hologram." *Deceptive Cadence, NPR Classical*, November 6, 2018.

https://www.npr.org/sections/deceptivecadence/2018/11/06/664653353/raising-the-dead-and-a-few-questions-with-maria-callas-hologram.

Ille, Megan Steigerwald. 2018. "Bringing Down the House: Situating and Mediating Opera in the Twenty-First Century." PhD diss., Eastman School of Music.

Kenmochi, Hideki. 2010. "VOCALOID and Hatsune Miku Phenomenon in Japan." InterSinging 2010—First Interdisciplinary Workshop on Singing Voice, October 1–2, 2010, Tokyo, Japan. https://www.isca-speech.org/archive/int_singing_2010/papers/isi0_001.pdf.

Kors, Stacey. 1999. "Monsters of Grace." *Salon*, July 21, 1999. https://www.salon.com/1999/07/21/monsters.

The Metropolitan Opera. 2020. "Press Release: The Met Announces Plans to Live-Stream an All-Star At-Home Gala on Saturday, April 25, at 1pm EDT." *The Metropolitan Opera*, April 13, 2020. https://www.metopera.org/about/press-releases/the-met-announces-plans-to-live-stream-an-all-star--at-home-gala/.

Opéra National de Paris. 2019. "Les Secrets du Palais Garnier | VR 360° 4K." YouTube video, 8:40. https://www.youtube.com/watch?v=kN6nh2dgPaM&t=347s.

Relative Motion. n.d. "Tosca VR." Accessed 15 July 2020. https://www.relativemotion.co.uk/tosca-vr.html.

Royal Opera House. 2016. "Join the Royal Opera Chorus in 360°." YouTube video, 2:33. https://www.youtube.com/watch?v=gCGO1txNyN8.

Salazar, Francisco. 2020. "Washington National Opera Announces Revised 2020–21 Season." *OperaWire*, July 23, 2020. https://operawire.com/washington-national-opera-announces-revised-2020-21-season/.

Schein, Esther. 2014. "Holographic Projection Systems Provide Eternal Life." *Society* 57, no. 7: 19–21. https://doi.org/10.1145/2617664.

Sgourev, Stoyan V. 2013. "The Dynamics of Risk in Innovation: A Premiere or an Encore?" *Industrial and Corporate Change* 22, no. 2: 549–575. https://doi.org/10.1093/icc/dts021.

Shaffer, Claire. 2020. "Hatsune Miku, Holographic Japanese Idol, Makes Her Coachella Debut." *Rolling Stone*, January 3, 2020. https://www.rollingstone.com/music/music-news/hatsune-miku-coachella-933263/.

The Parksville Murders. n.d. "The Parksville Murders." https://www.theparksville murders.com.

Vincent, Caitlin. 2020. "Giving It Away for Free—Why the Performing Arts Risks Making the Same Mistake Newspapers Did." *The Conversation*, June 4, 2020. https://theconversation.com/giving-it-away-for-free-why-the-performing-arts-risks-making-the-same-mistake-newspapers-did-139671.

Appendix 1

Digitally enhanced opera productions reviewed for this research

Opera	Composer	Director	Primary Presenting Company	Country	Year	Review Format
The Magic Flute	Mozart	C. Menzies	Australian International Opera Company	Australia	2016	Live
Lucia di Lammermoor	Donizetti	B. Wysocka	Bayerische Staatsoper	Germany	2015	Streaming
Angel's Bone	Du	M. J. McQuilken	Beth Morrison Projects/ Hong Kong New Vision Art Festival	Hong Kong	2018	Streaming
Dog Days	Little	R. Woodruff	Beth Morrison Projects/ LA Opera	USA	2015	Streaming
The Magic Flute	Mozart	S. McBurney	Dutch National Opera	Netherlands	2012	Streaming
Mefistofele	Boito	P. Himmelmann	Festspielhaus Baden-Baden	Germany	2016	Streaming
Don Giovanni	Mozart	J. Nikkilä	Finnish National Opera & Ballet	Finland	2020	Streaming
Florencia en el Amazonas	Catán	J. M. Condemi	Florida Grand Opera	USA	2018	Streaming
As One	Kaminsky	L. Thompson	Gertrude Opera	Australia	2020	Live
Vanessa	Barber	K. Warner	Glyndebourne Festival Opera	England	2018	Streaming

(Continued)

Opera	Composer	Director	Primary Presenting Company	Country	Year	Review Format
Turandot	Puccini	F. Aleu	Gran Teatre del Liceu	Spain	2019	Streaming
Bluebeard's Castle	Bartók	S.F. Weiss/ C. Vianello	Hungarian State Opera	Hungary	2011	Video Excerpts
The Magic Flute	Mozart	S. Andrade/B. Kosky	Komische Oper Berlin	Germany	2012	Live
Das Rheingold	Wagner	C. Padrissa	La Fura dels Baus	Spain	2007	DVD
Die Walküre	Wagner	C. Padrissa	La Fura dels Baus	Spain	2007	DVD
Silent Night	Puts	E. Simonson	Minnesota Opera	USA	2011	DVD
Il Trovatore	Verdi	H. De Ana	National Centre for the Performing Arts, Beijing	China	2019	Streaming
L'Enfant et les Sortilèges	Ravel	G. Pont/J. Bonas	Opéra de Lyon	France	2016	Streaming
La Bohème	Puccini	C. Guth	Opéra National de Paris	France	2017	Streaming
La Traviata	Verdi	S. Stone	Opéra National de Paris	France	2019	Streaming
Breaking the Waves	Mazzoli	J. Darrah	Opera Philadelphia	USA	2017	Streaming
Denis and Katya	Venables	T. Huffman	Opera Philadelphia	USA	2019	Streaming
Halka	Moniuszko	P. Passini	Polish National Opera	Poland	2019	Streaming
Tosca	Puccini	B. Wysocka	Polish National Opera	Poland	2019	Streaming
Cavalleria Rusticana	Mascagni	P. Stölzl	Salzburg Festival	Austria	2015	DVD
Pagliacci	Leoncavallo	P. Stölzl	Salzburg Festival	Austria	2015	DVD
Moby-Dick	Heggie	L. Foglia	San Francisco Opera	USA	2012	DVD
The Magic Flute	Mozart	H. Silverstein	San Francisco Opera	USA	2012	Video Excerpts
The Flying Dutchman	Wagner	P. Ionesco	San Francisco Opera	USA	2013	Video Excerpts
The (R)evolution of Steve Jobs	Bates	K. Newbury	Santa Fe Opera	USA	2017	Video Excerpts
Semele	Handel	T. Zvulun	Seattle Opera	USA	2015	Video Excerpts
Commute	Polias	C. Williams	Sydney Chamber Opera/ Carriageworks	Australia	2020	Streaming
Her Dark Marauder	Scott	D. Maas	Sydney Chamber Opera/ Carriageworks	Australia	2020	Streaming

Title	Composer	Director	Company / Venue	Country	Year	Format
The Invisible Bird	van Reyk	C. Williams	Sydney Chamber Opera/Carriageworks	Australia	2020	Streaming
The Tent	Macken	D. Maas	Sydney Chamber Opera/Carriageworks	Australia	2020	Streaming
Das Rheingold	Wagner	G. Cassiers	Teatro alla Scala	Italy	2010	DVD
The Magic Flute	Mozart	W. Kentridge	Teatro alla Scala	Italy	2011	DVD
Madama Butterfly	Puccini	A. Hermanis	Teatro alla Scala	Italy	2016	Streaming
The Perfect American	Glass	P. McDermott	Teatro Real de Madrid	Spain	2013	DVD
Brokeback Mountain	Wuorinen	I. van Hove	Teatro Real de Madrid	Spain	2014	Streaming
Turandot	Puccini	R. Wilson	Teatro Real de Madrid	Spain	2018	Streaming
The Cunning Little Vixen	Janáček	Y. Sharon	The Cleveland Orchestra	USA	2014	Video Excerpts
Doctor Atomic	Adams	P. Woolcock	The Metropolitan Opera	USA	2008	Streaming
Das Rheingold	Wagner	R. Lepage	The Metropolitan Opera	USA	2010	Streaming
Die Walküre	Wagner	R. Lepage	The Metropolitan Opera	USA	2011	Streaming
Faust	Gounod	D. McAnuff	The Metropolitan Opera	USA	2011	Streaming
The Enchanted Island	Various	P. McDermott	The Metropolitan Opera	USA	2011	Streaming
The Tempest	Adès	R. Lepage	The Metropolitan Opera	USA	2012	Streaming
The Nose	Shostakovich	W. Kentridge	The Metropolitan Opera	USA	2013	Streaming
Prince Igor	Borodin	D. Tcherniakov	The Metropolitan Opera	USA	2014	Streaming
La Donna del Lago	Rossini	P. Curran	The Metropolitan Opera	USA	2015	DVD
Lulu	Berg	W. Kentridge	The Metropolitan Opera	USA	2015	Streaming
Eugene Onegin	Tchaikovsky	D. Warner	The Metropolitan Opera	USA	2017	Streaming
Marnie	Muhly	M. Mayer	The Metropolitan Opera	USA	2018	Streaming
Akhnaten	Glass	P. McDermott	The Metropolitan Opera	USA	2019	Streaming
Don Giovanni	Mozart	K. Holten	The Royal Opera, Covent Garden	England	2014	DVD
King Roger	Szymanowski	K. Holten	The Royal Opera, Covent Garden	England	2015	Live
Lucio Silla	Mozart	T. Kratzer	Théâtre Royal de la Monnaie	Belgium	2017	Streaming
Frankenstein	Grey	A. Ollé	Théâtre Royal de la Monnaie	Belgium	2019	Streaming

(Continued)

Opera	Composer	Director	Primary Presenting Company	Country	Year	Review Format
The Tale of Tsar Saltan	Rimsky-Korsakov	D. Tcherniakov	Théâtre Royal de la Monnaie	Belgium	2019	Streaming
The Flying Dutchman	Wagner	R. Hodgman	Victorian Opera	Australia	2015	Live
Four Saints in Three Acts	Thomson	N. Black/K. Vincs	Victorian Opera	Australia	2016	Live
Das Rheingold	Wagner	F. Zambello	Washington National Opera	USA	2016	Video Excerpts

Appendix 2
Case study productions

The following productions serve as in-depth case studies for the use of digital scenography in opera. The creative teams for each production are listed below, as well as the production premiere date, any co-commissioning companies, and selected subsequent revivals by other companies. Both the order of credits and wording of credit titles are drawn from official company documentation, including playbills, production archives, and company websites.

Das Rheingold (The Metropolitan Opera)
Music and libretto by Richard Wagner.
In collaboration with Ex Machina
Production premiere: 2010
Production: Robert Lepage
Associate Director: Neilson Vignola
Set Designer: Carl Fillion
Costume Designer: François St-Aubin
Lighting Designer: Etienne Boucher
Video Image Artist: Boris Firquet
Subsequent revivals (select): The Metropolitan Opera, USA (2011, 2012, 2013, 2019)

Das Rheingold (Washington National Opera)
Music and libretto by Richard Wagner.
Co-production with San Francisco Opera
Production premiere: 2016
Director: Francesca Zambello
Associate Director and Choreographer: Denni Sayers
Set Designer: Michael Yeargan
Costume Designer: Catherine Zuber
Lighting Designer: Mark McCullough
Original Projections Designed by: Jan Hartley
New Projections Designed by: S. Katy Tucker
Remounted by: S. Katy Tucker
Subsequent revivals (select): San Francisco Opera, USA (2018)

Don Giovanni (The Royal Opera, Covent Garden)
Music by Wolfgang A. Mozart. Libretto by Lorenzo da Ponte.

Co-production with Israeli Opera, Gran Teatre del Liceu, and Houston Grand
  Opera
Production premiere: 2014
Director: Kasper Holten
Set Designer: Es Devlin
Video Designer: Luke Halls
Costume Designer: Anja Vang Kragh
Lighting Designer: Bruno Poet
Choreographer: Signe Fabricius
Subsequent revivals (select): Japan Performing Arts Foundation, Japan (2015); Gran
  Teatre del Liceu, Spain (2017); The Royal Opera, Covent Garden, UK (2018,
  2019); Houston Grand Opera, USA (2019)

Four Saints in Three Acts (Victorian Opera)
Music by Virgil Thomson. Libretto by Gertrude Stein.
Production premiere: 2016
Director: Nancy Black
Co-Director: Dr Kim Vincs
Light Designer: Peter Darby
Costume Supervisor: Candice MacAllister
Digital Scenography: Deakin Motion.Lab under the direction of Dr Kim Vincs
Technical Artists: Stephen Jeal, Casey Dalbo, Simeon Taylor, Peter Divers, Daniel
  Skovli
Programmers: Kieren Wallace, Thomas Ingram, John McCormick
Technical Supervisor: Richard Burt
Audiovisual Design: Jordan Kaye
Project Manager: Jordan Beth Vincent
Assistant Project Manager: Dee Czarnecki
Subsequent revivals (select): n/a

L'Enfant et les Sortilèges (Opéra de Lyon)
Music by Maurice Ravel. Libretto by Colette.
Commissioned in association with L'Auditori de Barcelona and Maestro Arts
Production premiere: 2016
Concept and video: Grégoire Pont
Spatial installation: James Bonas
Sets and Costumes: Thibault Vancraenenbroeck
Lighting: Christophe Chaupin
Subsequent revivals (select): Opéra de Lyon, France (2019); Royal Opera House
  Muscat, Oman (2019); San Francisco Symphony, USA (2019); Opéra de Limoges,
  France (2020); Théâtre de la Croix-Rousse, France (2021)

The Flying Dutchman (Victorian Opera)
Music and libretto by Richard Wagner.
Production premiere: 2015
Director: Roger Hodgman
Set & Visual Design: Matt Scott and Christina Smith
Costume Design: Teresa Negroponte

Lighting Designer: Matt Scott
3D Image Design & Creation: Deakin Motion.Lab—Professor Kim Vincs, Daniel
   Skovli, Simeon Taylor, Kieren Wallace, Peter Divers, Jacob Turoy
Assistant Director: Cameron Menzies
Subsequent revivals (select): n/a

The Magic Flute (Théâtre Royal de la Monnaie)
Music by Wolfgang A. Mozart. Libretto by Emanuel Schikaneder.
Co-production with Teatro alla Scala, Teatro di San Carlo, Opéra de Lille, and
   Théâtre de Caen
Production premiere: 2005
Director: William Kentridge
Assistant Director: Luc de Wit
Sets: William Kentridge, Sabine Theunissen
Lighting: Jennifer Tipton
Costumes: Greta Goiris
Video Controller: Catherine Meyburgh
Subsequent revivals (select): Opéra de Lille, France (2006); Teatro di San Carlo, Italy
   (2006); Brooklyn Academy of Music, USA (2007); Johannesburg Opera House,
   South Africa (2007); Cape Town Opera House, South Africa (2007); Théâtre de
   Caen, France (2007); Tel Aviv Opera House, Israel (2007); Théâtre Royal de la
   Monnaie, Belgium (2007); Festival d'Aix-en-Provence, France (2009); Teatro alla
   Scala, Italy (2011); Opéra de Rouen Haute-Normandie, France (2011); Théâtre des
   Champs-Elysée, France (2011); New National Theatre, Tokyo, Japan (2018)

The Magic Flute (San Francisco Opera)
Music by Wolfgang A. Mozart. Libretto by Emanuel Schikaneder.
Co-production with Washington National Opera, Opera Carolina, Opera Omaha,
   and Lyric Opera of Kansas City
Production premiere: 2012
Director: Harry Silverstein
Production Designer: Jun Kaneko
Lighting Designer: Paul Pyant
Choreographer: Lawrence Pech
Digital Animation: Clark Creative Group
Assistant Stage Director: Garnett Bruce
Costume Supervisor: Kirsti Johnson
Subsequent revivals (select): Opera Omaha, USA (2013); Lyric Opera of Kansas
   City, USA (2013); Opera Carolina, USA (2013); Washington National Opera,
   USA (2014); San Francisco Opera, USA (2015)

The Magic Flute (Komische Oper Berlin)
Music by Wolfgang A. Mozart. Libretto by Emanuel Schikaneder.
Production premiere: 2012
Director: Barrie Kosky and Suzanne Andrade
Animation: Paul Barritt
Conceived by: Barrie Kosky and 1927 (Suzanne Andrade and Paul Barritt)
Stage Design and Costumes: Esther Bialas

Dramaturgy: Ulrich Lenz

Lighting: Diego Leetz

Subsequent revivals (select): Opernhaus Düsseldorf, Germany (2013); LA Opera, USA (2013, 2016, 2019); Minnesota Opera, USA (2014, 2015); Edinburgh International Festival, UK (2015); Shanghai Grand Theatre, China (2015); Banlam Grand Theatre, China (2015); Guangzhou Opera House, China (2015); Teatro Real de Madrid, Spain (2016, 2020); Finnish National Opera, Finland (2016); Gran Teatre del Liceu, Spain (2016); Polish National Opera, Poland (2016); Bolshoi Theatre, Russia (2017); Cincinnati Opera, USA (2017); Opera Philadelphia, USA (2017); Opéra Comique, France (2017); Greek National Opera, Greece (2018); Teatro dell'Opera di Roma, Italy (2018); Hyogo Performing Arts Centre, Japan (2018); Auckland Festival, New Zealand (2019); Adelaide Festival, Australia (2019); Perth Festival, Australia (2019); National Kaohsiung Center for the Arts, Taiwan (2019)

The Magic Flute (Dutch National Opera)

Music by Wolfgang A. Mozart. Libretto by Emanuel Schikaneder.

Co-production with English National Opera and Festival d'Aix-en-Provence in collaboration with Complicité London

Production premiere: 2012

Stage Director: Simon McBurney

Set Designer: Michael Levine

Costume Designer: Nicky Gillibrand

Lighting Designer: Jean Kalman

Video Designer: Finn Ross

Sound Designer: Gareth Fry

Movement Director: Josie Daxter

Dramaturg: Simon McBurney and Klaus Bertisch

Subsequent revivals (select): English National Opera, UK (2013, 2019); Festival d'Aix-en-Provence, France (2014, 2018); Dutch National Opera, Netherlands (2015, 2018)

The (R)evolution of Steve Jobs (Santa Fe Opera)

Music by Mason Bates. Libretto by Mark Campbell.

Co-production with Seattle Opera, San Francisco Opera, and the Jacobs School of Music at Indiana University, with support from Cal Performances

Production premiere: 2017

Director: Kevin Newbury

Set Designer: Victoria 'Vita' Tzykun

Costume Designer: Paul Carey

Lighting Designer: Japhy Weideman

Projection Designer: 59 Productions—Benjamin Pearcy (Project Director), Tommy Lexen (Producer), Hannah Fasching (Design Assistant), David Curtis (Animator), Marcus Chaloner (Animator), Nick Corrigan (Assistant Video Designer), Brad Peterson (Assistant Video Designer)

Sound Design: Rick Jacobsohn

Choreographer: Chloe Treat

Subsequent revivals (select): Jacobs School of Music, Indiana University, USA (2018); Seattle Opera, USA (2019); San Francisco Opera, USA (2020, cancelled due to COVID-19); The Atlanta Opera, USA (2021/22)

The Cunning Little Vixen (The Cleveland Orchestra)
Music and libretto by Leos Janáček.
Production premiere: 2014
Director: Yuval Sharon
Animators: Walter Robot Studios—Bill Barminski and Christopher Louie
Projection and Lighting Designer: Jason Thompson
Costume Designer: Ann Closs-Farley
Mask Designer: Cristina Waltz
Subsequent revivals (select): The Cleveland Orchestra, USA (2017); Musikverein, Austria (2017); Göteborg Opera, Sweden (2020, cancelled due to COVID-19)

Appendix 3
Interview participants

The following individuals participated in one or more semi-structured interviews for this research. Each individual is noted below alongside the date of their interview(s), select digitally enhanced productions from their professional careers, and a link to their professional website, where available.

Interview Participant	Title	Interview Date(s)	Associated Digitally Enhanced Productions	Website
Directors and Designers				
Paul Barritt	Animator and Co-Artistic Director, 1927 Productions	June 17, 2017	Komische Oper Berlin's *The Magic Flute* (2012); Salzburg Festival/1927's *Golem* (2014); Komische Oper Berlin's *Petrushka and L'Enfant et les Sortilèges* (2017)	http://www.paulbarritt.com
Nancy Black	Stage Director	May 15, 2017	Victorian Opera's *Four Saints in Three Acts* (2016)	https://blackholetheatre.com.au/
Peter Divers	Former Animator and Virtual Production Supervisor, Deakin Motion.Lab	May 7, 2017	Victorian Opera's *The Flying Dutchman* (2015); Victorian Opera's *Four Saints in Three Acts* (2016); Australian International Opera Company's *Turandot* (2017)	n/a

(Continued)

Interview Participant	Title	Interview Date(s)	Associated Digitally Enhanced Productions	Website
Mark Grimmer	Company Director, 59 Productions	May 31, 2017; August 15, 2020	English National Opera/ Improbable's *Satyagraha* (2007); The Metropolitan Opera's *Dr Atomic* (2008); English National Opera's *Two Boys* (2011); English National Opera's *Marnie* (2017)	https://59productions. co.uk/ mark-grimmer/
Luke Halls	Filmmaker, Luke Halls Studio	August 29, 2017	The Royal Opera, Covent Garden's *Don Giovanni* (2014); The Royal Opera, Covent Garden's *King Roger* (2015); The Metropolitan Opera's *Otello* (2015); Bregenz Lake Stage's *Carmen* (2018); English National Opera's *Porgy and Bess* (2018)	https://lukehalls.com
Wendall K. Harrington	Projection Designer	June 27, 2017	Lyric Opera of Chicago's *A View from the Bridge* (1999); Opera Theatre of St. Louis' *Nixon in China* (2004); Minnesota Opera's *The Grapes of Wrath* (2007); Minnesota Opera's *Wuthering Heights* (2011); The Metropolitan Opera's *Werther* (2014)	http://www. wendallharrington. com

Interview Participant	Title	Interview Date(s)	Associated Digitally Enhanced Productions	Website
Roger Hodgman	Stage Director	June 11, 2017	Victorian Opera's *The Flying Dutchman* (2015)	https://shanahan.com.au/client/roger-hodgman/
Donald Holder	Lighting Designer	June 27, 2020	Dallas Opera's *Moby-Dick* (2010); English National Opera's *Two Boys* (2011); Gotham Chamber Opera's *Dark Sisters* (2011); The Metropolitan Opera's *Otello* (2015); English National Opera's *Porgy and Bess* (2018)	n/a
Elaine J. McCarthy	Projection Designer	May 23, 2020	New York City Opera's *Dead Man Walking* (2002); The Metropolitan Opera's *War and Peace* (2002); The Metropolitan Opera's *Mazeppa* (2006); Dallas Opera's *Moby-Dick* (2010); Dallas Opera's *Tristan und Isolde* (2012); Dallas Opera's *Everest* (2015)	http://www.ejmdesign.net
Katie Mitchell	Stage Director	March 10, 2018	Royal National Theatre's *Waves* (2006); English National Opera/Young Vic's *After Dido* (2009); Berlin State Opera/Salzburg Festival's *Al gran sole carico d'amore* (2012); Salzburg Festival's *The Forbidden Zone* (2014)	https://theagency.co.uk/the-clients/katie-mitchell/

(Continued)

Interview Participant	Title	Interview Date(s)	Associated Digitally Enhanced Productions	Website
Sven Ortel	Projection Designer	May 21, 2020	Broadway's *The Woman in White* (2005); Mariinsky Theater's *Ring* cycle (2009); Broadway's *Women on the Verge of a Nervous Breakdown* (2010); Broadway's *Newsies* (2012); Polonsky Shakespeare Center's *A Midsummer Night's Dream* (2013); Alliance Theater's *Candide* (2018)	https://www.svenortel.com
Grégoire Pont	Animator	August 13, 2020	Opéra de Lyon's *L'Enfant et les Sortilèges* (2016)	https://www.gregoirepont.com
Tobias Ribitzki	Former Assistant Stage Director, Komische Oper Berlin	September 13, 2016; February 19, 2019; April 1, 2019	Komische Oper Berlin's *The Magic Flute* (2012); Komische Oper Berlin's *The Magic Flute—*Revivals at LA Opera (2013), Minnesota Opera (2014), Teatro Real de Madrid (2016), Finnish National Opera (2016), Opera Philadelphia (2017), Greek National Opera (2018), Perth Festival (2019), Adelaide Festival (2019)	https://www.theapolis.de/de/profil/tobias-ribitzki

Interview Participant	*Title*	*Interview Date(s)*	*Associated Digitally Enhanced Productions*	*Website*
Finn Ross	Video Designer	September 12, 2016; June 20, 2017; September 25, 2018	Dutch National Opera's *The Magic Flute* (2012); Theatre an der Wien's *Béatrice et Bénédict* (2013); The Metropolitan Opera's *Eugene Onegin* (2013); English National Opera's *Benvenuto Cellini* (2014); Broadway's *The Curious Incident of the Dog in the Night-Time* (2014); The Royal Opera, Covent Garden's *The Rise and Fall of the City of Mahagonny* (2015); Dutch National Opera's *Hansel and Gretel* (2015); Broadway's *Harry Potter and the Cursed Child, Parts One and Two* (2018)	https://www. scottmarshall. co.uk/creatives/ finn-ross/
Sabine Theunissen	Set Designer	June 10, 2017; May 1, 2018	Théâtre Royal de la Monnaie's *The Magic Flute* (2005); The Metropolitan Opera's *The Nose* (2010); The Metropolitan Opera's *Lulu* (2015); Salzburg Festival's *Wozzeck* (2017)	https:// sabinetheunissen. weebly.com

(*Continued*)

Interview Participant	Title	Interview Date(s)	Associated Digitally Enhanced Productions	Website
S. Katy Tucker	Video and Projection Designer	September 21, 2017; September 5, 2018	San Francisco Opera's *The Flying Dutchman* (2013); The Metropolitan Opera's *Prince Igor* (2014); Washington National Opera's *Florencia en el Amazonas* (2014); Washington National Opera's *Ring* cycle (2016); Washington National Opera's *Don Giovanni* (2020)	http://www. skatytucker.com
Victoria 'Vita' Tzykun	Production Designer	August 28, 2018; September 8, 2020	The Metropolitan Opera's *Mazeppa* (2006); Dallas Opera's *Tristan und Isolde* (2012); Wolf Trap Opera's *Don Giovanni* (2012); Seattle Opera's *Semele* (2015); Indianapolis Opera's *The Man Who Mistook His Wife For A Hat* (2015); Santa Fe Opera's *The (R)evolution of Steve Jobs* (2017)	https://www. vitavision.net

Interview Participant	Title	Interview Date(s)	Associated Digitally Enhanced Productions	Website
Japhy Weideman	Lighting Designer	June 1, 2020	Broadway's *Macbeth* (2013); Broadway's *Dear Evan Hansen* (2016); Santa Fe Opera's *The (R)evolution of Steve Jobs* (2017); Broadway's *Charlie and the Chocolate Factory* (2017)	http://www. japhyweideman. com

Administrators and Performers

Interview Participant	Title	Interview Date(s)	Associated Digitally Enhanced Productions	Website
Yarmila Alfonzetti	Executive Director, State Opera of South Australia	February 28, 2019	Komische Oper Berlin's *The Magic Flute*—Revival at Adelaide Festival (2019)	https://stateopera. com.au
Carolyn Chard	Executive Director, West Australian Opera	February 18, 2019	Komische Oper Berlin's *The Magic Flute* – Revival at Perth Festival (2019)	https://www.waopera. asn.au
Aaron Blake	Performer	February 28, 2019	Komische Oper Berlin's *The Magic Flute*— Revivals at Minnesota Opera (2014), Cincinnati Opera (2017), Hyogo Performing Arts Centre, Japan (2018), Perth Festival (2019), Adelaide Festival (2019)	https://www. aaronblaketenor. com
Beth Moxon	Performer	September 28, 2020	Opéra de Lyon's *L'Enfant et les Sortilèges* (2016)	https://www.beth- moxon.co.uk

Index

Note: Page numbers followed by "n" denote endnotes.